# IN SEARCH OF THE SOUL

## FOUR VIEWS OF THE MIND-BODY PROBLEM

EDITED BY **JOEL B. GREEN**

WITH CONTRIBUTIONS BY **KEVIN CORCORAN, STEWART GOETZ, WILLIAM HASKER AND NANCEY MURPHY**

WIPF & STOCK · Eugene, Oregon

Wipf and Stock Publishers
199 W 8th Ave, Suite 3
Eugene, OR 97401

In Search of the Soul
Perspectives on the Mind-Body Problem
By Green, Joel B.
Copyright©2005 by Green, Joel B.
ISBN 13: 978-1-60899-473-1
Publication date 11/1/2010
Previously published by InterVarsity Press, 2005

# CONTENTS

# 1  BODY AND SOUL, MIND AND BRAIN

## CRITICAL ISSUES
*Joel B. Green*

*Then God said, "Let us make humankind in our image, according to our like-ness; and let them have dominion over the fish of the sea, and over the birds of the air, and over the cattle, and over all the wild animals of the earth, and over every creeping thing that creeps upon the earth."*

*So God created humankind in his image, in the image of God he created them; male and female he created them.*

*God blessed them, and God said to them, "Be fruitful and multiply, and fill the earth and subdue it; and have dominion over the fish of the sea and over the birds of the air and over every living thing that moves upon the earth."*

GENESIS 1:26-28

*We are machines built by DNA whose purpose is to make more copies of the same DNA. . . . This is exactly what we are for. We are machines for propagat-ing DNA, and the propagation of DNA is a self-sustaining process. It is every living object's sole reason for living.*

RICHARD DAWKINS, "GROWING UP IN THE UNIVERSE"

In a characteristically provocative, some might say insolent, fashion, evolu-tionary biologist Richard Dawkins articulates a scientific view of humanity that contrasts sharply with the perspective of Christian Scripture and the Christian tradition. His is the sort of viewpoint that many Christians fear when the natural sciences enter the conversation. Not only have we become "machines" in Dawkins's reckoning, but the purpose of our lives, individually and collectively, has been reduced to accommodating those impulses arising at the level of our molecular biology.

Although for many the threat to traditional views of personhood may appear to originate in evolutionary biology, today the frontier of human definition is defined more particularly by study of the central nervous system, especially the brain: its systems, networks and neuronal interactions. "Bit by experimental bit," writes philosopher Patricia Churchland, "neuroscience is morphing our conception of what we are."[1] This includes dispensing with the "soul" in favor of biologically anchored processes. As a recent *New York Times* article reported, "Neuroscientists have given up looking for the seat of the soul, but they are still seeking what may be special about human brains, what it is that provides the basis for a level of self-awareness and complex emotions unlike those of other animals." Noting the now-common view that morality and reason grow out of social emotions and feelings that are themselves linked to brain structures that map the body, the article suggests that, maybe, what makes us human is all in the wiring of the brain.[2] If the Christian tradition has typically located human distinctiveness—indeed, the human sense of "self"— in human possession of a "soul," then it is no surprise that science might be regarded by some as a spiritually caustic agent.

What does it mean to be human? In what ways, if any, is our essential humanity tied to body and soul, mind and brain? This is not the stuff of mere curiosity. A host of pressing issues is at stake:

- What distinguishes us from nonhuman animals?

- Is there anything about humans that our mechanical creations, our innovations in artificial intelligence, will be unable to duplicate?

- What view of the human person is capable of funding what we want to know about ourselves theologically—about sin, for example, as well as moral responsibility, volition, repentance, joy and growth in grace?

- How do we explain our actions? Am I free to do what I want, or is my sense of decision making a ruse?

- What portrait of the human person is capable of casting a canopy of sacred worth over human beings, so that we have what is necessary for discourse concerning morality and for ethical practices regarding "human dignity" and "sacred worth," not least on beginning- and end-of-life issues?

- If humans, like sheep, can be cloned, will the resulting life form be a "person"?

---

[1]Patricia Smith Churchland, *Brain-Wise: Studies in Neurophilosophy* (Cambridge, Mass.: MIT Press, 2002), p. 2.
[2]Sandra Blakeselee, "Humanity? Maybe It's All in the Wiring," *New York Times*, December 9, 2003, F1.

- How should we understand "salvation"? What needs to be "saved"? What does salvation entail? Salvation of my "soul"? If so, does this entail a denial of the world and embodied life, focusing instead on my internal, spiritual life and the life to come? What view of salvation is funded by a given view of humanity?

- How ought the church to be extending itself in mission? Mission to what? The spiritual or soulish needs of persons? Society at large? The cosmos?

- What about pastoral ministry? Given that the role of the pastor has historically been defined as "soul care," what happens to the pastoral vocation if there is no "soul"?

- What is the nature and role of the church? How is our understanding of the church implicated in different views of what it means to be human? What is the role of the church in the formation of human persons?

- What happens when we die? What view(s) of the human person is consistent with Christian belief in life after death?

For many, and not least for many Christians, the traditional answer to the question, what makes a human genuinely human? has been the identification of the human person with his or her soul. Although the origin of the soul was debated among Christian theologians as early as the second century,[3] it was nonetheless clear to most by the postapostolic period that, as the *Letter to Diognetus* puts it, "the soul dwells in the body, yet is not of the body" (1.27). Exegesis of the Genesis account of the creation of humanity generally focused on God's breathing into Adam "the breath of life" (Gen 2:7)—that is, the placing of the living soul into what had been formed from dust[4]—with the result that the first human being, and all persons to appear subsequently, is a human person by virtue of the possession of a soul. "Without the soul, we are nothing," wrote Tertullian.[5] Writing in the early fourth century, Lactantius is even more clear: "The body can do nothing without the soul. But the soul can do many and great things without the body."[6] Dogmatic or systematic theology concerned with the doctrine of humanity has traditionally discussed the unique-

---

[3] Are souls created by God ex nihilo at the moment of their infusion into the body (Lactantius, Thomas Aquinas, Peter Lombard)? Are body and soul formed together (Tertullian, Martin Luther)? Are souls pre-existent (Origen)?

[4] For an accessible compilation of relevant texts, see Andrew Louth, ed., *Genesis 1—11*, Ancient Christian Commentary on Scripture, Old Testament 1 (Downers Grove, Ill.: InterVarsity Press, 2001), pp. 50-53.

[5] Tertullian *Soul's Testimony* 6.

[6] Lactantius *Divine Institutes* 7.12.

ness of humanity in two theological loci, human creation in the divine image and the human possession of a soul.[7] Often these two are reduced to one, with the soul understood as the particular consequence of creation in God's image.

For persons of faith—Christians included, but many others besides—the idea of a soul separable from the body is not only intuitive but has contributed a great deal. We have regularly appealed to the soul as proof that humans are not mere animals, and thus as a foundation for our views of human dignity and the sacredness of human life; we have imagined that human possession of a soul has immediate and far-reaching consequences for the burgeoning and troubled arena of bioethics.[8] Moreover, Christians generally have derived from belief in the existence of the soul their affirmation of the human capacity to choose between good and ill, as free moral agents. Further, since it is with regard to the soul that the divine image shared by human beings comes into clearest focus, the soul provides the necessary (though not sufficient) ground of human spirituality, of one's capacity to enter into and enjoy a relationship with God. Still further, the existence of a nonphysical soul, distinct and separable from the body, is typically regarded as the means by which human identity can cross over the bridge from this life to the next; indeed, traditional Christian thought has tended to regard the body as frail and finite and the soul as immortal.

These are important matters, but they are also complex. Many voices are needed if these issues are to be explored fully. In this volume, we hear particularly from Christian philosophers who, in various ways and to varying degrees, are themselves in conversation with other disciplines.[9] The purpose of this opening chapter is to provide orientation to the larger discussion concerning the nature of the human person by (1) introducing the range of options championed today for portraying what it means to be human, together with

---

[7]For example, H. Wheeler Robinson, *The Christian Doctrine of Man*, 3rd ed. (Edinburgh: T & T Clark, 1926); and, more recently, Paul K. Jewett, *Who We Are: Our Dignity as Human: A Neo-Evangelical Theology*, ed. Marguerite Shuster (Grand Rapids: Eerdmans, 1996).

[8]This is recently argued in J. P. Moreland and Scott B. Rae, *Body and Soul: Human Nature and the Crisis in Ethics* (Downers Grove, Ill.: InterVarsity Press, 2000).

[9]For multidisciplinary perspectives, see the following collections: Warren S. Brown, Nancey Murphy and H. Newton Malony, eds., *Whatever Happened to the Soul? Scientific and Theological Portraits of Human Nature*, Theology and the Sciences (Minneapolis: Fortress, 1998); Joel B. Green, ed., *What About the Soul? Neuroscience and Christian Anthropology* (Nashville: Abingdon, 2004); Niels Henrik Gregersen et al., eds., *The Human Person in Science and Theology*, Issues in Science and Theology (Grand Rapids: Eerdmans, 2000); Malcolm A. Jeeves, ed., *From Cells to Souls: Changing Portraits of Human Nature* (Grand Rapids: Eerdmans, 2004); Robert John Russell et al., eds., *Neuroscience and the Person*, Scientific Perspectives on Divine Action 4 (Vatican City State: Vatican Observatory, 1999).

some of the vocabulary typically associated with these options; (2) presenting a series of compass points we Christians need to consider as we contemplate these options; and (3) sketching some representative issues that together underscore why discussions about body and soul, mind and brain are so significant and controversial.

In the essays and responses that make up the heart of this book, philosophers Stewart Goetz, William Hasker, Nancey Murphy and Kevin Corcoran demonstrate how each portrait of the human person they champion accounts for many of these issues. Of course, given the constraints of space imposed on our contributors, we can hardly expect them to address all of the pertinent concerns. Even so, the astute reader may be able to extrapolate from what the contributors are able to discuss to how they might further their arguments; moreover, we may follow the paths of their thinking in their own additional publications and in other materials they cite.

### Portraits of the Human Person: Options and Definitions

To many Christians, the range of possible ways of giving an account of the human person may be surprising, and the assumptions and vocabulary that characterize the discussion can be off-putting, if not downright overwhelming. In a recent introduction to the debate, Corcoran concluded that "the mind-body problem remains wide open."[10] This would come as a surprise to mid-twentieth-century readers of one of the early histories of neurology, wherein Walther Riese confidently asserts that the human soul, a stranger to the anatomical structures of the cerebrum, had been eliminated in the 1800s by philosophers, naturalists and physicians.[11] More recently, Dawkins confidently pronounced over the demise of the idea of a human soul, "Good riddance."[12] Nevertheless, standard textbooks on the philosophy of mind continue to discuss a range of options for articulating the nature of the relationship of mind and brain, just as neurobiologists admit to the persistence of an "explanatory

---

[10]Kevin Corcoran, introduction to *Soul, Body and Survival: Essays on the Metaphysics of Human Persons*, ed. Kevin Corcoran (Ithaca, N.Y.: Cornell University Press, 2001), p. 11.

[11]Walther Riese, *A History of Neurology* (New York: MD Publications, 1959), pp. 19-48.

[12]Richard Dawkins and Steven Pinker, "Is Science Killing the Soul?" (The Guardian-Dillons Debate, chaired by Tim Radford, Westminster Hall, London, February 10, 1999), *Edge* 53 (April 8, 1999), <http://www.edge.org/documents/archive/edge53.html>, accessed on January 2, 2004).

gap" regarding how the physical correlates of a phenomenal state are related to our subjective feelings of that state.[13]

Unrest around these issues, especially among philosophers, has yielded a plethora of options, including, for example, substance dualism, naturalistic dualism, holistic dualism, emergent dualism, two-aspect monism, reflexive monism, constitutional materialism, nonreductive physicalism and eliminative materialism.[14] With this renaissance in philosophical attention, the debate has come full circle, since, in Western thought, its beginnings can be traced to the dualism of Plato (c. 429-347 B.C.), the monism of Aristotle (384-322 B.C.) and the range of metaphysical permutations aligned along this continuum.[15] Even as early as the late fifth century B.C., however, treatises written by (and attributed to) Hippocrates, the famous physician of classical antiquity, weighed in on the relation of σῶμα (sōma, "body") and ψυχή (psychē, "soul," "self," "personality"); and historically the terms of this debate have been correlated with anatomical and physiological factors, especially as these have been related to concerns of a religious sort. That is, the mind-body problem has long been the gathering point for wide-ranging perspectives—philosophy, theology, the natural sciences and the psychological sciences, among the most prominent.

In the chapters that follow, the contributors devote considerable attention

---

[13]See Joseph Levine, "Materialism and Qualia: The Explanatory Gap," *Pacific Philosophical Quarterly* 64 (1983): 354-61; Susan Greenfield, "Soul, Brain and Mind," in *From Soul to Self*, ed. M. James C. Crabbe (London: Routledge, 1999), pp. 108-25.

[14]For substance dualism, see, e.g., Richard Swinburne, *The Evolution of the Soul*, rev. ed. (Oxford: Clarendon, 1997). For naturalistic dualism, see David J. Chalmers, *The Conscious Mind: In Search of a Fundamental Theory* (Oxford: Oxford University Press, 1996). For holistic dualism, see John W. Cooper, *Body, Soul and Life Everlasting: Biblical Anthropology and the Monism-Dualism Debate*, 2nd ed. (Grand Rapids: Eerdmans, 2000). For emergent dualism, see William Hasker, *The Emergent Self* (Ithaca, N.Y.: Cornell University Press, 1999). For two-aspect monism, see Malcolm A. Jeeves, *Human Nature at the Millennium: Reflections on the Integration of Psychology and Christianity* (Grand Rapids: Baker, 1997). For reflexive monism, see Max Velmans, *Understanding Consciousness* (London: Routledge, 2000). For constitutional materialism, see Kevin J. Corcoran, "Persons and Bodies," *Faith and Philosophy* 15 (1998): 324-39; Lynne Rudder Baker, *Persons and Bodies: A Constitution View*, Cambridge Studies in Philosophy (Cambridge: Cambridge University Press, 2000). For nonreductive physicalism, see Nancey Murphy, "Nonreductive Physicalism: Philosophical Issues," in *Whatever Happened to the Soul? Scientific and Theological Portraits of Human Nature*, ed. Warren S. Brown, Nancey Murphy and H. Newton Malony, Theology and the Sciences (Minneapolis: Fortress, 1998), pp. 127-48. For eliminative materialism, see Paul M. Churchland, *The Engine of Reason, The Seat of the Soul: A Philosophical Journey into the Brain* (Cambridge, Mass.: MIT Press, 1995).

[15]For historical perspective, see John P. Wright and Paul Potter, eds., *Psyche and Soma: Physicians and Metaphysicians on the Mind-Body Problem from Antiquity to Enlightenment* (Oxford: Clarendon, 2000); Paul S. MacDonald, *History of the Concept of Mind: Speculations about Soul, Mind and Spirit from Homer to Hume* (Aldershot, U.K.: Ashgate, 2003).

to introducing their respective positions and attendant vocabulary. By way of anticipating those more expansive discussions, it may be helpful to provide some linguistic and conceptual orientation.

Arranged along a continuum, perspectives championed today can be characterized as more or less materialist, more or less dualist. On the extreme poles are two positions, (reductive) materialism and radical dualism, both of which are difficult to square with Christian theological commitments. Dispersed between these two poles are other generous categories within which the debate among Christians tends to be localized.

*Reductive materialism* has it that the human person is a physical (or material) organism whose emotional, moral and religious experiences will ultimately be explained by the natural sciences. People are nothing but the product of organic chemistry. As Francis Crick has famously remarked, " 'You,' your joys and your sorrows, your memories and your ambitions, your sense of identity and free will, are in fact no more than the behavior of a vast assembly of nerve cells and their associated molecules."[16]

*Radical dualism* puts forward the view that the soul (or mind) is separable from the body, having no necessary relation to the body, with the human person identified with the soul. Apart from further qualification or explanation, in this view the soul acts apart from bodily processes, and the body is nothing more than a temporary and disposable holding tank for the soul.

*Holistic dualism* in its various renditions qualifies as a form of substance dualism, but it posits that the human person, though composed of discrete elements, is nonetheless to be identified with the whole, which then constitutes a functional unity. "The soul and the body are highly interactive, they enter into deep causal relations and functional dependencies with each other, the human person is a unity of both."[17] As will become clear in the essays that follow, the substance dualism of Goetz (chap. 2) and the emergent dualism of Hasker (chap. 3) can be located within this broad category.

Various forms of *monism* defended among Christians require no second metaphysical entity, such as a soul or spirit, to account for human capacities and distinctives, while insisting that human behavior cannot be explained exhaustively with recourse to genetics or neuroscience. Using various models, these monists argue that the phenomenological experiences that we label

---

[16]Francis Crick, *The Astonishing Hypothesis: The Scientific Search for the Soul* (New York: Simon & Schuster, 1994), p. 3.

[17]J. P. Moreland, "Restoring the Substance to the Soul of Psychology," *Journal of Psychology and Theology* 26 (1998): 35.

"soul" are not reducible to brain activity and represent essential aspects or capacities of the self, rather than a substantial, ontological entity such as a "soul." Two of those models are presented in this book: Murphy's nonreductive physicalism (chap. 4) and Corcoran's constitution view of the human person (chap. 5).

Although sometimes presumed in popular discussion, a *tripartite* view of the human person is only rarely found in biblical studies or in the theological literature; according to this view, the human being is made up of three ontologically separate entities—body, soul and spirit.[18]

### *Theology, Christian Scripture and Science: Points of Departure*

One of the first sets of questions that we who are interested in understanding the human person from a Christian vantage point must address has to do with the sources of our knowledge. Whatever else Christians do, we work with constraints such as Scripture, experience and the Christian tradition. Of these, the last is the only one that has, until recently, spoken with almost one voice; Christian tradition is practically univocal in its presumption of some form of anthropological dualism.[19] Much less easy to summarize is how Christians will account for the findings of the natural sciences, since Christians have embraced different approaches.[20]

*Anthropology and science.* What, then, of the natural sciences? Should neuroscience, in particular, provide yet another constraint in Christian anthropology? In fact, the concept of God's "two books," the Bible and the natural world, was a regular fixture in seventeenth-century English natural theology. Accordingly, science and religion could not be viewed as antagonists, for science was simply an investigation into God's creation. As Augustine had written centuries earlier, "Some people read books in order to find God. But the very appearance of God's creation is a great book." He advised, "Ponder heaven and earth religiously."[21]

---

[18]In propagating this view, the work of Watchman Nee has been surprisingly influential. See his *The Spiritual Man*, 3 vols. (New York: Christian Fellowship, 1968). See now John C. Garrison, *The Psychology of the Spirit: A Contemporary System of Biblical Psychology* (n.p.: Xlibris, 2001); cf. Edward J. Cumella, "Bio-Psycho-Social-Spiritual: Completing the Model," *Remuda Review* 1, no. 1 (2002): 1-5.

[19]That the earliest tradition was marked by some diversity at this point is suggested in Etienne Gilson, *The Spirit of Medieval Philosophy* (New York: Charles Scribner's Sons, 1936), p. 172.

[20]For an overview and a compelling argument concerning the hyperbole of reported tensions between science and Christian faith, see Denis Alexander, *Rebuilding the Matrix: Science and Faith in the Twenty-first Century* (Grand Rapids: Zondervan, 2001).

[21]Augustine *Sermo Mai* 126; English translation in Karlfried Froehlich, " 'Take Up and Read': Basics of Augustine's Biblical Interpretation," *Interpretation* 58 (2004): 12.

Science must be taken seriously, first, on account of our doctrine of creation. This means that, for the Christian, inquiry starts not from "science," but from the Christian tradition in its understanding of nature in its creatureliness. Of course, until the modern era, there was no need for navigating science-theology relations, since science, philosophy and religion composed the same vocation, proceeded from the same intellectual impulses and focused on the same subject matter. On account of the Christian doctrine of creation, theology is an all-encompassing enterprise, so that the subsequent segregation of science from theology could never mean that science would fall outside the purview of theology. Insofar as science is present as one of the sources for the theological enterprise, theology remains open to the possibility of reformulation on account of scientific discovery. It is not only that our doctrine of creation urges a unitary approach to knowledge, pressing us to account for natural science in our theological work, however. There are also considerations of an epistemological sort—considerations, that is, which focus on how we know what we know. Accordingly, we must account for the reality that natural science is, and has always been, part of our worldview. The two, science and theology, interact in a more organic way than we often acknowledge, with the result that it is virtually impossible to extricate the one influence from the other. This is true of the "science" presumed of the biblical writers and of the "science" presumed of biblical interpreters and theologians from the second century onward. We have before us a long history of interpreters of biblical texts who have engaged those texts on the basis of scientific views of the human person pervasive in the worlds of the interpreters.

What is contemporary science telling us about the human person? Neuroscientists almost exclusively speak of human life in terms of embodiment as physical persons. Typically, they do this on account of the complex and subtle dependencies of our thought processes on the state and functioning of our brains. They might draw attention to any variety of research reports from the last year or two, including the following:

- experimental data demonstrating that the psychological pain of social loss, such as the loss of a loved one, has neural correlates in the prefrontal cortex and the anterior cingulate cortex, suggesting a "human sadness system" in the brain[22]

- the use of functional magnetic resonance imaging (fMRI) to show that the

---

[22]Naomi I. Eisenberger et al., "Does Rejection Hurt? An fMRI Study of Social Exclusion," *Science* 302, no. 5643 (2003): 290-92.

orbital and medial prefrontal cortex and the superior temporal sulcus regions of the brain play a central role in humans' moral appraisals, demonstrating a neural substrate for the emotions by which we assign moral values to events, objects and actions[23]

- research, popularized in *Newsweek*, indicating that when a person intends to suppress unwanted memories, his or her prefrontal cortex is involved in dampening activity in the hippocampus, a subcortical structure implicated in memory retrieval[24]

- evidence that communicative intention between persons is signaled by the activation of two common brain regions (namely, the paracingulate cortex and temporal poles bilaterally), the same areas of the brain that are activated when people are asked to consider the mental states of others[25]

- research, also popularized in *Newsweek*, showing that the experience of motherhood triggers morphological and hormonal alterations in the brain, effecting reductions in anxiety and stress responsiveness[26]

- indications that emotion-induced memory gains and losses depend on a common neurobiological mechanism that can be manipulated by the pharmacological agent propranolol or by damage to the amygdala[27]

- support for the hypothesis that gray matter volume differences in motor, auditory and visual-spatial brain regions (comparing professional musicians with amateur and nonmusicians) is due to structural adaptations in the brain in response to long-term skill acquisition and repetitive rehearsal of those skills[28]

- a study establishing that the brain's anterior cingulate cortex is impli-

[23]Jorge Moll et al., "The Neural Correlates of Moral Sensitivity: A Functional Magnetic Resonance Imaging Investigation of Basic and Moral Emotions," *Journal of Neuroscience* 22, no. 7 (2002): 2730-36.

[24]M. C. Anderson et al., "Neural Systems Underlying the Suppression of Unwanted Memories," *Science* 303, no. 5655 (2004): 232-35; cf. Mary Carmichael, "An Irrepressible Idea," *Newsweek*, January 19, 2004, p. 10.

[25]Knut K. W. Kampe et al., " 'Hey John': Signals Conveying Communicative Intention Toward the Self-Activate Brain Regions Associated with 'Mentalizing,' Regardless of Modality," *Journal of Neuroscience* 23, no. 12 (2003): 5258-63.

[26]Jennifer Wartella et al., "Single or Multiple Reproductive Experiences Attenuate Neurobehavioral Stress and Fear Responses in the Female Rat," *Physiology & Behavior* 79, no. 3 (2003): 373-81; cf. Mary Carmichael, "Mother Knows Best," *Newsweek*, November 17, 2003, p. 8.

[27]B. A. Strange et al., "An Emotion-Induced Retrograde Amnesia in Humans Is Amygdala- and β-Adrenergic-Dependent," *Proceedings of the National Academic of Sciences* 100, no. 23 (2003): 13626-31.

[28]Christian Gaser and Gottfried Schlaug, "Brain Structures Differ between Musicians and Non-Musicians," *Journal of Neuroscience* 23, no. 27 (2003): 9240-45.

cated in monitoring the consequence of one's actions[29]

- confirmation that long-term depression can reshape the brain, shrinking the hippocampus, a subcortical structure implicated in memory[30]

These research results may be combined with often dramatic clinical stories of a patient's altered sense of self due to brain lesion and with related research unveiling the role of the brain in emotion and volition.[31] These data (and their less sophisticated precursors over the past 300 years) have generally led scientists away from belief in a nonmaterial entity, such as a soul, as a way of explaining the human self. And the fact that these research results are increasingly finding their way into the popular press leads us to anticipate that the population at large, including the churched population, will increasingly begin to contemplate their ramifications for what it means to be human.

As a whole, those neuroscientists who are Christians champion the notion of psychosomatic unity, too, though they are careful to avoid the reduction of mental states or spiritual awareness, for example, to neuronal interaction.[32] Evidence of this sort has led theologian Wolfhart Pannenberg to conclude that the close mutual interrelations of physical and psychological occurrences have robbed of their credibility traditional ideas of a soul distinct from the body. "When the life of the soul is conditioned in every detail by bodily organs and processes, how can it be detached from the body and survive without it?"[33]

How will such research results as these be factored into the philosophical and theological debate on the mind-brain, body-soul problem? Will science join Scripture, the Christian tradition and experience as constraints on the discussion?

[29]Shigehiko Ito et al., "Performance Monitoring by the Anterior Cingulate Cortex During Saccade Countermanding," *Science* 302, no. 5642 (2003): 120-22.

[30]Constance Holden, "Future Brightening for Depression Treatments," *Science* 302, no. 5646 (2003): 810-13.

[31]These connections were suggested in the cases described over three decades ago in Oliver Sacks, *The Man Who Mistook His Wife for a Hat and Other Clinical Tales* (New York: Simon & Schuster, 1970). More recently, see Antonio R. Damasio, *Descartes' Error: Emotion, Reason and the Human Brain* (New York: Putnam, 1994); idem, *The Feeling of What Happens: Body and Emotion in the Making of Consciousness* (New York: Harcourt, 1999); Todd E. Feinberg, *Altered Egos: How the Brain Creates the Self* (Oxford: Oxford University Press, 2001). On emotion and volition, see also Joseph LeDoux, *The Emotional Brain: The Mysterious Underpinnings of Emotional Life* (London: Weidenfeld & Nicolson, 1998); Elkhonon Goldberg, *The Executive Brain: Frontal Lobes and the Civilized Mind* (Oxford: Oxford University Press, 2001); Benjamin Libet et al., eds., *The Volitional Brain: Towards a Neuroscience of Free Will* (Thorverton: Imprint Academic, 1999).

[32]Most recently, cf. Jeeves, ed., *From Cells to Souls*.

[33]Wolfhart Pannenberg, *Systematic Theology* (Grand Rapids: Eerdmans, 1994), 2:182.

*Anthropology and Scripture.* What of Scripture? Does the Bible teach either monism or body-soul dualism? Any number of texts could be marshaled in support of a manifestly affirmative response on behalf of dualism: for example, "Do not fear those who kill the body but cannot kill the soul; rather fear him who can destroy both soul and body in hell" (Mt 10:28) or "Then Jesus, crying with a loud voice, said, 'Father, into your hands I commend my spirit' " (Lk 23:46).

Until recently, the view of many theologians would have been that the Old Testament assumes or bears witness to anthropological monism, whereas the New Testament supports a dualist rendering of the human person, body and soul. Biblical scholars who have addressed the question, on the other hand, are almost unanimous in their conclusion that both Old and New Testaments assume or testify to an anthropological monism. This is not because biblical scholars have been influenced by neuroscientific research, but rather because of shifts in the discipline of biblical studies itself, among which two are especially important.

First, we now recognize that the longstanding and pervasive view that posited a dichotomy between Hebrew thought (which affirmed some form of monism) and Greek thought (which affirmed some form of dualism) was a gross caricature. This is because, on the one hand, Greek thought was more variegated on the nature of the soul than a reading focused on Plato (or on some first-century Neo-Platonists) would allow. There simply was no singular conception of the soul among the Greeks, and the body-soul relationship was variously assessed among philosophers and physicians in the Hellenistic period.[34] For example, Heinrich von Staden summarizes "the belief cluster" shared by philosophers and physicians of the Hellenistic period by noting, among other things, that the "soul" is corporeal, and that the "soul" is generated with the "body" and neither exists before the body nor is separable from it after the body's demise. That is, "the soul does not exist independently of the body in which it exists."[35] What happens after we die? It may be useful to refer to Cicero, who summarizes the two primary competing views: either the body and soul are annihilated at death or the soul separates from the body.[36] This is

---

[34]See, e.g., Wright and Potter, eds., *Psyche and Soma;* Dale B. Martin, *The Corinthian Body* (New Haven, Conn.: Yale University Press, 1995), pp. 3-37.

[35]Heinrich von Staden, "Body, Soul and Nerves: Epicurus, Herophilus, Erasistratus, the Stoics and Galen," in *Psyche and Soma: Physicians and Metaphysicians on the Mind-Body Problem from Antiquity to Enlightenment,* ed. John P. Wright and Paul Potter (Oxford: Clarendon, 2000), pp. 79-116 (79).

[36]Cicero *Tusculan Disputations* 1.11.23-24.

hardly the dualism widely assumed to characterize "the Greeks" in the Hellenistic and Roman periods.

On the other hand, one must speak of the complex relationship of Hellenism and Judaism characterizing the centuries after the military successes of Alexander the Great in the Near East in the last half of the fourth century B.C.—relationships of acculturation, to be sure, but otherwise on a continuum between resistance and integration. Consequently, the environment within which the New Testament was taking shape provided for the presence of a variety of views, both within Roman Hellenism and within Hellenistic Judaism. For both of these reasons, it is erroneous to allege that the New Testament authors lived in a milieu pervaded by body-soul dualism. For these reasons, too, it is easy to understand how Graham Warne could reach the conclusion that the apostle Paul was a monist but Philo the Alexandrian Jew a dualist, in spite of the fact that these two Jewish writers lived at approximately the same time and under similar religious and philosophical influences.[37]

Second, advances in linguistics, following the work of Ferdinand de Saussure in the early twentieth century, disallow the confusion between words and concepts, and thus call into question the erroneous view that, say, the Greek term ψυχή *(psychē) means* "soul" and therefore refers to (something like) an ontological entity separate from the σῶμα *(sōma,* "body"). Although ψυχή *could* refer to "soul," understood within the framework of a body-soul dualism, this *cannot* be presumed on lexical grounds. Aristotle, for example, devotes an entire treatise to "the soul" (ΠΕΡΙ ΨΥΧΗΣ, "On the Soul"), and defines ψυχή in terms of what we today would designate a physicalist account of human nature, just as the Septuagint, a Greek translation of Israel's Scriptures dating from the Hellenistic period, typically translates the Hebrew נֶפֶשׁ *(nepeš,* "vitality") with ψυχή, without thereby introducing anthropological dualism into the Old Testament. In fact, נֶפֶשׁ occurs almost 800 times in the Old Testament, with the primary meaning of "throat" or "gullet" (very much a physical referent!) and with the extended sense of "vitality" or "the impulse of life over against death." When used anthropologically, its typical use is with reference to the entire human being, not to a portion of the person. Persons in the Old Testament "do not think of themselves in a subject-object relationship (spirit and soul); the subject in particular is not thematic. On the basis of being alive, of individuation within life, of perceiv-

---

[37]Graham J. Warne, *Hebrew Perspectives on the Human Person in the Hellenistic Era: Philo and Paul* (Lewiston, N.Y.: Mellen, 1995).

ing life as an in-and-out rhythm (breathing?), they find themselves to be living quanta with respect to *hayyîm*, life."[38]

Of course, we should acknowledge the ease with which we in the modern era might read a Cartesian interest in "the mind" back into the Bible. Given the importance of the horizons of our own assumptions in acts of reading and interpretation, and given the pervasive influence of the Cartesian idea of a disembodied mind even today, it is no surprise that many readers of the Bible have found body-soul dualism in its pages. We can illustrate the problem with reference to Western medicine, where the Cartesian mind-body split is so fully on display. Only with slight hyperbole can Trinh Xuan Thuan remark, "To this day, the brain and mind are regarded as two distinct entities in Western medicine. When we have a headache, we consult a neurologist; when we are depressed, we are told to see a psychiatrist."[39] Given this way of structuring reality, why would we not unreflectively segregate healing (biomedical) from salvation (spiritual)?[40] In the Old Testament, however, the identity of God as "healer" is preeminently focused on deliverance for the people of God; "I, Yahweh, am your healer," God's people are told, following the narration of the incredible lengths to which Yahweh has gone to liberate Israel from Egypt (Ex 15:26, my translation; see 2 Kings 5:7). In Scripture as a whole, when it comes to Yahweh's saving acts on behalf of his people, we find little room indeed for segregating the human person into discrete, constitutive "parts," whether "bodily" or "spiritual" or "communal."

Persons who find evidence for dualism in the Scriptures sometimes point to evidence of a different sort—to a biblical eschatology that requires a disembodied intermediate state, for example, or to the story of the witch of Endor in 1 Samuel 28, which seems to require the presence of Samuel's "soul" at Endor. With regard to 1 Samuel 28, however, Bill Arnold has cataloged evidence especially from the early history of Christian interpretation of this story demonstrating that no consensus has emerged that would defend a traditional dualism. Although he is himself cautious about what conclusions might be reached about the anthropology assumed by this text, he does observe that those interpretations assuming a physicalist approach are closer to the ancient Israelite

---

[38]H. Seebass, "נֶפֶשׁ," in *Theological Dictionary of the Old Testament*, vol. 9, ed. G. Johannes Botterweck et al. (Grand Rapids: Eerdmans, 1998), pp. 503-4; see Seebass's excursus, "The Translation 'Soul,'" pp. 508-10.

[39]Trinh Xuan Thuan, *Chaos and Harmony: Perspectives on Scientific Revolutions of the Twentieth Century* (Oxford: Oxford University Press, 2001), p. 294.

[40]For a prominent example of this bifurcation, see John Wilkinson, *The Bible and Healing: A Medical and Theological Commentary* (Grand Rapids: Eerdmans, 1998).

worldview.[41] Regarding the intermediate state, the evidence is also less than straightforward whether Scripture and/or its earliest interpreters assumed or taught an intermediate state or, if an intermediate state is presumed, whether it would be disembodied.[42]

In short, simple appeal to "what the Bible teaches" will not resolve those anthropological questions arising from discussion of body and soul, mind and brain. It is worth asking, though, whether a reading of the narrative of Scripture as a whole accounts best for a view of the human person characterized by dualism or by monism. Theological interpretation of Scripture will need more textured attention than it has generally attracted if the biblical materials are to speak faithfully to these issues.

*Anthropology and experience.* In discussion of Christian anthropology generally, appeal is made to two kinds of human experience: (1) I am more than my body, and (2) I experience all manner of sensations in a unified way. Both have to do with our experience of a subjective inner life—the perceptions, thoughts, feelings and awareness of my experiences, including what it is like to be a cognitive agent. This subjective, firsthand quality of experience goes by the shorthand "consciousness,"[43] and, for most of us, it is difficult to believe that our first-person experiences of embarrassment or fulfillment, love or hate, and smells or colors are nothing more than brain states.

How do we explain consciousness? How can I be aware that, at this very moment, I am crafting this sentence and employing a word processor, without being aware of the underlying neural processes at work in my doing so? Simply put, no one knows, and this has led to two different sorts of approaches. One is to posit the existence of a soul, by which I recognize as a singular, unified experience what is otherwise a fractured and complex set of interactions and sensations. In order to explain my experience of a unified consciousness, that is, something beyond the physical is required. In the absence of an accepted neuroscientific explanation, the appeal to a non-material solution is especially attractive, though, of course, one of the possibilities in this argument of which we should be wary is the devolution of the whole discussion into a soul-of-the-gaps explanation: since it cannot be

---

[41]See Bill T. Arnold, "Soul-Searching Questions About 1 Samuel 28: Samuel's Appearance at Endor and Christian Anthropology," in *What About the Soul? Neuroscience and Christian Anthropology,* ed. Joel B. Green (Nashville: Abingdon, 2004), pp. 75-83.

[42]See, e.g., Brian Edgar, "Biblical Anthropology and the Intermediate State," *Evangelical Quarterly* 74 (2002): 27-45, 109-21; Joel B. Green, "Eschatology and the Nature of Humans: A Reconsideration of the Pertinent Biblical Evidence," *Science & Christian Belief* 14 (2002): 33-50.

[43]I have borrowed this attempt at definition from Chalmers, *Conscious Mind.*

explained by the natural sciences, it must be supernatural.

Of course, the lack of an explanation for consciousness is not regarded as a deterrent by persons otherwise convinced by nondualist anthropologies. How might conscious selfhood, comprising subjective experience and autonomous agency, arise from causal chains of events in the material world? Thomas Metzinger, a German philosopher who has written extensively on the matter, replies that, in reality, there are no autonomous selves in the physical world; rather, our "selves" are ongoing processes that allow each of us to conceive of ourselves as wholes, thus enabling us to interact causally with our inner and outer environments in an entirely new, integrated and intelligent manner.[44] Antonio Damasio, seeking the neurobiological underpinnings of consciousness, speaks not of a single neural site or center of "the self," but rather of one's sense of self arising through a complex of crossregional integrations of neural activity; other neuroscientists similarly present models of consciousness that depend on an intricate choreography of distributed populations of neurons and neuronal systems.[45] In these discussions, it is not uncommon to hear talk of emergent capacities, even of "soul" in the sense of powers of mind that arise from our bodies and brains (rather than as an entity distinct from the body).[46]

One of the crucial factors urging a nested, physicalist understanding of consciousness is evidence from lesion studies that consciousness is abolished by widely distributed damage rather than by localized cortical damage to the brain. The failure or alteration of the experience of selfhood (as this is experienced by most of us) among those whose brains are damaged by traumatic injury or disease—the reality, for example, of persons who experience themselves as being nonexistent (Cotard's syndrome), of persons who fail to recognize a part of their own bodies or who totally reject it (asomatognosia),

---

[44]Thomas Metzinger, *Being No One: The Self-Model Theory of Subjectivity* (Cambridge, Mass.: MIT Press, 2003). For extensive discussion on a variety of approaches to the question of consciousness, see Metzinger's edited volumes: *Conscious Experience* (Paderborn: Schöningh, 1995) and *Neural Correlates of Consciousness: Empirical and Conceptual Questions* (Cambridge, Mass.: MIT Press, 2000).

[45]Damasio, *Feeling of What Happens*. Compare, e.g., Wolf Singer, "Phenomenal Awareness and Consciousness from a Neurobiological Perspective," in *Neural Correlates of Consciousness: Empirical and Conceptual Questions*, ed. Thomas Metzinger (Cambridge: MIT Press, 2000), pp. 121-37; Gerald M. Edelman and Giulio Tononi, "Reentry and the Dynamic Core: Neural Correlates of Conscious Experience," in *Neural Correlates of Consciousness: Empirical and Conceptual Questions*, ed. Thomas Metzinger (Cambridge, Mass.: MIT Press, 2000), pp. 139-51.

[46]From different perspectives, e.g., Jeffrey M. Schwartz and Sharon Begley, *The Mind and the Brain: Neuroplasticity and the Power of Mental Force* (New York: HarperCollins, 2002); Keith Ward, *In Defence of the Soul* (Oxford: OneWorld, 1992); Fraser Watts, *Theology and Psychology*, Ashgate Science and Religion Series (Aldershot, U.K.: Ashgate, 2002).

of persons whose sense of relatedness to others is severely compromised (e.g., Capgras syndrome), and of persons who experience the presence of two purposeful minds (some callosotomy patients)—argues strongly for taking seriously the importance of the brain in explaining the experience of unitary consciousness. Nevertheless, for the majority of us, it remains difficult to overcome the sense that bodies and brains are just different sorts of things than feelings and thoughts and intentions, and, undoubtedly, this is one reason for the persistence of a dualist accounting of the human person.

## Body and Soul: Complexities and Controversies

These ruminations have suggested the complexity of the issues before us, particularly with regard to the range of considerations bearing on Christian thinking about the nature of humanity. What role will these sources of knowledge play? What ought one to make of the Christian tradition with its staunch testimony to some form of body-soul dualism? How will Scripture inform the discussion? What is one to make of mounting evidence from the natural sciences? What role might our experience of conscious selfhood play?

Having placed these considerations side by side in this way, I hope that I have demonstrated why the debate is ongoing. Whether one is thinking, say, of Scripture or human experience, we find no knockdown arguments favoring one view to the exclusion of another. Instead, we press ahead by insisting that all of the relevant data be considered and that those who join the conversation make plain how these different sources of knowledge are to be heard and mobilized.

It remains, finally, to sketch a series of questions that make so important the present discussion concerning the nature of the human person. I want to develop a selection of such issues briefly in order to underscore what is at stake in the debate and why Christians need to be fully engaged in it.

*Are we (only) animals?* When confronted with the sorts of issues with which this book is concerned, many persons who are new to the discussion are stunned by the presumed inference of monism that we are nothing but animals. Apart from the soul, what is it that separates us from cats and dogs, monkeys and shrimp other than, perhaps, the complexity of our brains? In his first novel, *Watchers,* Dean Koontz, famous for his fictional explorations of the paranormal, introduces a genetically engineered golden retriever, Einstein, who complains about the tattoo identification in his ear. It "marked him as mere property, a condition that was an affront to his dignity and a violation of his rights as an intelligent creature." In reply, Nora, his human conversation partner, observes, " 'I do understand. You are a . . . a *person,* and a person with'—this was the first time she had thought of this aspect of the situation—

'a soul.' " She continues, "If you've got a soul—and I know you do—then you were born with free will and the right to self-determination."[47] We may be stunned by this attribution of a soul to a dog, even a genetically enhanced one, or we may puzzle over the ready conclusion that free will and self-determination are necessarily tied to the canine possession of a soul. What may be even more interesting, though, is how statements of this sort find their way into best-selling books in the late twentieth century. After all, only three decades before, in *I, Robot*, Isaac Asmiov had portrayed robots with traits that others might have reserved for humans. Robbie the robot, for example, wants to "hear a story," is "faithful and loving and kind" and is even called "my friend . . . not no machine" by his young companion, Gloria. Gloria's mother is nonetheless clear that Robbie is "nothing more than a mess of steel and copper in the form of sheets and wires with electricity." "It has no soul" and so should never be confused with a human being.[48] Apparently, how to draw the line between humans and other animals or between humans and machines, or whether there are such lines to be drawn, is on the minds of folks around us.

We know that from a genetic perspective, humans and chimpanzees share some 99 percent of their genetic sequences, with significant differences between them expressed in nuclear transport and olfaction.[49] We have evidence that brown capuchin monkeys are capable of demanding equitable exchanges and that monkeys engage in goal-oriented decision making.[50] And now we are told that fish have some level of consciousness—a sense of awareness, though not an awareness of self.[51] Scripture itself teaches us that we are made of the stuff of the earth, like other animals; that we are given the breath of life (נֶפֶשׁ, *nepeš*, "vitality," sometimes translated "soul") just as other animals are; and that our destiny is enmeshed with that of the rest of creation (Gen 1—2; Rom 8:19-23). If, in the mind of many, what distinguishes the human person from other creatures is human possession of the soul, what are we to make of the singular lack of support for this view in Scripture itself? How might a portrait of the human person answer the question, Are we nothing but animals?

---

[47]Dean Koontz, *Watchers* (New York: Berkley, 1987), p. 434.
[48]Isaac Asimov, *I, Robot* (New York: Doubleday, 1950), pp. 5, 9, 23.
[49]Andrew G. Clark et al., "Inferring Nonneutral Evolution from Human-Chimp-Mouse Orthologous Gene Trios," *Science* 302, no. 5652 (2003): 1960-63.
[50]S. Milius, "Unfair Trade: Monkeys Demand Equitable Exchanges," *Science News* 164 (2003): 181; Kenji Matsumoto et al., "Neuronal Correlates of Goal-Based Motor Selection in the Prefrontal Cortex," *Science* 301, no. 5630 (2003): 229-32.
[51]James Gorman, "Fishing for Clarity in the Waters of Consciousness," *The New York Times*, May 13, 2003, <www.nytimes.com/2003/05/13/science/life/13ESSA.html?ei+5070&en =75a4c333c9e>, accessed on June 6, 2003.

*Are we of sacred worth?* It has often been imagined, and has now been stringently argued by J. P. Moreland and Scott Rae, that body-soul dualism, with the person identified with soul, is necessary if we are to confer on humans, and especially the most vulnerable among us, a protective canopy.[52] Those in a persistent vegetative state, the comatose, those with advanced dementia—such persons are worthy of all of the moral consideration and standing we might confer on the healthy because the soul remains. That belief in an immaterial soul identifiable with the real person has served to extend sacred worth to human beings is undeniable.[53] Is this necessarily so? Human history demonstrates that this is not the case; witness, for example, the appeal to a person's not having a soul as a means of legitimating the oppression and abuse of human slavery, whether in Roman antiquity or in early America. If human dignity and worth are not tied to human possession of a soul, as monists might want to argue, for what reasons might we extend sacred worth to persons? Particularly, on what basis might we extend love to the most imperiled among us?

*Do I have a choice?* Whether one turns to Steven Spielberg's *Minority Report* or the Wachowski brothers' *Matrix* trilogy, in many corners today we find popular expression of the public unease with reports, often alleged to represent science, of human determinism. Unless we are seeking to befuddle a jury in a legal case, we resist a bottom-line conclusion that "my genes made me do it." Simple notions of genetic determinism are universally rejected,[54] but the possibility of libertarian free will, the exercise of volition outside the realm of causation, continues to be discussed. It is especially here, on the battlefield of free will, that various forms of dualism and varieties of monism remain locked in struggle. This is not surprising, perhaps, given David Hume's judgment that the problem of free will is "the most contentious question of metaphysics, the most contentious science."[55] Generally speaking, for the dualist, the only way to preserve free will—at least, that variety of free will worth having—is to posit a nonmaterial entity, the soul, that is not caught in the chain of cause and effect.

Of course, body-soul dualism thus brings up a further problem: namely,

---

[52]Moreland and Rae, *Body and Soul*.

[53]See, e.g., Stephen G. Post, "A Moral Case for Nonreductive Physicalism," in *Whatever Happened to the Soul? Scientific and Theological Portraits of Human Nature*, ed. Warren S. Brown, Nancey Murphy and H. Newton Malony, Theology and the Sciences (Minneapolis: Fortress, 1998), pp. 195-213 (esp. pp. 197-202).

[54]Compare Ted Peters, *Playing God? Genetic Determinism and Human Freedom* (New York: Routledge, 1997); Daniel C. Dennett, "The Mythical Threat of Genetic Determinism," *Chronicle of Higher Education*, January 31, 2003, B7-9.

[55]David Hume, *Enquiry Concerning Human Understanding* (Oxford: Clarendon, 1975), p. 95.

how an immaterial soul can interact with and guide the activity of a material body. Interestingly, whereas many recent substance dualists are happy to leave the problem of body-soul interaction in the realm of the mysterious, or even to dismiss its force altogether, one of the key figures in the history of neuroscience, Emanuel Swedenborg (1688-1772), regarded agnosticism on this matter as the path to atheism. Though known today primarily for his theological mysticism and the church that bears his name, this polymath devoted his whole life, he tells us, to "the search for the soul," which in turn led him to an exhaustive analysis of all that was currently known about the brain. By the turn of the eighteenth century, Descartes's hypothesis that the "seat of the

soul" was localized in the pineal gland had given way to an alternative hypothesis, focused on the cerebrospinal fluid in the brain's ventricles. Swedenborg's examination of all available physiological data led him to conclude, rather, that "it is the cerebrum through which the intercourse between the soul and the body is established; for it is as it were the link and the uniting medium."[56] Interestingly, Swedenborg's dualism did not lead to the free will so important to many dualists. Rather, since influx from God flows into the soul and from the soul into the mind, which in turn activates the body, in the end

free will is an illusion, for it is actually God's will that activates the body through the conduit of the soul.

Attempts to account for human volition among nondualists have been extensive and varied, with many adopting a compatibilist form of free will, arguing that deliberation and volition may coexist with causal chains. In a collection of studies published under the title *The Volitional Brain: Towards a Neuroscience of Free Will*, scholars representing diverse fields report on the neurobiology of volition and present psychological and philosophical perspectives as well as contributions from physics. The correlation of the exercise of volition with neural mechanisms located in the prefrontal cortex and, conversely, observations that persons with symptoms of a "sick will" (e.g., inactivity, lack of ambition, autistic behavior, depressive motor and behavioral inhibition) demonstrate subnormal activity in the prefrontal cortex suggest a neural substrate for decision making. Interestingly, in one set of reported ex-

---

[56]Emanuel Swedenborg, *The Brain: Considered Anatomically, Physiologically and Philosophically*, ed. R. L. Tafel, 4 vols. (London: James Speirs, 1882), 1:67 (italic in original). For an introduction to Swedenborg's neurology, see Martin Ramström, *Emanuel Swedenborg's Investigations into Natural Science and the Basis for His Statements Concerning the Function of the Brain* (Uppsala: University of Uppsula Press, 1910). On the search for "the seat of the soul," see more fully, G. W. Bruyn, "The Seat of the Soul," in *Historical Aspects of the Neurosciences: A Festschrift for Macdonald Critchley*, ed. F. Clifford Rose and W. F. Bynum (New York: Raven, 1982), pp. 55-81.

periments, electroencephalograph monitoring of brain waves suggested that the awareness of decision making occurred *subsequent to the action itself.*[57]

In *Neurophilosophy of Free Will*, philosopher Henrik Walter argues that a "moderate version of free will" is compatible with what we are learning from neuroscience, whereas in another monograph psychologist Daniel Wegner speaks frankly of "the illusion of conscious will," insisting that "although the experience of conscious will is not evidence of mental causation, it does signal personal authorship of action to the individual and so influences both the sense of achievement and the acceptance of moral responsibility."[58] Owen Flanagan, another philosopher who has worked to take seriously what we know from neuroscience, insists "there is a robust conception of free agency that does not require us to be metaphysically free." The scenario he paints is one in which "genes and life experiences feed into a brain that has, as one of its properties, the capacity to process and access information consciously or subconsciously in a way that is one important contribution to, possibly the proximate cause of, a decision."[59] Coming at the issue from an altogether different vantage point, from the perspective of game theory, Paul Glimcher argues that the whole debate about decision making has been hampered by the incapacity of either classic dualism or monism to account for behavior in all of its complexity. Glimcher's research allows him actually to monitor the path of decision making in the brain as the decision is in process, and it leads to a description of our subjective experience of decision making as a mixed strategy solution requiring the activation of a lawful neuronal randomizer. Like many who have joined this debate, Glimcher urges that our experiences and ideas about free will are the consequence of longstanding cultural explanations and that these are in need of reexamination. He concludes that "real animals must be both physical and indeterminate, a possibility Descartes never considered."[60]

Clearly, the last word on the question of free will has not been written. In fact, when it comes to squaring long-held beliefs about our abilities to choose with what we find to be the case in brain research, the first pages are only now being penned. It is manifestly important for all but the most deterministic versions of Christian theology that God has endowed human beings with the ca-

---

[57]Libet et al., eds., *Volitional Brain;* cf. also Goldberg, *Executive Brain.*

[58]Henrik Walter, *Neurophilosophy of Free Will: From Libertarian Illusions to a Concept of Natural Autonomy* (Cambridge, Mass.: MIT Press, 2001); Daniel M. Wegner, *The Illusion of Conscious Will* (Cambridge, Mass.: MIT Press, 2002), p. 318.

[59]Owen Flanagan, *The Problem of the Soul: Two Visions of Mind and How to Reconcile Them* (New York: Basic, 2002), p. 116.

[60]Paul W. Glimcher, *Decisions, Uncertainty and the Brain: The Science of Neuroeconomics* (Cambridge, Mass.: MIT Press, 2003), p. 345.

pacity to choose (and do) evil as well as good. What sort of free will this necessitates, whether this requires a nonmaterial soul, and how this resonates with the natural sciences remain contentious areas of discussion.

*What does it mean to be saved? What is the mission of the church?* In the face of budget cuts in the municipal area where my family and I live, the Lexington-Fayette Urban County Government faced hard decisions about competing priorities for funding the arts and social services. The ensuing headline in the *Lexington Herald-Leader* could have appeared in many a congregational newsletter: "Feed the Soul or Feed the Hungry?"[61] This way of thinking is one expression of a longstanding dualism segregating the needs of the body from those of the soul, a dualism easily mapped onto the church's words and practices of Christian mission. There are contrary voices, of course; one thinks, for example, of the Fuller Theological Seminary theologian William A. Dyrness, whose publications have included *Let the Earth Rejoice! A Biblical Theology of Holistic Mission* and, more recently with James Engel, *Changing the Mind of Missions: Where Have We Gone Wrong?*[62] However, there has been very little work indeed on the implications of our portraits of the human person for our vision and practices of evangelism and mission.[63] Instead, the longstanding and widespread assumption that the real person is to be identified with the soul has resulted in the primary attribution of missional interest to the saving of lost souls. Addressing physical needs, in this rendering, has sometimes become a means to an end; witness, for example, the practice of some emergency-relief organizations, which require that the hungry listen to a sermon before partaking of the promised free meal. Without prejudging whether body-soul dualism must lead to a relative deprecation of the body, we can observe nonetheless that body-soul dualism historically has done so when it comes to talk about salvation and practices of Christian mission. Versions of dualism that are more emphatic in their functional holism may have the resources to overcome these tendencies.

Christian monists would take a different viewpoint, since, in their rendering, salvation would be defined in terms of human restoration; and, since the human being is inextricably bound up with the human family and with

---

[61]Rich Copley, "Feed the Soul or Feed the Hungry?" *Lexington Herald-Leader,* June 16, 2002, D1.

[62]William A. Dyrness, *Let the Earth Rejoice! A Biblical Theology of Holistic Mission* (Westchester, Ill.: Crossway, 1983); James F. Engel and William A. Dyrness, *Changing the Mind of Missions: Where Have We Gone Wrong?* (Downers Grove, Ill.: InterVarsity Press, 2000).

[63]See now, however, Michael A. Rynkiewich, "What About the Dust? Missiological Musings on Anthropology," in *What About the Soul? Neuroscience and Christian Anthropology,* ed. Joel B. Green (Nashville: Abingdon, 2004), pp. 133-44.

God's created order, then salvation would of necessity be explicated as fully embodied, as oriented toward human community and as cosmological in scope. "Healing," in this portrait, could not segregate mind and brain, body and soul, person and community, or human and cosmos, with the result that Christian mission would have to be worked out in terms of practices that promote human recovery in the fullest terms. When it comes to "salvation," one could speak only of "human needs" and "human wholeness," and not of "spiritual needs" (as if these could be distinguished). Of course, this would require transformations in other areas of life as well. The rigidly bio-medical model used by most physicians and psychiatrists in the West, the work of pastoral care, practices associated with teaching and learning—these and many others would need re-envisioning in order to address human persons (and not bodies or souls or intellects) in community (and not as isolated agents).[64]

Either way, dualism or monism, those engaged in the discussion about the nature of the human person would do well in serving the church if they were to engage more self-consciously the implications of their work for our understanding of salvation and our words and practices of Christian mission.

*What about life after death?* As numerous Christian interpreters have noted, debate on the reality of a human soul is intricately woven into our hope of immortality. Perhaps the most widespread view has been and still is that personal identity, vested in the soul, is dissociated from the physical body at death; that the soul survives death; and that this makes possible life after death. In most versions of dualism, the presumption at work here is that the soul is able to survive death because it is itself immortal.

At the same time, as Caroline Walker Bynum has demonstrated, Christian belief concerning the resurrection has stubbornly focused on the physicality of both resurrection and ultimate salvation,[65] and today this interest has led to a

---

[64]Compare, e.g., Paul R. McHugh, "Treating the Mind as Well as the Brain," *Chronicle of Higher Education*, November 22, 2002, B14; Virginia T. Holeman, "The Neuroscience of Christian Counseling?" in *What About the Soul? Neuroscience and Christian Anthropology*, ed. Joel B. Green (Nashville: Abingdon, 2004); Stuart L. Palmer, "Pastoral Care and Counseling Without the 'Soul': A Consideration of Emergent Monism," in *What About the Soul? Neuroscience and Christian Anthropology*, ed. Joel B. Green (Nashville: Abingdon, 2004), pp. 159-70.

[65]Caroline Walker Bynum, *The Resurrection of the Body in Western Christianity, 200-1336* (New York: Columbia University Press, 1995). She concludes "that a concern for material and structural continuity showed remarkable persistence even where it seemed almost to require philosophical incoherence, theological equivocation, or aesthetic offensiveness. . . . The materialism of [traditional Christian] eschatology expressed not body-soul dualism but rather a sense of self as psychosomatic unity" (p. 11).

renewed emphasis on the resurrection *of the body,* as the Apostles' Creed has it, as opposed to the immortality of the soul. This view has raised rather difficult questions of its own, since the natural decay of the body, the observable frailty of our physicality, seems to vacate the doctrine of bodily resurrection of all sensibility. In reply, Christian theologians and scientists alike have emphasized that Scripture holds forth no belief that inherent in some part of the human person is the quality of immortality; rather, Scripture teaches that the hope of life after death is rooted solely in the gracious intervention of God to bring forth life. As John Polkinghorne reasons,

> It seems a coherent belief that God will remember and reconstitute the pattern that is a human being, in an act of resurrection that takes place beyond present history. Thus the Christian hope centers on a real death followed by a real resurrection, brought about through the power and merciful faithfulness of God. Christianity is not concerned with a claim that there is human survival because there is an intrinsically immortal, purely spiritual, part in our being. The ground of hope for a destiny beyond death does not lie in human nature at all, but in divine, steadfast love.[66]

If not through persistence of this body, how might continuity of personal identity, from death to life after death, be guaranteed? How can I be sure that the *me* that enjoys eternal life is really *me?* Here we raise the question of personal identity in general and the possibility of the survival of personal identity in particular—an issue that has suggested to some that the hope of resurrection turns after all on anthropological dualism: mortal body, immortal soul. Given the self-evident finality of death for the physical body, without recourse to a separate entity or personal "essence" (that is, a soul, which constitutes the real *me*) that survives death, how can we maintain a reasonable doctrine of the afterlife? If, instead of *possessing* a body, I *am* a body, then when my body dies, do I not likewise cease to exist?

For Christian belief the hope of resurrection, grounded in God's raising Jesus from the dead, is nonnegotiable. For we Christians, then, any satisfying portrait of the human person will need to narrate how I—*me* and not some

---

[66]John Polkinghorne, *Science and Theology: An Introduction* (London: SPCK, 1998), p. 115. See also Murray J. Harris, "Resurrection and Immortality in the Pauline Corpus," in *Life in the Face of Death: The Resurrection Message of the New Testament,* McMaster New Testament Studies, ed. Richard N. Longenecker (Grand Rapids: Eerdmans, 1998), pp. 147-70; Richard N. Longenecker, "Is There Development in Paul's Resurrection Thought?" in *Life in the Face of Death: The Resurrection Message of the New Testament,* McMaster New Testament Studies, ed. Richard N. Longenecker (Grand Rapids: Eerdmans, 1998), pp. 171-202; Ted Peters et al., eds., *Resurrection: Theological and Scientific Assessments* (Grand Rapids: Eerdmans, 2002).

other, *my* particular identity as a person—might cross the bridge from this life to the next.

## Epilogue

Well known in the annals of the relationship between scientific innovation and theology are the revolutionary proposals of Copernicus and Charles Darwin. Historically, we humans have preferred to locate ourselves in a place of indisputable honor, at the center of the cosmos. Consequently, we have found ourselves humbled by scientific discovery: in the modern age, first by Copernicus, who demonstrated that our planet and, thus, we who inhabit the earth, are not the center around which the universe pivots; second, by Darwin and evolutionary biology, who have located *Homo sapiens* within the animal kingdom with a genetic make-up that strongly resembles the creatures around us.

At the turn of the third millennium, a further scientific innovation, this one arising from within neurobiology, has the potential to be just as sweeping in its effects among theologians and within the church. Indeed, quantum leaps in our understanding of the brain in the last three decades are rewriting our understanding of who we are, and these are of immediate consequence for the centuries-old quest for answers to basic, human questions: Who am I? Why am I here? For Christians more specifically, these basic questions expand to include concerns about the God-given capacity to choose (and do) evil as well as good, about the meaning and purpose of salvation, about the hope of resurrection and life after death, and more.

In this emerging context, reflective and spirited discussion, not faint-heartedness, is the order of the day. Rather than giving these concerns over to the natural sciences and retreating into a cave of fideism, rather than repeating our beliefs over and over like a mantra, it is important that we engage these questions actively, working self-consciously from within the Christian tradition. The result may be that new light is cast on long- and deeply held theological claims, perhaps even providing new images and metaphors that help to carry forward the enterprise of articulating the faith within the community of God's people and communicating the faith to the unchurched. Alternatively, recognizing with Augustine that "the very appearance of God's creation is a great book" to be pondered religiously, we recognize that our theology remains open to the possibility of reformulation on account of scientific discovery.[67]

---

[67]See the helpful essay by Michael Fuller, "A Typology for the Theological Reception of Scientific Innovation," *Science & Christian Belief* 12 (2000): 115-25.

How these multiple voices—Scripture, the neurosciences and related disciplines, the Christian tradition, and our experience—will learn to serve in the same choir remains to be seen. What is clear is that we would be foolish to turn a deaf ear to any one of them.

# 2 SUBSTANCE DUALISM

### Stewart Goetz

The philosopher Roderick Chisholm has written that we should take seriously "certain things we have a right to believe about ourselves" and "be guided in philosophy by those propositions we all do presuppose in our ordinary activity."[1] Although I am unclear about whether I have a right to believe certain things about myself, it is clear to me that I just find myself having such beliefs, and it is not possible for me to stop having them unless I am provided with a good reason to think that they are questionable or false. One of the things that I, as an ordinary person, believe about myself is that I am a soul that is distinct from my physical (material) body. Hence, I am what philosophers and theologians term a substance dualist or, more simply, a dualist.

Because my belief that dualism is true is ordinary in nature, it is shared by many others. As the philosopher William Lyons has recently stated, the view "that humans are bodies inhabited and governed in some intimate if mysterious way by minds (souls), seemed and still seems to be nothing more than good common sense."[2] Thus, we find this common sense was manifested in the ordinary beliefs of people in first-century Palestine. For example, when Jesus asked his disciples who people thought he was, some thought he was John the Baptist, others that he was Elijah and others that he was Jeremiah or one of the prophets (Mt 16:13-14). Even Herod, who had John the Baptist executed, wondered if Jesus was John (Mt 14:2). Given that it is reasonable to assume that John the Baptist's body could easily be located, it only makes sense to conclude that people thought that Jesus might be John's soul reembodied.[3] In our own day, J. K. Rowling makes effective use of dualism in

---

[1]Roderick M. Chisholm, *Person and Object* (LaSalle, Ill.: Open Court, 1976), p. 15.

[2]William Lyons, *Matters of the Mind* (New York: Routledge, 2001), p. 9.

[3]As N. T. Wright meticulously demonstrates (*The Resurrection of the Son of God* [Minneapolis: Fortress, 2003], chap. 4), the mainstream Jewish view in the immediate centuries leading up to and including the life of Jesus was that bodily resurrection presupposed the existence of the soul in an intermediate state which was united with a new physical body in a new world that God would make in the future when he would vindicate all of the righteous members of Israel against their enemies. The fact that Herod says Jesus is John the Baptist who "has been raised from the dead" (Mt 14:2) does not entail that Herod was expressing a view of

her hugely popular Harry Potter novels, in which the worst death one can die is to have one's soul sucked out of one's body by the kiss of a being called a dementor. And the contemporary nondualist philosopher John Searle reports that "when I lectured on the mind-body problem in India [I] was assured by several members of my audience that my views must be mistaken, because they personally had existed in their earlier lives as frogs or elephants, etc."[4]

Given, then, that ordinary people are dualists, it should come as no surprise that the Christian intellectual tradition, like other religious traditions, has been on the side of ordinary belief with its affirmation of the soul-body distinction. As Kevin Corcoran, who is not a dualist, has recently noted, "Most, if not all, orthodox Christian theologians of the early church were anthropological *dualists*."[5] The consensus, moreover, remained on the side of dualism from medieval time right up to the twentieth century. One must, however, be careful here. Although the Christian intellectual tradition has sided with dualism, it is a mistake to think that Scripture itself explicitly teaches or defends dualism. Through the years, much ink has been spilt on the issue of what the Bible has to say about anthropology: some writers argue that it teaches that the soul exists and dualism is true, and others claim that it teaches a monistic, Hebrew

---

resurrection at odds with this dominant view. Given that John and Jesus were extraordinary individuals with strong messages about righteousness and that Herod was personally involved in John's murder, it makes perfect sense (ibid., pp. 411-14) to think Herod was speculating that God was especially vindicating John as a righteous sufferer by resurrecting him then as opposed to in the future.

The expression "the resurrection of the dead" warrants one further comment. As Wright points out elsewhere (*The New Testament and the People of God* [Minneapolis: Fortress, 1992], pp. 320-34), one must be careful about using linguistic expressions as the basis for determining what people believe about the nature of the afterlife. Wright notes that just as it is possible to use language about the soul and life after death to refer to the idea of physical resurrection, so is it possible to use language about physical resurrection to refer to the idea of the soul and life after death. Thus, it is erroneous to conclude that because the Pharisees are consistently described in the Gospels and extrabiblical sources as believing in the resurrection of the dead that they did not believe in the existence of a soul that would receive a new body in the future. They did believe in the soul's existence and its future reembodiment, as Wright notes with the support of various texts, and it should not go unmentioned at this point that the apostle Paul was a Pharisee.

Finally, although Herod was wrong about Jesus' being John reembodied, Herod got the embodiment part right. Jesus was the incarnation (embodiment) of God, an idea that is far more intelligible on a dualist understanding of the person than on a materialist view.

[4] John R. Searle, *The Rediscovery of the Mind* (Cambridge, Mass.: MIT Press, 1992), p. 91.

[5] Kevin Corcoran, "Dualism, Materialism and the Problem of Post Mortem Survival," *Philosophia Christi* 4 (2002): 414 (emphasis in original). Compare Caroline Walker Bynum, *The Resurrection of the Body in Western Christianity, 200-1336* (New York: Columbia University Press, 1995), pp. 57-58.

mind-body holism.[6] As Joel Green points out, however, the "biblical writers never explicitly take up the problem of the construction of the human person as a topic."[7] The writers of Scripture never explicitly addressed the issue because they were not writing a philosophical or anthropological text. Rather, they were writing as ordinary people to other ordinary people about the gospel and its implications for living everyday life in a hostile world.[8] When it came to addressing concerns about ordinary but important desires for personal happiness, salvation from evil and justice—none of which is fully satis-

---

[6]Those who believe that Scripture teaches a Hebrew holism often suggest that dualism is a Greek idea imported by the early church fathers. Dualism, however, is not a Greek idea but is also found, for example, in India (in Hinduism and Buddhism). As I have suggested and will elaborate on below, the idea of the soul is one that is had by an ordinary person, and it is its ordinariness that explains its presence in both Greece and India. Thus, although the early church fathers might have drawn on Greek philosophical reflection about the soul (e.g., when they wrote the creeds), they, like the authors of Scripture, did not need to go any further than ordinary human belief to come up with the ideas of the soul and dualism. Moreover, dualism does not entail that the soul is an immortal entity that exists independently of God's creative activity. It is important to remember this point, given all of the abuse of dualism by biblical scholars in recent decades.

[7]Joel Green, "'Bodies—That Is, Human Lives': A Re-examination of Human Nature in the Bible," in *Whatever Happened to the Soul? Scientific and Theological Portraits of Human Nature*, ed. Warren S. Brown, Nancey Murphy and H. Newton Malony, Theology and the Sciences (Minneapolis: Fortress, 1998), p. 154.

[8]I can do no better than quote John Cooper on this matter: "The New Testament writers are primarily interested in the proclamation of the gospel and not in promoting a particular theoretical anthropology. But it might nonetheless be true that they express the gospel in terms of a worldview, including a view of human nature, which at least in general presupposes or implies positions on philosophical issues. . . . Scripture presents a nontheoretical, 'commonsense' vision of the afterlife which nevertheless has ontological presuppositions and implications. . . . It is legitimate and nonspeculative to identify these assumptions and to make inferences from the teachings of Scripture using the laws of logic" (*Body, Soul and Life Everlasting: Biblical Anthropology and the Monism-Dualism Debate* [Grand Rapids: Eerdmans, 1989], pp. 112, 197). Not surprisingly, Cooper maintains that the view of human nature presupposed by Scripture is dualism.

The point that Scripture simply assumes what the ordinary person believes is bolstered by comments of C. S. Lewis, who points out that early Christians, including Jesus, were not teaching a theoretical morality, but simply presupposed knowledge of the moral law held by their hearers: "The idea . . . that Christianity brought a new ethical code into the world is a grave error. If it had done so, then we should have to conclude that all who first preached it wholly misunderstood their own message: for all of them, its Founder, His precursor, His apostles, came demanding repentance and offering forgiveness, a demand and an offer both meaningless except on the assumption of a moral law already known and already broken. . . . A Christian who understands his own religion laughs when unbelievers expect to trouble him by the assertion that Jesus uttered no command which had not been anticipated by the Rabbis—few, indeed, which cannot be paralleled in classical, ancient Egyptian, Ninevite, Babylonian, or Chinese texts" ("On Ethics," in *Christian Reflections*, ed. Walter Hooper [Grand Rapids: Eerdmans, 1967], pp. 46-47). Just as Christianity did not bring a new ethical code into the world, so also it did not bring a new anthropology.

fied on this earth—the biblical writers simply drew on the ordinary human being's belief that we are souls that can continue to exist after death and have
these desires fulfilled. The belief that we are souls, moreover, sometimes manifested itself with the authors of Scripture in the conviction that it is possible
to become disembodied before death. Thus, when Paul boasted to the Corinthians that he was caught up into paradise, though he cannot remember
whether it was in his body or out of it (2 Cor 12:2-4), he was simply presupposing that he was a soul that could exist outside his body.[9]

## What Is a Soul?

In light of the fact that ordinary people believe in a soul-body distinction, it is
helpful to state briefly with some degree of precision what the soul is. In the
simplest terms, the soul is a substance. What, however, is a substance? A substance is a particular entity or thing, whether material (e.g., a table or a tree) or
immaterial (e.g., a soul) which has or exemplifies essential properties or characteristics that it cannot lose without ceasing to exist. These essential properties include powers to act and capacities (propensities) to be acted upon. When
a soul exercises one of its powers, it is an agent, and when it has one of its capacities actualized, it is a patient. A soul has various essential psychological
powers, including the power to think about, consider or focus on different issues (e.g., I can think about the soul-body distinction) and the power to choose
to act (e.g., I can choose to become a Christian). Essential capacities of the soul
include the capacity to experience pleasure (e.g., I experience pleasure while
reading Harry Potter books and when playing baseball), the capacity to experience pain (e.g., I experience pain when hit by a pitched ball), and the capacities to desire (e.g., I desire a drink of water after a hard workout) and to believe (e.g., I believe that writing this essay is hard work). Given this
characterization of a soul in terms of its essential psychological powers and capacities, it is important to make two additional points.

First, one should recognize that, although the power to think is an essential
property of the soul, the soul need not continuously exercise this power in order to exist. Moreover, a particular thought, such as that the Yankees will win
the World Series, if it is had by a soul, might not have been had by it and yet it

---

[9]Other examples where Scripture presupposes dualism include Paul's desire to depart this
life and be with Christ (Phil 1:21-24), because to be away from the body is to be at home with
the Lord (2 Cor 5:8) before final re-embodiment at the general resurrection of the righteous.
Then there are the various admonitions against the spiritualist or occult practice of contacting the dead (Lev 19:31; 20:6; Deut 18:11; Is 8:19-20), as well as the story of Saul's contacting
the witch of Endor before warring with the Philistines (1 Sam 28).

would still have been the same soul. Similarly, though a soul might have chosen as a way of life to forego performing certain kinds of action (e.g., watching sexually explicit and violent movies) as ways of fulfilling its desire for pleasure, it might have chosen a different way of life. Still, it would have been the same soul. The idea, here, is that particular exercisings of the powers of thought and choice are nonessential or accidental in nature, and it is because they are that we believe that we could have thought and chosen different things and still have been the same soul. This point about the accidental nature of particular thoughts and choices accounts for the ordinary belief I have that, although I chose to be a college professor, I might have chosen instead to have been a lawyer or a member of the clergy and still have been the same soul. Similarly, because particular thoughts, choices and personality traits are accidental in nature, we believe that a person who enters prison as a bitter, cold-blooded killer can exit as a thankful, kind-hearted, individual who works on behalf of the well-being of others.

Second, one must be equally mindful that, although the soul has multiple, essential psychological powers and capacities, these powers and capacities are not themselves substances (i.e., they are not substantive). Because they are properties and not substances, powers and capacities cannot be separated from and exist independently of the soul such that they are able (have the capacity) to become parts of other substances. They are not substantive, separable parts of the soul in the way that a portion of the table on which I am writing (e.g., the top or a leg) is a substantive, separable part of the table that can exist independently of the table and become a part of another substance (e.g., a leg of a table can become a leg of a chair). Thus, a table, unlike a soul, is a complex entity or thing in virtue of the fact that it is made up of parts that are themselves substances (substantive parts). Physical scientists inform us that a table is actually a lattice structure of molecules bound together by attractive powers affecting appropriate capacities and that when this lattice structure is broken by a sufficient force, the table breaks. Unlike a table, and material objects in general, a soul is not a complex entity because it has no substantive parts. Instead, it is substantively simple in nature. Thus, complexity at the level of propertyhood is compatible with simplicity at the level of thinghood.[10]

---

[10]A soul is immaterial (not material or physical). To be immaterial, however, is not to be composed of immaterial stuff. It is not to be composed of any stuff at all. See Roderick M. Chisholm, "On the Simplicity of the Soul," *Philosophical Perspectives* 5 (1991): 168. In order to deflect standard criticism, I should make it clear that value judgments, such as that the soul is good and the material world is evil, are not part of dualism per se. One can be a dualist and not believe any such idea. As a dualist, I certainly do not believe any such idea.

## Belief That the Soul Exists Is Basic

So far, I have focused on the ordinary person's belief that she or he is a soul and on what a soul is. At this point, it is relevant to ask whether ordinary persons hold the belief that they are souls on the basis of an argument. In other words, do ordinary persons think about themselves and what they are, and conclude from other beliefs of theirs that they are souls? I think it is plausible to maintain that an ordinary person's belief that he or she is a soul is basic in nature in the sense that it is not inferred or derived from any other belief that he or she has.[11] In addition, a person's belief that he or she is a soul is found near the bottom of his or her system of beliefs. One of the many things of which the philosopher Alvin Plantinga has reminded us is that our belief structures are analogous to the structures of buildings. Thus, some of our beliefs are more foundational than, and provide the basis for, other beliefs that we have.[12] Given this hierarchical structure, Plantinga also points out that a belief has a feature that he terms its depth of ingression, which is measured by how much reverberation or impact its loss would have on the rest of a person's belief structure.[13] The more peripheral the belief, the less its depth of ingression. For example, although I believe that the Philadelphia Eagles have a home game tomorrow, my finding out that they are playing in Indianapolis would not have extensive reverberations throughout my belief structure. The depth of ingression of my belief about the Eagles' schedule is low. Because my belief that I am a soul is not only basic but also at the center of my belief structure,

---

[11] Dean Zimmerman ("Christians Should Affirm Mind-Body Dualism," in *Contemporary Debates in Philosophy of Religion,* ed. Michael Peterson and Raymond J. Vanarragon [Oxford: Blackwell, 2003], pp. 314-27) suggests that most Christians believe in the soul's existence on the basis of their religious convictions, which are rooted either in what the church teaches (in the case of Roman Catholics) or in what Scripture assumes or teaches (in the case of both Roman Catholics and Protestants). On my view, belief that I am a soul is basic and explains why it is plausible both for the church to teach that the soul exists and for the writers of Scripture to assume that it exists. Zimmerman notes that adherents of other religions believe that the soul exists because of their religious convictions. I think it is plausible to maintain that other religious traditions affirm the soul's existence because belief in its existence is basic and prior to religious belief.

[12] Though Alvin Plantinga has written extensively on the issue of belief, I will refer to his essay "Reason and Belief in God," in *Faith and Rationality,* ed. Alvin Plantinga and Nicholas Wolterstorff (Notre Dame, Ind.: University of Notre Dame Press, 1983), pp. 16-93. As an indication of the foundational nature of the ordinary person's belief that she or he is a soul, Thomas Nagel points out that no matter what empirical (scientific) discoveries we make, it might very well be impossible for us to give up what he calls the simple view of ourselves ("Brain Bisection and the Unity of Consciousness," in *Mortal Questions* [Cambridge: Cambridge University Press, 1979], p. 164).

[13] Plantinga, "Reason and Belief in God," p. 50.

an undermining of it would have extensive reverberations throughout my belief system. For example, its loss would undermine both my belief that certain accounts of my origin are false (e.g., the standard Darwinian account of my, and everyone else's, origination in terms of random mutations and natural selection assumes that I am a material being) and my conviction that I can survive death and experience beatitude in the presence of God. The depth of ingression of my belief that I am a soul is, therefore, high.

The fact that the belief that I am a soul—a simple substance with psychological properties—is basic does not imply that the belief is groundless in the sense that there is no experience or awareness of mine that explains my having it.[14] The logical question at this point, then, is, what experience explains my having the belief that I am a soul? The most plausible answer is that the experience in question is just my inner or introspective awareness of myself as a simple substance that exemplifies psychological properties. Some thoughts of the philosopher René Descartes about his awareness of himself as a soul can serve as our guide at this point:

> When I consider the mind [soul], that is to say, myself inasmuch as I am only a thinking thing, I cannot distinguish in myself any parts, but apprehend myself to be clearly one and entire; and although the whole mind seems to be united to the whole body, yet if a foot, or an arm, or some other part, is separated from my body, I am aware that nothing has been taken away from my mind. And the faculties [powers and capacities] of willing, feeling, conceiving, etc., cannot be properly speaking said to be parts, for it is one and the same mind which employs itself in willing and in feeling and understanding.[15]

Descartes notes that, when he introspectively considers himself, he apprehends himself to be one and entire, by which he seems to mean that he is aware that he has no substantive parts. He is careful to make clear that the lack of such parts does not imply a lack of a multiplicity of properties (of which he is also aware) because simplicity at the level of thinghood is compatible with complexity at the level of propertyhood. Moreover, because Descartes is aware that he is a substantively simple soul, when he, for example, thinks about what he is, he is aware that all of him thinks. He thinks as a whole or in his entirety because as an entity that lacks substantive parts, it is not possible for one part of him to think while another does not. And when he simultaneously thinks

---

[14]Ibid., pp. 78-79.

[15]René Descartes, *Meditations*, Sixth Meditation, in *The Philosophical Works of Descartes*, vol. 1, trans. Elizabeth S. Haldane and G. R. T. Ross (Cambridge: Cambridge University Press, 1911), p. 196.

about his being a soul, hopes that he will survive death and feels pain in his
foot, he is aware that it is one and the same soul in its entirety that is the subject
of each event.

To clarify Descartes's position, it is helpful to consider the following objection raised by the philosopher David Armstrong:

> Descartes seems to be moving illegitimately from the fact that the mind is a *single*
> thing to the conclusion that it is a *simple* thing. And introspection would seem to
> go against Descartes here. We can be aware of multiple processes coexisting in
> our minds [souls]. Indeed, Plato argues in the *Republic* (434d-441c) for parts of the
> soul on the ground that we can entertain inconsistent desires. He gives the exam-
> ple of a man torn between his desire to gaze at corpses lying beside the road and
> his feeling that this is a shameful desire to indulge.[16]

Is Descartes making the illegitimate inference that Armstrong suggests?
This is doubtful. Descartes would likely respond that, although he sometimes has inconsistent desires (desires such that the fulfillment of one excludes the fulfillment of the other), the loss of one or both of them (which is
a common experience) does not result in a diminishment of him in the sense
that he loses substantive parts. All of him remains after their loss. Hence,
Armstrong has not provided a good reason to think that Descartes starts
with the general belief that he is a single thing and infers the specific belief
that he is a simple thing.

There is an additional Armstrongian kind of argument in the offing
against the view that a person is introspectively aware of himself or herself
as a simple substance with multiple properties.[17] The opponent of this view
(a materialist or physicalist) begins by conceding that the soul seems or appears to itself to be substantively simple. The materialist points out, however, that what is thought to be an awareness of what is X (simple) can be and
is sometimes confused with the lack of an awareness of what is Y (complex)
and a passage to the belief in the absence of Y or the presence of X. Such a
passage, although legitimate in some cases (for example, the failure to find
an elephant in one's kitchen warrants the conclusion that there is no elephant
in the kitchen) is illegitimate in others (for example, the failure to see a pin
on the floor of a room cluttered with objects does not warrant the conclusion
that there is no pin on the floor). The operative principle in failure-to-be-
aware reasoning seems to be something like the following: The passage from

---

[16]David Armstrong, *The Mind-Body Problem: An Opinionated Introduction* (Boulder, Colo.:
Westview, 1999), p. 23 (emphasis in original).
[17]Ibid., pp. 27-30.

a failure to be aware of Y in context C to the conclusion that Y is absent and/
or X is present is warranted only if it is reasonable not only to think that in
C one could, but also to think that in C one would, be aware of Y if it were
there. The materialist's position about the soul and self-awareness is that the
believed awareness of the soul's substantive simplicity is confused with the
failure to be aware of the soul's substantive complexity, and the subsequent
passage from the failure to be aware of its substantive complexity to the belief that it is substantively simple is unreasonable because it is not possible
to be aware of its substantive complexity, even if it is there. Hence, although
materialism is not bolstered by the seemingly noncomplex nature of the soul
as a substance, neither is it undermined.

What is important to consider at this juncture is what, if any, justification
there is for maintaining that the soul is not aware of its substantive simplicity,
but is confusing such awareness with the failure to be aware of its substantive
complexity and then making the accompanying illegitimate inference to its
substantive simplicity. Armstrong, after acknowledging that our mental lives
have an appearance of simplicity that is "hard to shake off," provides an argument against belief in the reality of this apparent simplicity. This argument
makes use of an appearance of simplicity in ordinary perception that is supposedly equally hard to shake off.

> For instance, we see pictures on a television screen, but we *are not able* to see the
> complex structures of little pixels that actually make up the images. We *are not
> perceptually aware of* this complexity. The real structure of the pictures does not ap-
> pear. Perhaps introspective awareness is also like this. Mental phenomena ap-
> pear to introspection to be far more simple than they really are.[18]

This argument, when conjoined with the alleged confusion between an
awareness of X and the failure to be aware of Y, yields an argument against
belief in the self's substantive simplicity that goes something like this:
Though we think we are aware of the soul's substantive simplicity, we con-

---

[18]Ibid., p. 30 (emphasis added). Although I am concerned with the apparent simplicity of the
substantive self, it should not be overlooked that philosophers like Armstrong readily admit that psychological events (e.g., believing, desiring, experiencing pain) also seem to us
to lack parts. Colin McGinn makes the following general point about the nature of our conscious lives: "It is precisely [spatially defined properties] that seem inherently incapable of
resolving the mind-brain problem: we cannot link consciousness to the brain in virtue of
spatial properties of the brain. . . . Consciousness defies explanation in such terms. Consciousness does not seem made up out of smaller spatial processes. . . . Our faculties bias us
towards understanding matter in motion, but it is precisely this kind of understanding that
is inapplicable to the mind-body problem"(*The Problem of Consciousness* [Oxford: Basil
Blackwell, 1991], pp. 11-12, 18 n. 21).

fuse this believed awareness with the lack of an awareness of the soul's substantive complexity and an illegitimate passage from this lack of awareness
to a belief in the soul's substantive simplicity. It is reasonable to think that
this confusion occurs in this case because of the existence of cases (e.g., a
television picture) in which a substance that is complex is not perceived to
be so and an inference is made to its simplicity, and this inference is illegitimate because there is no reason to think that one could be aware of that
substance's complexity even though it is there.

In response to this Armstrongian argument, it is reasonable to question
whether the alleged confusion and illegitimate inference occur in the case of
the television picture. It is important to realize that the television picture
seems to have substantive parts insofar as it is a scene composed of things
like mountains, people, cars, and so on; it does not appear to be substantively simple. What, then, about a particular part of the scene—say, a solid
blue hat on the head of a person who is looking at a mountain? Does the picture of the hat appear to be substantively simple? In a certain but relative
sense, yes, it does. Relative to other objects in the picture of the same scale
or size that comprise parts (the car in the picture is made up of tires, a
bumper, a hood, etc.), the hat appears to be a noncomplex basic building
block of the picture. What, then, about the Armstrongian argument vis-à-vis
the hat in the picture? The argument is persuasive at this point only if it is
plausible to maintain that our failure to perceive the substantive complexity
(the compositional pixels) of the picture of the hat leads to our having a
(hard to shake) belief that the picture is substantively simple in a nonrela-
tive, absolute sense. It is, however, implausible to maintain this. We are not
led to have a belief that the picture of the hat is absolutely substantively
simple (it has no substantive parts of any size), i.e., even though we do not
perceive the picture's substantive parts. Instead, in light of our awareness
of certain properties of the picture, we are led to believe that it does have
substantive, though unobserved, parts. Because of our awareness of its spatial extension, shape and solidity, we are led to believe that it is material in
nature and occupies space in virtue of (unperceived) substantive parts of it
occupying distinct regions of space. In light of my apprehension of my soul,
not only do I have no reason to think that I have unperceived substantive
parts, but also I have reason to think that I do not have such parts. Most interesting for the present discussion (beyond the apparent simplicity of the
soul) is that, although I seem to have the property of occupying certain regions of space, I seem to occupy those regions in virtue of all of me (not substantive parts of me) being present at the different points of the space that I

occupy. I will have more to say about the apparent spatial nature of the soul below.[19]

In summary, it is reasonable to think that material objects have substantive parts even when we are not aware of them. It is reasonable for us to think this in light of our awareness of certain properties that they do have. Therefore, unless a materialist can provide some other reason for thinking that materialism is true that is sufficiently compelling to undermine the ground for believing that one is a simple substance,[20] he or she has not given a good reason to doubt that a self is aware of its substantive simplicity.

So far, then, I do not think there is any reason to doubt that a basic belief that one is a soul is grounded in an introspective awareness of oneself as a soul.[21] Someone whose belief that the soul exists is basic in nature might be called an "antecedent soulist."[22] Given that I am an antecedent soulist, the following is

---

[19]I can think of one way in which I might legitimately infer the picture's substantive simplicity from my failure to perceive its substantive complexity. My inference at this point requires that I abandon my belief that the hat is material and composed of substantive parts that occupy distinct regions of space and suppose that it occupies space in the way that I seem to occupy space, which is by my being present in my entirety at each point in space that I occupy. The trouble now is that my making the inference in question presupposes and is based on my belief that I am substantively simple and occupy space in the way that I do. It in no way undermines that belief.

[20]Armstrong's independent reason for thinking that materialism is true is the belief that natural science is our best guide to the nature of reality, where the principles of explanation of natural science exclude any appeal to minds and their purposes. (See his "Naturalism, Materialism and First Philosophy," *Philosophia* 8 [1978]: 261-76). Below, I examine and respond to scientific considerations that supposedly make problematic the idea that a soul causally interacts with its physical body. It must be remembered, however, that even if dualist responses to these arguments fail, it does not follow that materialism is true. The falsity of dualism is compatible with the truth of idealism, which is the view that only souls and other nonphysical entities exist.

[21]What about commissurotomy cases in which the cerebral commissures connecting the two halves of the brain are severed with the result that it can seem to observers that there are two minds—one aware of what the other is not? (See Nagel, "Brain Bisection.") Without being dismissive, the answer is that no one knows what is going on in such cases. At best, we can be sure about what is not going on: namely, a soul is not being divided.

[22]John Perry calls himself an "antecedent physicalist" about the self, a person "who is committed to physicalism in the sense that she or he sees some compelling reasons for it and will not give it up without seeing some clear reason to do so" (*Knowledge, Possibility and Consciousness* [Cambridge, Mass.: MIT Press, 2001], p. 27). Though, like Perry, a physicalist (materialist), David Papineau is rightly skeptical that anyone starts out or is antecedently a materialist about the self: "I don't take materialism to be obvious. . . . On the contrary, I regard it as a rather eccentric position, which stands in need of some argumentative support. (Certainly it is a minority attitude from a historical point of view. Few philosophers or scientists have been materialists about consciousness until relatively recently.)" (*Thinking About Consciousness* [Oxford: Clarendon, 2002], p. 8).

a simple argument (call it the "Simple Argument"[23]) for dualism:

1. I (my soul) am (is) essentially a simple entity (I have no substantive parts).

2. My body is essentially a complex entity (my body has substantive parts).

3. If "two" entities are identical, then whatever is a property of the one is a property of the other.

4. Therefore, because I have an essential property that my body lacks, I am not identical with my body.

The Simple Argument makes use of antecedent soulism. There are many dualist philosophers, however, who either maintain that antecedent soulism is false and that belief that the soul exists is (or must be) inferred from other beliefs or concede that antecedent soulism is true or at least plausible but maintain it is possible (and, perhaps, desirable) to provide an argument either to bolster one's own belief in the soul's existence or to convince others of its existence. For example, some dualists argue that it is reasonable to believe that one is a soul and that dualism is true on the basis of the ability to conceive of or imagine one's disembodiment. This modal argument (*modal* means something like "concerned with what is possible") goes as follows: I can conceive of myself existing disembodied;[24] therefore, it is reasonable to believe that it is possible for me to exist disembodied. Because it is a necessary truth that no physical body is able to become or exist disembodied (i.e., a physical body is essentially a physical body), it follows that I am a soul and not identical with my (or any) physical body. Thus, I am a soul and dualism is true.[25]

The problem with the modal argument is that, although it is true that I can conceive of my disembodiment, there is a distinction between a weak and a strong form of conceivability that is a function of the distinction between the weak (failure to be aware) and strong (awareness of) forms of awareness just discussed. Before explaining the role this distinction plays in the context of the

---

[23]Stewart Goetz, "Modal Dualism: A Critique," in *Soul, Body and Survival: Essays on the Metaphysics of Human Persons,* ed. Kevin Corcoran (Ithaca, N.Y.: Cornell University Press, 2001), pp. 89-104.

[24]Typically, the conceivable disembodiment involved in the modal argument is disembodiment from one's animal body. For example, I can conceive of myself floating above and looking down at my body on an operating table. Strictly speaking, however, the conceivable disembodiment is disembodiment in *any* form. Thus, in response to a physicalist who maintains that I am identical with my brain, the proponent of the modal argument argues that it is reasonable to believe that I am not my brain on the grounds that I can conceive of being disembrained.

[25]Charles Taliaferro defends the modal argument in his excellent book *Consciousness and the Mind of God* (Cambridge: Cambridge University Press, 1994).

modal argument, it is necessary to make clear that if it is possible for me to exist disembodied, then the relationship between my body and me is contingent in nature. That is, although I actually exist in a relationship to my body (for simplicity's sake, call it the "embodiment relationship"), which guarantees that this relationship is possible (nothing can be actual without being possible), it is also possible that I exist without this embodiment relationship. The question, now, is whether I can be aware of this contingent relationship between my body and me, if it is real.

On the one hand, if I cannot be aware of whether or not the embodiment relationship is contingent, then, although I can conceive of my being disembodied, I am unwarranted in concluding from what I can conceive that I can exist disembodied and, thereby, am a soul. This conclusion is unwarranted because what I can conceive of is explainable in terms of my failure to be aware of the nature (contingent or necessary) of the embodiment relationship, which might, for all I know, be a necessary relationship that I have with my body (e.g., I am necessarily embodied because I am identical with my body). Failure to be aware of the nature of the embodiment relationship sustains only a *weak* form of conceivability.[26]

On the other hand, if I am aware of the contingent nature of the embodiment relationship, then a problem of circularity arises for the proponent of the modal argument. Although it is true that I can conceive of my disembodiment in virtue of being aware of the contingency of the embodiment relationship, my being aware of this contingency requires that I be aware that I am a substance that is distinct from my physical body.[27] In other words, awareness of my being contingently related to my physical body presupposes that I am aware that I am a soul. Thus, this awareness of myself as a soul that exists in a contingent embodiment relationship with my body sustains a *strong* form of conceivability of disembodiment, but it does so at the price of presupposing that the soul exists, which was supposedly the conclusion of the modal argument, not its starting point.

---

[26]Thomas Nagel acknowledges that, so far as the ordinary concept of the self is concerned, its only essential properties are psychological in nature. Thus we are able to conceive of disembodiment (disembrainment). Nagel argues, however, that our having this concept is explained by the fact that we fail to be aware of the hidden nature of the self which includes necessary truths about our identity with our brain (*The View from Nowhere* [Oxford: Oxford University Press, 1986], pp. 37-49).

[27]Awareness that I am a substance that is distinct from my physical body can be accounted for either by awareness of my exemplifying the property of being simple or by awareness of my exemplifying a psychological property (or properties) that only a soul can exemplify. A problem with the latter alternative is that a proponent of the modal argument, like Taliaferro, maintains that psychological properties can be exemplified by the same entity that exemplifies physical properties (*Consciousness*, pp. 54, 57, 84, 161).

Though proponents of the modal argument and antecedent soulists disagree about whether it is possible to argue for the soul's existence from what is conceivable, they do agree that if a belief in the soul's existence is inferable, it is not a certain kind of inferred belief, namely, a hypothesis or theory that is put forth to account for empirical or observational data with which one starts. Nancey Murphy argues against dualism by claiming that "we need not postulate the existence of an entity such as a soul or mind in order to explain life and consciousness."[28] According to Murphy, we start with the observed data of life and consciousness and hypothesize (erroneously, she thinks) that a soul must exist to account for them. This is not where we start, however. If I am correct, a person starts with the basic belief that she or he exists as a conscious soul. Although an individual might postulate the existence of a soul other than one's own to account for the life and behavior of another physical body that she or he observes is similar to one's own, one does not hypothesize that she or he is a soul.

## The Problem of Causal Interaction

If an ordinary person starts with the basic belief that he or she is a soul and infers the truth of dualism according to the Simple Argument, why all of the fuss? Why is there a need for an essay such as this one about the nature of human beings? The answer to this question is something like the following: An ordinary person rarely pauses to think about the implications of the soul's existence and the truth of dualism that are theoretical in nature. He or she does not need to think about such implications in order to get on with the concerns of everyday life. What philosophers do is wonder about the deeper implications of an ordinary view like dualism, and what many of them have concluded is that some of the implications of dualism create serious problems for the view itself. Indeed, these philosophers have argued that dualism is burdened with such serious problems that it must be false. Someone who is convinced of this (a nondualist) and is also a Christian might try to argue that, unlike ordinary people, the writers of Scripture were not really dualists. Because I am a dualist and a Christian, the only alternative for me is to ask whether the objections to dualism raised by these philosophers are sound. In this section, I will consider the most frequently

---

[28]Nancey Murphy, "Human Nature: Historical, Scientific and Religious Issues," in *Whatever Happened to the Soul? Scientific and Theological Portraits of Human Nature*, ed. Warren S. Brown, Nancey Murphy and H. Newton Malony, Theology and the Sciences (Minneapolis: Fortress, 1998), p. 18.

raised objection to dualism, namely, the problem of causal interaction.[29]

The heading of this section suggests that there is only one problem of causal interaction. In reality, however, the problem is raised in different forms, leading one to wonder whether it is not analogous to a genus of which there are various species. I will consider three versions of the problem,[30] two of which can, in principle, be raised against any form of dualism and one of which is special to a particular kind of dualism. I will begin with the two that can be raised against dualism per se.

The first version of the problem of causal interaction arises because of the principle of the causal closedness of the physical order, which according to defenders of the principle is not only a fundamental metaphysical truth but also a necessary methodological assumption of the practice of science (the scientific method). According to the principle of causal closedness, only physical events (or the physical properties of physical events) can be invoked in ultimate or final explanations of the occurrence of other physical events. Thus, according to the principle of the causal closure of the physical world, final or ultimate psychological (mental) explanations of physical events that refer to purposes of minds are in principle unacceptable and must not be invoked.[31]

To put some flesh on the bones of the implications of the causal closure principle, consider its employment in the following example, developed by Jaegwon Kim, about a hypothetical neuroscientist who is studying what goes on in people's physical bodies when they raise their arms.[32] Suppose that you are a patient of this neuroscientist. Presumably, on an occasion when you move your fingers and raise your arms, there are nerve impulses that reach appropriate muscles and make those muscles contract with the result that your fingers move and your arms go up. And these nerve signals presumably originated in the activation of certain neurons in your brain. What caused those neurons to fire? According to Kim, we now have a quite detailed understand-

---

[29]Strictly speaking, the objection is raised against one type of dualism—namely, causal interactionist dualism. There are other kinds of dualism (e.g., preestablished harmony, occasionalism), but here I am only concerned with causal interactionist dualism.

[30]A clear and concise statement of them can be found in Armstrong, *Mind-Body Problem*, pp. 19-20.

[31]Karl Popper says that "the physicalist principle of the closedness of the physical [world] . . . is of decisive importance, and I take it as the characteristic principle of physicalism or materialism" (Karl R. Popper and John C. Eccles, *The Self and Its Brain* [New York: Routledge, 1977], p. 51). Popper adds, and then argues for the view, that "there is no reason to reject our prima facie view [the view that the physical world is open to mental, purposeful explanations]; a view that is inconsistent with the physicalist principle."

[32]This example can be found in Jaegwon Kim, *Philosophy of Mind* (Boulder, Colo.: Westview, 1996), pp. 131-32.

ing of the process that leads to the firing of a neuron in terms of complex electrochemical processes involving ions in the fluid inside and outside a neuron,
differences in voltage across cell membranes, and so forth. In other words, we
have a pretty good picture in terms of the laws of physics, chemistry and biology of the processes at the microphysical level that explain the movements of
your fingers and the raising of your arms. If, by hypothesis, you are a soul in
which occur nonphysical events, at least one of which is capable of causing a
neuron to emit a signal (or prevent it from doing so), then if this event is to produce the movements of your fingers and arms, it must somehow intervene in
these electrochemical processes. But how can this happen? How can an event
involving a soul causally influence the state of some molecules? Does it elec-
trically charge them or nudge them this way or that way? Surely, says Kim, in
order to have a complete explanation of the complex processes that lead to the
movements of your fingers and arms, the neuroscientist does not believe that
she or he needs to include reference to a nonphysical event that causally influences the molecular processes involved. Even if, adds Kim, the idea of an event
of a soul influencing the motion of a molecule is intelligible, the postulation of
such an event is neither necessary nor helpful (methodologically) in explaining why and how your fingers and arms move.

Kim's final point about the lack of a need to invoke your soul's activity to
explain the movements of your fingers and arms is counterintuitive, given the
assumed coherence of the idea of a soul's ability to causally interact with its
body. To understand why this final point is counterintuitive, let us fill out his
example a bit more. Suppose that you have been typing (which requires moving your fingers) for several minutes. You are tired and feel tight in your back,
so you raise your arms. It is commonsensical to explain both movements in
terms of purposes which, in this case, might be respectively to type a letter and
to relax. Reference to these purposes seems not only helpful, but also necessary for understanding why your fingers move and your arms go up. If we assume, as Kim does for the sake of discussion, that you cause your arms to
move (I will set aside moving your fingers, for the sake of brevity) by directly
causing neural events in the motor section of your brain, then when you raise
your arms for the purpose of relaxing, you (some nonphysical event involving
you) must cause initial neural events that ultimately lead to the rising of your
arms. Kim argues that in order to have a complete understanding of what goes
on when you raise your arms, a neuroscientist, because of his or her assumption of the causal closedness of the physical world, believes that he or she does
not need to include reference to you, a soul, and your purpose for raising your
arms, which is to relax. Why, however, would or should anyone think that this

is the case, given that it is so highly counterintuitive?

At this point, let us distinguish between a neuroscientist qua ordinary human being and a neuroscientist qua physical scientist. Surely a neuroscientist qua ordinary human being who is trying to understand why your arms go up after you have been typing for some time must and would refer to you and your reason for acting in a complete account of why your arms rise. Must he or she, however, qua physical scientist, avoid making such a reference? Kim claims that he or she must avoid such a reference because, qua physical scientist, he or she must make an assumption about the causal closedness of the physical world that conflicts with his or her commitment, qua ordinary person, to the causal openness of the physical world to explanatory purposes. Is Kim right about this?

In order to answer this question, it is necessary to consider what it is about physical entities that a physical scientist is trying to discover in his experimental work. Kim's neuroscientist qua physical scientist is trying to discover the capacities of particles or microphysical entities such as neurons to be causally affected (moved) by exercised causal powers of other physical entities including other neurons. For example, in his pioneering work on the brain, Wilder Penfield stimulated cortical motor areas of patients' brains with an electrode, resulting in movements of their limbs.[33] As Penfield observed the neural impulses that resulted from stimulation by the electrode, he had to assume that during his experiments the patients' brains were causally closed to other causal influences. Otherwise, he could not conclude that the electrode causally affected the neurons' capacities to be moved and that their causal impulses causally affected the capacities of neurons further down the causal chains. There is no reason, however, to think that because Penfield's investigation of the brain required the assumption of causal closedness in the context of his experiments that he had to be committed qua physical scientist to the assumption that the physical world is universally causally closed such that the capacities to be moved of microphysical entities can be actualized only by other physical entities. That is, there is no reason to think that because a neuroscientist like Penfield must assume causal closedness in his or her experimental work in order to discover how physical entities causally interact with each other that he or she must be committed qua physical scientist to the nonexistence of souls that act for purposes and also have the power to causally affect those entities. All that a neuroscientist such as Penfield must be committed to, qua physical scientist, is that souls, if they exist, are not causally actualizing

---

[33]Wilder Penfield, *The Mystery of the Mind* (Princeton: Princeton University Press, 1975).

the capacities to be moved of the relevant neurons during his experiments. If the neuroscientist makes the methodological presupposition that microphysical entities can have their capacities to be moved actualized only by other physical entities, then he or she does so not qua physical scientist but qua metaphysical materialist or naturalist.

In assessing the causal closedness argument, it is important to emphasize that, in seeking to understand how different physical entities affect the capacities of microparticles to be moved, a neuroscientist is seeking to learn about properties of these entities that are essentially conditional or iffy in nature. To see this, consider the following description of basic particles provided by David Chalmers:

> Basic particles . . . are largely characterized in terms of their propensity to interact with other particles. Their mass and charge is specified, to be sure, but all that a specification of mass ultimately comes to is a propensity to be accelerated in certain ways [moved at certain rates] by forces, and so on. . . . Reference to the proton is fixed as the thing that causes interactions of a certain kind that combines in certain ways with other entities, and so on.[34]

What Chalmers describes as a "propensity" of a particle to be moved is a capacity of it to be moved which is such that if it is actualized by an exercised power (a force) of another entity (whether physical or nonphysical in nature), it will be necessitated to move in a certain way. There is nothing, however, in the nature of the propensity or capacity of that particle that requires that it be actualized in accordance with physical laws such that the physical world is closed to causal influence by nonphysical souls performing mental acts (e.g., choices) for purposes. Hence, the actualization of a microparticle's capacity to be moved by a soul on an occasion when it makes a choice to act for a purpose is not excluded by anything that needs to be assumed for a scientific study of that capacity. And it is precisely on an occasion like that noted by Kim, when an arm movement occurs for a purpose, that a neuroscientist qua anything except metaphysical materialist or naturalist will reasonably believe that the originative microphysical movements are traceable to the causal activity of a soul.

My response to the causal closedness argument is premised on an assumption that Kim himself makes, which is that causation is a productive or generative relationship wherein the cause produces its effect. Some have argued that this conception of causation is outdated and that the fundamental laws of phys-

---

[34]David J. Chalmers, *The Conscious Mind: In Search of a Fundamental Theory* (Oxford: Oxford University Press, 1996), p. 153.

ics do not mention causality.[35] Rather, laws of physics about properties such as mass, electrical charge and motion are expressed in terms of mathematical relationships. Moreover, the properties of souls—what I have termed their psychological powers and capacities, at least one of which must be causally productive of physical events when exercised if dualism is true—are not mathematically representable. Hence, because physics does not employ a productive view of causation, it excludes or is closed to the explanatory relevance of souls.

Like Kim, I am not a physicist, and therefore, like him, I am hesitant about engaging the critic at this point for fear that I appear to be spouting off about matters beyond my intellectual purview. Nevertheless, I find Kim's own responses to this argument persuasive and summarize two of his points in what immediately follows.[36] First, Kim suggests that if there is no productive causation anywhere, then there is no mental causation or human agency of any kind.[37] This not only is unbelievable, but also seems self-refuting. After all, does not the proponent of the argument that causation is not a productive relation believe that he is trying to produce a belief in his listeners or readers that there is no productive causality? Second, Kim points out that the fact that causality is not mentioned in the fundamental laws of physics, or that the word *cause* does not appear in the statements of these laws, does not show that the concept of productive causation is absent from physics. There are the mathematical laws and then there is our interpretation or understanding of those laws:

> My impression is that disputes about the interpretation of quantum mechanics, for example, are replete with causal concepts and causal considerations; e.g., measurement (as in a measurement "having an outcome"), . . . observation (as having a perturbational influence on the system observed), interference, etc. . . . Entries on "force" in science dictionaries and encyclopedias typically begin like this: "In dynamics, the physical agent which causes a change of momentum.". . . A force causing a body to accelerate strikes me as an instance of productive causation par excellence.[38]

---

[35]See Barry Loewer, review of *Mind in a Physical World* by Jaegwon Kim, *Journal of Philosophy* 98, no. 6 (2001): 315-24.

[36]Jaegwon Kim, "Book Symposia: *Mind in a Physical World*: Responses," *Philosophy and Phenomenological Research* 65, no. 3 (2002): 674-77.

[37]Kim's response on behalf of the reality of mental causation appears puzzling until one realizes that he believes mental causation is ontologically reducible to productive physical causation ("Book Symposia: *Mind in a Physical World*: Précis," *Philosophy and Phenomenological Research* 65, no. 3 [2002]: 642).

[38]Kim, "Book Symposia: *Mind in a Physical World*: Responses," p. 676. One might add that the concept of the mass of an object, when expressed numerically, is typically interpreted as a function of that entity's *resistance* to acceleration by a *force*. The italicized terms seem part and parcel of the idea of causation as productivity.

Before proceeding to the second version of the problem of causal interaction, it is important to make clear that the argument from causal closedness against dualism is also used against Christian theists who believe that God exists and acts in this world. Thus, Douglas Futuyma and Matthew Bagger, respectively, set forth the implications of causal closure for explanations of certain events (e.g., the resurrection of Jesus, the healings performed by Jesus) that refer to God.

> Science is the exercise of reason, and so is limited to questions that can be approached by the use of reason, questions that can be answered by the discovery of objective knowledge and the elucidation of natural laws of causation. In dealing with questions about the natural world, scientists must act as if they can be answered without recourse to supernatural powers . . . of God.[39]

> We can never assert that, in principle, an event resists naturalistic [physical] explanation. A perfectly substantial, anomalous event, rather than providing evidence for the supernatural, merely calls into question our understanding of particular laws. In the modern era, this position fairly accurately represents the educated response to novelty. Rather than invoke the supernatural, we can always adjust our knowledge of the natural in extreme cases. In the modern age in actual inquiry, we never reach the point where we throw up our hands and appeal to divine intervention to explain a localized event like an extraordinary experience.[40]

Though God's powers vastly exceed those of a human soul, they are exemplified by a psychological, nonphysical, simple substance. Therefore, if the argument from the alleged causal closedness of the physical world against dualism cannot be answered, there is no room for God and his purposes to enter the explanatory fray. Christian theists would do well to think twice about jettisoning dualism because of the causal closedness argument while trying to preserve explanatory space for God. Any sophisticated materialist will quickly point out that if the assumption of causal closedness is justified, then not only does it undermine the truth of dualism, but also it defeats the truth of Christian theism.

If we assume for the sake of discussion, then, that the soul can causally interact with its body in the brain, then the second version of the problem of causal interaction asks, where does the interaction occur in the brain? Descartes (for reasons that need not be discussed here) claimed that the interaction

---

[39]Douglas J. Futuyma, *Science on Trial: The Case for Evolution* (New York: Pantheon, 1982), pp. 169-70.
[40]Matthew Bagger, *Religious Experience, Justification and History* (Cambridge: Cambridge University Press, 1999), p. 13. I am indebted to Charles Taliaferro for this reference.

occurred in the pineal gland. The late neurophysiologist Sir John Eccles, who was a dualist, suggested that the point of interaction is "where the firing or inhibition of neurons might occur as a result of small changes in electrical discharge."[41] Eccles's thesis was that the changes in discharge could be the direct effects or direct causes of events in the soul. In light of the speculations of Descartes and Eccles about the location of causal interaction, Armstrong makes the argumentative claim that the dualist urgently needs some scientific theory about the point of causal interaction and, ideally, a theory that can be empirically tested.[42]

Why, however, think that the dualist needs at all, let alone urgently needs, an empirically testable scientific theory about the location of causal interaction between a soul and its body? After all, a belief in the soul's existence is an introspective, not an empirical, matter, so why is it important to locate the point of causal interaction? Does Armstrong think that if a dualist could point to activity at a spot in the brain that neuroscience indicates is where arm movements typically originate, then there would finally be empirical evidence for the truth of dualism? Surely, however, Armstrong qua metaphysical physicalist would question whether it would be reasonable to believe that the indicated brain activity was caused by the action of a soul. Moreover, how might a dualist "prove" to Armstrong that it was? By pointing out that neuroscientists have been unable to find any physical cause of that brain activity? Surely Armstrong would argue that the failure to find a physical cause of that activity is no reason to think that it does not exist. By now, the reader should be well aware of the argumentative dialectic that involves a failure to be aware when it comes to issues pertaining to the existence of the soul.

In the end, there is no harm in a dualist speculating about and/or empirically looking for the locus of causal interaction. To think, however, that the believability of dualism is tied to the discovery of this locus is sheer confusion. If, by hypothesis, numerous theories about the place of causal interaction were advanced and all of them proved fruitless, dualism would not in the least be undermined, since the basis for belief in the soul's existence is not empirical in nature and nothing about the nature of the scientific method is incompatible with the truth of dualism.

The third version of the problem of causal interaction concerns Descartes's form of dualism (Cartesian dualism) in particular. For the sake of space, Des-

---

[41] Armstrong, *Mind-Body Problem*, p. 19; with reference to John C. Eccles, *The Neurophysiological Basis of Mind* (Oxford: Clarendon, 1953), chap. 8.

[42] Armstrong, *Mind-Body Problem*, p. 19.

cartes's view can briefly be summarized as follows: Any substance that is in space is physical, and any physical substance is extended. In addition, any substance that is extended is divisible into substantive parts. Thus, if the soul were in space, it would be divisible into such parts. Because the soul is simple, however, it is not divisible into substantive parts. Therefore, it cannot be physical and, thus, cannot be located in space.

Many have argued that the idea of a nonspatial entity causally interacting with a spatial entity is too problematic. The heart of the objection is that for any two entities to interact causally, they must stand in a relation to each other which is such that the substance acted upon (the patient) is accessible to the agent's exercised causal power. And it is simply impossible to conceive how a spatial substance and a nonspatial substance can stand in the requisite accessibility relationship.[43] Hence, whatever reasons one might have for thinking that Cartesian dualism is true, the problem of causal interaction defeats them. Two responses on behalf of the dualist are in order at this point.

First, if C, the Cartesian dualist, is convinced that C's reasons for believing that C is a nonspatial soul and causally interacts with C's spatial physical body are better than those reasons C is given for believing that there can be no accessibility relation between the soul and physical body, then C is justified in believing in the existence of such an accessibility relation, even though C cannot conceive of what it is.[44]

Second, one might concede the force of the argument from causal interaction against Cartesian dualism and embrace a non-Cartesian dualism. Or one might find a non-Cartesian dualism more compelling from the outset. For example, Philip Quinn has suggested that, because an individual's perceptual perspectives on the physical world are spatially located, it is preferable to think that the soul is a conscious, unextended, simple substance that occupies a spatial point inside its physical body, most likely the brain.[45] William Hasker

---

[43]It seems to me that the lack of the requisite accessibility relation is at the heart of the objection to Cartesian dualism. Sometimes, however, one finds the argument stated in the more general terms of the lack of the requisite likeness relationship between mind/soul and body. According to this statement of the objection, the mind/soul and body are so extremely unlike each other (one example of this unlikeness being that the soul is nonspatial while the body is spatial) that it is metaphysically impossible for the two to interact causally. As C. D. Broad pointed out, however, in his work *The Mind and Its Place in Nature* ([Paterson, N.J.: Littlefield, Adams, 1960], pp. 97-98), who is to say how alike two things must be in order to conclude that two entities cannot enter into a causal relation because they lack the requisite likeness?

[44]For more about this issue, see my "Dualism, Causation and Supervenience," *Faith and Philosophy* 11, no. 1 (1994): 92-108.

[45]Philip Quinn, "Tiny Selves: Chisholm on the Simplicity of the Soul," in *The Philosophy of Roderick M. Chisholm*, ed. Lewis Edwin Hahn (Chicago: Open Court, 1997), pp. 55-67.

has defended a view similar to that suggested by Quinn, except that Hasker claims that the space within which the soul is located must be at least as large as the space of those parts of the brain with which the soul causally interacts.[46] Yet another alternative is one suggested by Immanuel Kant: that the soul is present in its entirety at each point in space where it is natural to locate any one of its sensations, which, for all intents and purposes, means the soul is located as a whole in every part of space occupied by its physical body.[47] In short, then, it does not follow that if the problem of causal interaction makes Cartesian dualism too problematic, then dualism is false. There are non-Cartesian dualisms.

The idea of a non-Cartesian dualism, specifically one where the soul is present in its entirety at each point in space where it is natural to locate any of its sensations (which for all intents and purposes is the space occupied by its intact body), provides the framework for one final objection to dualism that is not a species of the causal interaction genus. A proponent of this last objection can concede that the dualist has adequate answers to the problems associated with causal interaction, but insist that the most serious problem for dualism is its counterintuitive character in light of the basic belief that one is one's physical body. For example, Peter van Inwagen has claimed that "when I enter most deeply into that which I call *myself*, I *seem* to discover that I am a living animal. And, therefore, dualism seems to me to be an unnecessarily complicated theory about my nature."[48] In other words, van Inwagen seems to hold that his belief that he is his living body is basic and grounded in an introspective awareness of his identity with his living body. In light of my claim that I have the basic belief that I am a soul that is grounded in an introspective awareness of myself, what is one to make of van Inwagen's claim? Can both of us be correct?[49] If not, why not?

Beyond merely pitting my word against van Inwagen's, I think two points are particularly relevant. First, though philosophical argumentation is not a function of counting heads, the vast majority of human beings have believed

---

[46]William Hasker, *The Emergent Self* (Ithaca, N.Y.: Cornell University Press, 1999), p. 192.

[47]C. D. Broad summarizes Kant's view about the spatial location of the soul in his *Religion, Philosophy and Psychical Research* (New York: Harcourt, Brace, 1953), pp. 130, 132. Recently, J. P. Moreland and Scott Rae (*Body and Soul: Human Nature and the Crisis in Ethics* [Downers Grove, Ill.: InterVarsity Press, 2000]) have defended a Thomistic view of the soul as fully present at each point occupied by its physical body.

[48]Peter van Inwagen, "Dualism and Materialism: Athens and Jerusalem?" *Faith and Philosophy* 12, no. 4 (1995): 476 (emphasis in original).

[49]The idea of a basic belief is one that is person-relative in the sense that a belief that is basic for one person might not be for another.

that the soul exists. Thus, van Inwagen's belief strikes one as puzzling in a way that mine does not. Most materialists do not start with a belief in materialism, as van Inwagen does, but end up there on the grounds that there are too many problems with dualism.[50] Hence, what I have done in this section is try to respond to what materialists take to be good reasons for abandoning dualism.

Second, although recognizing that there is little, if anything, one can do to persuade another person that his or her basic belief is mistaken, one can try to find ground that both acknowledge and which might be erroneously interpreted by one individual as support for his or her view. In the case of van Inwagen, I would concede to him that, when I enter most deeply into myself, I too discover in a certain sense that I am a living animal. What I discover is that, as Kant suggested, I seem to occupy the space that is occupied by my physical body (e.g., proprioceptively, I seem to be simultaneously present in my foot, torso and head). In Descartes's words, "I am very closely united to it [my body], and so to speak so intermingled with it that I seem to compose with it one whole."[51] To this extent, I seem to be a living animal. Though I seem to fill the space of my physical body, what makes it impossible for me to think that I am identical with it is the fact that I also seem to be a simple entity that has no substantive parts. Hence, although my physical body occupies a certain region of space in virtue of its substantive parts occupying distinct portions of that space, I occupy that same space in a different way by being present in my entirety at each point of the space that I occupy. It is beyond the scope of this paper to defend what I will term "holistic dualism," the view that the soul is present in its entirety at each point in space that it experiences sensations. However, as a holistic dualist I wonder whether van Inwagen infers that he is his animal body from being aware of himself as filling the space of his physical body, where such an awareness at least fails to include an awareness of his having substantive parts, or whether he is actually aware of himself as having substantive parts when he enters most deeply into himself.

## Dualism and Free Will

Just as I find myself having the basic belief that I am a soul, so also I find myself

---

[50]In commenting on a paper by Taliaferro, I once pointed out to an audience that included van Inwagen that every introductory philosophy book I had read that discussed personal identity and the mind-body problem started with dualism as the ordinary view and then went on to point out problems with it. Van Inwagen conceded the point but maintained that this approach by the authors of such books was no more than "intellectual posturing." Given what I find out about myself in my own self-awareness, I find this suggestion hard to believe.

[51]Descartes, Sixth Meditation, p. 192.

having the basic belief that I have freedom of the will in the libertarian sense that I am free to make undetermined choices for purposes. Moreover, just as my basic belief that I am a soul is grounded in an awareness of myself as a soul, so also my basic belief that I have libertarian free will is grounded in an awareness of my making such choices. There is a link between these two basic beliefs that has not gone unnoticed by philosophers. Searle has described this link in the following way:

> If there is any fact of experience that we are all familiar with, it's the simple fact that our own choices . . . seem to make a difference to our actual behavior. . . . We know we could have done something else, because we chose one thing for certain reasons. But we were aware that there were also reasons for choosing something else, and indeed, we might have . . . chosen that something else. . . . Human freedom is just a fact of experience. . . . In order for us to have radical [libertarian] freedom, it looks as if we would have to postulate that inside each of us [our physical bodies] was a self that was capable of interfering with the causal order of nature. That is, it looks as if we would have to contain some entity [substance] that was capable of making molecules swerve from their paths.[52]

After noting that the possession of libertarian freedom requires the existence of the self (soul), Searle goes on to raise the problem of causal interaction, stating that, although dualist interactionism might be intelligible, "it's certainly not consistent with what we know about how the world works from physics."[53] In light of the considerations discussed in the previous section, there is no reason to think that there is a decisive problem of causal interaction for dualism. It is helpful at this point to consider briefly what happens to our possession of libertarian freedom, given a denial of the soul's existence.

The most popular contemporary alternative to dualism is the general ontological thesis that reality is a multilayered hierarchy consisting of levels of entities with their characteristic properties and events. According to this view, the lowest, fundamental or bottom level of reality consists of microphysical particles. On top of this lowest level are higher, intermediate-level entities (e.g., chemical, biological) with their distinctive properties and events. Psychological properties and events are properties of human beings (brains or central nervous systems) that are higher (highest?)-level macroentities. There is a dependency relationship between the lower-level, physical properties and events of microobjects and the higher-level psychological properties and events of human be-

---

[52]John R. Searle, *Minds, Brains and Science* (Cambridge, Mass.: Harvard University Press, 1984), pp. 87-88, 92.
[53]Ibid., p. 92.

ings: no human being can have psychological properties unless he or she has physical properties, and the lower-level physical properties and events determine the higher-level psychological properties and events in the sense that nothing can be just like a given human being physically without its also being just like it psychologically. There is a primacy of the physical over the psychological, and physical indiscernibility (two entities are physically identical) entails psychological indiscernibility (two entities are psychologically identical).

The deterministic dependency relationship of the psychological on the physical world is typically characterized as a supervenience relationship: higher-level psychological properties and events supervene on physical properties and events.[54] Because a choice is a psychological event, it supervenes on a physical event. This implies that a choice is determined to occur by that on which it supervenes. No choice occurs indeterministically and is explained by a purpose for which it is made. In short, there seems to be no room for libertarian freedom of the will given the supervenience of the psychological on the physical. Given the supervenience of the psychological on the physical, it seems that at best we can have compatibilist freedom in which one and the same choice is both determined and free.

Some who deny the existence of the soul try to keep space for the reality of libertarian freedom by invoking the idea of the emergence of psychological properties from physical properties. For example, Timothy O'Connor has defended a form of property emergentism according to which irreducible higher-level psychological properties emerge when the appropriate fundamental physical conditions obtain.[55] According to O'Connor, a property like the power to choose[56] is an emergent property such that a choice can float free from (not be determined by) its fundamental physical conditions and produce events in or involving the object in which the fundamental physical conditions obtain, in this case the brain or human nervous system. O'Connor has described emergentism in terms of supervenience. On this account, an emergent

---

[54]Strictly speaking, the supervenience relation is not a dependency relation, but is no more than an extensional, co-variance relation (cf. Goetz, "Dualism," and Kim, *Philosophy of Mind*, p. 11). Because so many proponents of the supervenience of the mental on the physical build the notion of dependency into their materialistic view, I simplify things for the sake of discussion and assume that supervenience is a dependency relation.

[55]Timothy O'Connor, "Emergent Properties," *American Philosophical Quarterly* 31, no. 2 (1994): 91-104; and *Persons and Causes: The Metaphysics of Free Will* (Oxford: Oxford University Press, 2000), pp. 110-25.

[56]Strictly speaking, O'Connor talks about the emergence of an agent-causal capacity or power, and not the emergence of the power to choose (cf. *Persons and Causes*, p. 121). For present purposes, however, the distinction is inconsequential.

property $P$ (e.g., the power to choose) is an emergent causal property (power) of an object $O$ that has substantive parts if and only if

1. $P$ supervenes on properties of the parts of $O$;

2. $P$ is not had by any of $O$'s parts;

3. $P$ is simple or partless;

4. $P$ has direct, downward, determinative influence on the pattern of behavior involving $O$'s parts.

O'Connor points out that there are ways to avoid acknowledging the existence of emergent properties. For example, one might posit the presence of additional and hitherto undetected microproperties (properties of which, up to now, we have failed to be aware) that manifest themselves in highly complex systems of certain kinds by giving rise to $P$ in such a way that $P$ is constituted by, as opposed to emergent from, them (thus, P is not simple or partless). O'Connor responds to this proposal by saying that "the only motivation one could have for postulating a (rather elusive) microproperty is a very strong methodological principle to the effect that one is to avoid emergentist hypotheses at all costs, which by my lights is not a reasonable one."[57]

Three points are relevant to evaluating the emergentist position. First, in light of the ordinary person's belief in dualism, it is instructive to reflect on O'Connor's response to the non-emergentist's suggested positing of additional and hitherto undetected mircroparticles as constituents of $P$. O'Connor claims that the only motivation for postulating such microproperties is the methodological principle that one must avoid emergentism at all costs. At this point, it is just as plausible for a dualist to respond to the emergentist that it seems as if the only motivation for postulating emergent properties is the very strong methodological principle that one must avoid dualism at all costs.

Second, and also in light of the ordinary person's belief in dualism, one wonders why it is necessary to abandon dualism in favor of emergentism. O'Connor notes the objection to dualism from causal interaction without commenting on its force.[58] If he thinks it has some force, then it is appropriate to point out that it cuts against his own view. As Kim makes clear, how a property such as $P$ emerges from the physical "will forever remain a mystery; we have no choice but to accept it as an unexplainable brute fact."[59] Moreover, once $P$ has emerged, its direct downward determinative influence (see point 4, above)

---

[57]O'Connor, "Emergent Properties," p. 99.
[58]O'Connor, *Persons and Causes*, p. 119.
[59]Kim, *Philosophy of Mind*, p. 229.

is brute, and if the emergentist believes dualism is suspect because of the problem (mystery) of causal interaction, then it is incumbent on him or her to explain why downward causation is less problematic (mysterious).

Third, the emergentist view, insofar as it assumes that a person is a biological entity with substantive parts (see point 1),[60] conflicts with my earlier point that I am aware of myself as an entity that lacks substantive parts. Without some convincing reason for doubting the reliability of this introspective awareness, the emergentist view of the self is simply at odds with my experience of myself.

## Conclusion

I exist and am a soul. Does my existence require an explanation? It is reasonable to think that it does because, although I exist, and thus my existence is possible (what is actual must be possible), I also might not exist. Thus, my existence is contingent in nature, and what is contingent in nature must have an explanation for its existence. Complex substances are what I will call "naturally contingent" in the sense that their existence is explained by the coming together of their substantive parts. Because the soul has no such parts, it cannot come into existence in this way and, thereby, its existence is not naturally contingent. Instead, its existence is what I will call "metaphysically contingent," where metaphysically contingent entities come into being out of nothing or ex nihilo. Given, however, that it is plausible to think that nothing can just pop into existence out of nothing, what is metaphysically contingent must have a cause of its existence. What kind of cause? If it is reasonable to think that I exist for the purpose of experiencing perfect happiness (and this seems reasonable to me because my own perfect happiness is what I most deeply desire), then it is reasonable to think that the cause of my existence must be a soul which created me for that purpose. And this soul is what we call God. As John Calvin wrote, "No man can survey himself without forthwith turning his thoughts toward the God in whom he lives and moves."[61]

---

[60]O'Connor, *Persons and Causes*, p. 73.

[61]John Calvin *Institutes of the Christian Religion* 1.1.1.

I want to thank Craig Blomberg, Win Guilmette, J. P. Moreland and Dean Zimmerman for reading earlier drafts of this paper and making several helpful comments.

# AN EMERGENT DUALIST RESPONSE

*William Hasker*

$A$s I read Stewart Goetz's essay I am reminded once again of the mediating position occupied by emergent dualism among theories of the mind. I find myself quite comfortable with much of what Goetz has written; a great many (but not all) of his assertions about the soul are consistent with my own view. On the other hand, though, I believe I am better able than Goetz is to address the sorts of concerns that motivate materialists such as Nancey Murphy and Kevin Corcoran. To be sure, such a mediating stance by no means assures one of success. Many a thinker has set out to get the best of both worlds and ended up with the worst of both.

The most interesting feature of Goetz's paper, to my reading, is a certain disagreement that emerges between him and Corcoran—or perhaps I should say, between Goetz, Corcoran and Peter van Inwagen. Each of the three claims to have a "basic belief"—one not inferred from other beliefs that he holds—about his own nature as a human person. Corcoran has a basic belief that he is a material thing, and van Inwagen has a similar belief about himself. Goetz, in contrast, has a basic belief that he is an immaterial soul. Corcoran says little about the source of his belief, but van Inwagen states (echoing David Hume) that "when I enter most deeply into that which I call *myself*, I *seem* to discover that I am a living animal." Goetz understands this as meaning that van Inwagen's "belief that he is his living body is basic and grounded in an introspective awareness of his identity with his living body." Goetz himself, in sharp contrast, claims to have "an inner or introspective awareness of myself as a simple substance that exemplifies psychological properties." Here then, we have a striking difference between the claimed introspective awarenesses of two competent philosophers. What are we to make of this conflict?

One possible answer is that there is really no conflict. All of the claims being made are correct. Corcoran and van Inwagen are indeed aware of being purely material beings, and Goetz, for his part, is aware of being an immaterial soul.

These men simply are differently constituted in this respect, just as some people are right-handed and others are left-handed. I suppose, however, that this will please no one, so we must look for another solution.

Let me clarify things by stating my own view up front: I am very suspicious of *both* sorts of claims to introspective awareness of one's "true nature." My view is that the issues concerning the nature of human beings must be resolved by broad empirical and theoretical considerations (the sorts of considerations that figure prominently in all the essays in this book), and that any attempt to settle the questions by an appeal to "direct awareness" is unlikely to be successful. Since Goetz has spelled out his claim in more detail (and since it is his essay I am discussing), my principal question here will be, are we directly aware of being immaterial souls?

In order to get this question in focus, it is important to be clear about what Goetz claims as the content of this introspective awareness. As noted above, he says it is an awareness "of myself as a simple substance that exemplifies psychological properties." Subsequently, Goetz expands on the implications of this. René Descartes, he says, is "aware that he has no substantive parts." Furthermore, "when he . . . thinks about what he is, he is aware that *all* of him thinks. He thinks as a *whole* or in his *entirety* because as an entity that lacks substantive parts, it is not possible for one part of him to think while another does not" (emphasis added). (One would assume this means also that it is not possible for one part to think *some particular thing* while another does not. If so, then if there is such a thing as a "subconscious mind," which thinks things that the conscious mind either disbelieves or is ignorant of, such a subconscious mind is no part of the self.) A further implication is that my body is no part of myself. For I am aware of myself as something which has no parts, but if my body is part of me then I do have parts. (Along with the body itself, all of its parts will be parts of me.) But while my body is not part of me, I (that is, my soul) do "seem to have the property of occupying certain regions of space"; nevertheless, "I seem to occupy those regions in virtue of *all of me* . . . being present at the different points of the space that I occupy." A rather rich and complex sort of awareness, to be sure.

Goetz lays quite a lot of emphasis throughout his essay on the alleged fact that ordinary people are dualists and agree with his view as against materialism. No doubt it is true that dualism in some form or other is very widespread in human cultures. But I think there is a good deal of evidence against the claim that all or most ordinary people share the intuition of the self, as it is described by Goetz. A great many people, I am convinced, would react with incredulity to the claim that one's body is no part of oneself. (The book title *Our Bodies, Our Selves* was not, I think, widely perceived as an oxymoron.) Belief in the subconscious mind is not, I suppose, universal in all human cultures, but it is pretty deeply ingrained in our own culture (and supported with quite a lot of evidence), and the suggestion that one's subconscious mind is no part of oneself is hard to take seriously. I personally have known quite a few ordinary Christians who claim to be "trichotomists," that is, to believe that human beings consist of three parts—body, soul (or mind) and spirit—where soul and spirit are in some strong sense distinct parts of the person. Then there is Plato's famous division of the soul into reason, "spirit" and appetite. It is just possible that neither of these divisions (by Plato and the trichotomists) should count as division into "substantial parts"; without further analysis, it is difficult to be sure. But it seems unlikely that a believer in the simplicity of the soul, as endorsed by Goetz and Descartes, would have spoken in either of these ways. Perhaps most interesting of all, however, is Goetz's reference to the kiss of the dementors in the Harry Potter books. If what the dementor "sucks out" of its victim is a Cartesian soul, then the "kiss" would amount to death; it would leave behind, if not a lifeless body, at least one entirely devoid of consciousness. On the contrary, the dementor's victim still retains a kind of awareness, including a terrible sense of emptiness consequent on the departure of the soul.[1] It certainly looks as though both the soul that has been taken away and that which is left behind are thought of as being "parts" of the self. To be sure, Goetz could claim that all of the persons mentioned do indeed share his "Cartesian" intuition of the self as simple, but that they are merely confused and have failed to draw the appropriate conclusions from this awareness. But to the extent that their beliefs do not correspond to the content of his claimed awareness, the significance of their support for his position is weakened.

As I have already stated, I am skeptical about claims to intuition made by either materialists or dualists. Now Goetz has given an explanation for (what he takes to be) van Inwagen's mistaken interpretation of his experience of embodiment. So in order to restore symmetry, it will be helpful if I can give an explanation for (what I take to be) Goetz's own mistake. I propose that the intuition of the soul claimed by Goetz is nothing more nor less than the experience of the unity of consciousness, as set forth in my essay (and at greater length in

---

[1] [Harry asks,] "What—they kill—?"

"Oh no," said Lupin. "Much worse than that. You can exist without your soul, you know, as long as your brain and heart are still working. But you'll have no sense of self anymore, no memory, no . . . anything. There's no chance at all of recovery. You'll just—exist" (J. K. Rowling, *Harry Potter and the Prisoner of Azkaban* [New York: Scholastic, 1999], p. 247).

my book).[2] It often happens that we experience, all at once, a fairly complex array of data of different kinds. It occurs to us that this complex experience is nevertheless a unity in being experienced by a single subject; the experience cannot exist "parceled out" among distinct chunks of matter, as it would have to be if the subject were a complex whole consisting of physical parts. Thus we conclude, somewhat as Goetz concludes, that the subject of experience cannot be a physical thing and that there must exist a single, unified subject of consciousness (namely, the emergent self).

I would acknowledge that the unity-of-consciousness argument has certain drawbacks as compared with Goetz's Simple Argument. It is considerably more complex and difficult, especially in its fully developed form. And the conclusions it reaches, while similar, are less sweeping than those of the Simple Argument. (While the conscious self does not consist of parts, it does not follow that it cannot be divided into parts, much less that all of myself is involved in thinking whatever I am conscious of at a given moment.) I take these "drawbacks" as strengths rather than weaknesses of the unity-of-consciousness argument. By eschewing reliance on an overly strong claim to intuitive awareness, and by limiting its conclusions to those genuinely supported by the evidence, the argument (I would claim) reaches its goal more securely and confers greater warrant on its conclusions. As the tortoise said to the hare, "Slow and steady wins the race."

---

[2]William Hasker, *The Emergent Self* (Ithaca, N.Y.: Cornell University Press, 1999).

# A NONREDUCTIVE PHYSICALIST RESPONSE

*Nancey Murphy*

I begin with thanks to Stewart Goetz for providing an interesting and innovative argument for the dualist position. I assume that my assignment, though, is not to commend his work but to attempt to explain our differences.

I mention in my essay (in chapter four) that I expected my approach to philosophy to be different from some of my fellow contributors. To respond to Goetz's essay I need to explain some of the differences.

René Descartes, considered the founder of modern philosophy, is famous for having set out to doubt everything that he had learned from the philosophical tradition in order to place knowledge on a new and certain foundation. He believed that if everyone followed his method, they all would come to the same conclusions. He began with introspection, asking what ideas he could find in his mind that he was unable to doubt. His criterion was that any idea that appeared clearly and distinctly to him must be true.

The problem many have noted with Descartes's method is that what appears clear and distinct to one person sometimes turns out not to be so to others. For example, a "clear and distinct" premise of one of his arguments for the existence of God is that "it is manifest by the natural light that there must be at least as much reality in the efficient and total cause as in its effect."[1] This idea is not at all clear to people today; in fact, it is so unclear that we might want to say that it is neither true nor false.

Another example of such conflicting philosophical intuitions, of course, appears in Goetz's essay. He begins by stating his own belief that he is a soul, distinct from his body, but he also reports Peter van Inwagen's contrary intuition: "when I enter most deeply into that which I call *myself*, I *seem* to discover that I am a living animal."

Many philosophers have concluded that such intuitions are unreliable

---

[1] René Descartes, *Meditations on First Philosophy*, Third meditation.

grounds for philosophy simply because of such conflicts. In addition, they believe it is possible to explain the source of (many) such intuitions. Wallace Matson says that the thing Descartes failed to doubt was his own language—not his Latin or French (whatever that could mean), but rather what twentieth-century philosopher Ludwig Wittgenstein would call the *grammar* of his language. Grammar in this special sense refers to the implicit rules for the use of central concepts. The grammar of scholastic language allowed for using the word *real* in a comparative manner, whereas ours allows us to say only that something is real or unreal. This accounts for the fact that Descartes's intuition was clear and distinct to him while it makes no sense to us.[2]

An interesting fact about contemporary culture is that we have competing systems of language available for talking about ourselves. We still have the traditional language of bodies and souls, which allows us to say, for instance, that "when my body dies I shall be with God." However, new ways of talking have been developing for some years now, largely as a result of developments in science.

If our most basic intuitions about ourselves are dependent on the kind of language we have learned, this seems to call for ways to evaluate the language itself. One way is to examine the sources of the different linguistic systems. If recent scientific theories are a major source of the new physicalist language, where did the dualist language come from? I believe that it, too, comes from theories—theories developed in the distant past. One suggestion is that dualist theories were devised for ethical reasons. It is clear that people do not receive just rewards and punishments in this life. Thus, it was hypothesized that there must be another life apart from the body in which justice is done. For some Greek philosophers the concept of the soul served various explanatory purposes. One was to account for the differences between living and nonliving things. It did not appear possible to account for the special powers of animals or humans in terms of the potentials of matter, so a nonmaterial principle or component seemed a necessary postulate.

Goetz's comment on an earlier remark of mine reflects our different understandings on the relations between language and experience. Goetz says that

> according to Murphy, we start with the observed data of life and consciousness and hypothesize (erroneously, she thinks) that a soul must exist to account for them. This is not where we start, however. If I am correct, a person starts with the basic belief that she or he exists as a conscious soul.

---

[2]Wallace I. Matson, *A New History of Philosophy*, 2 vols. (San Diego: Harcourt Brace Jovanovich, 1987), 2:276-80.

I agree that an individual in a given era may simply find that he or she has such basic beliefs, but such beliefs may be artifacts of one's linguistic resources. The important question for philosophy, then, is the source of the linguistic resources, and whether those habitual or newly minted forms of language are congruent with the way things really are. This requires, in turn, that one ask whether the theories of, say, Plato or Aristotle are better supported than contemporary neuroscientific theories about the sources of our capacities for cognition, emotion and all of the other faculties that earlier theorists had attributed to the soul or mind.

So I conclude that Goetz's finding that he has the belief that he is a soul should carry little weight as grounds for an argument about whether humans in fact have (or are) souls. First, others who are probably just as introspectively keen have opposite beliefs. Second, if I am correct about a common source of such philosophical intuitions being the language we speak, and about the language we speak being conditioned by past or present theories about the way things are, then it is circular to argue on the basis of these intuitions for one or the other of the theories. Instead we have to look at the weight of evidence for the theories influencing our language and thereby our intuitions and even our subjective experiences of ourselves.

I turn now to Goetz's claim about his subjective experience of himself as a "simple substance." This will provide an opportunity for me to illustrate the sort of empirical approach that I advocate. I want to consider briefly some of the empirical research that may be relevant to explaining Goetz's experience of himself as a simple substance.

Since I do not share Goetz's experience I shall have to speculate a bit. I suspect that his experience is based on the experience we all have (at least most of the time) of the unity of consciousness (so what I say here will be relevant also to a critique of William Hasker's argument, which is based on the indivisibility of consciousness). In fact, there are interesting arguments in the philosophical and scientific literature over the question of whether consciousness *is* unified or not.[3] Some argue that our consciousness is in fact "gappy" and provide interesting studies from the psychology of perception to suggest that we would notice this gappiness if we were more attentive. It seems better, to me, to concede the common subjective experience of unified consciousness, but to use evidence from perceptual studies to show that the subjective unity must be *constructed* by means of sophisticated neural processes. The argument would

---

[3]See, e.g., the exchange between Daniel Dennett and Owen Flanagan, *The Nature of Consciousness: Philosophical Debates*, ed. Ned Block et al. (Cambridge, Mass.: MIT Press, 1997), pp. 83-93.

go something like this: Consciousness arises from brain processes. We know that the brain lacks a great deal of the sensory input needed for providing unified consciousness. Therefore, the brain has methods of constructing a unified experience of a unified world out of its gappy bits and pieces of information. An important research project (well underway) is to come to understand how it does so.

In this context, however, such an argument will backfire! A dualist, assuming that it is the soul that perceives the world, might say this: Given that the world itself is a continuous whole, that I am (veridically) conscious of it as a coherent whole, then the fact that the brain has access only to bits and pieces is grounds for arguing that it cannot be the brain that gives rise to such (veridical) consciousness. Examples of cases where we *erroneously* perceive continuity, then, are more useful here. One simple example is the fact that when two lights within a certain distance from one another flash in quick succession, we see not two flashes but a single light moving from the first location to the second. The physicalist can explain this easily as of a piece with the general continuity-constructing capacities of the brain (as when we see continuous motion in a movie constructed from a series of still frames). The dualist, I expect, will have to resort to ad hoc explanations for the soul's misperception of the world *in just these special cases.* This is an illustration of my general contention that physicalism provides excellent resources for guiding scientific research programs, while dualism is sterile in this regard.[4]

---

[4]See Nancey Murphy, "Nonreductive Physicalism: Philosophical Issues," in *Whatever Happened to the Soul? Scientific and Theological Portraits of Human Nature*, ed. Warren S. Brown, Nancey Murphy and H. Newton Malony, Theology and the Sciences (Minneapolis: Fortress, 1998), pp. 127-48.

# A CONSTITUTIONAL RESPONSE

*Kevin Corcoran*

Stewart Goetz is an ordinary guy. He is a dualist, after all. Although I believe that lots of "ordinary" people are dualists, I believe that I am, in the relevant sense, an ordinary guy too. But I am no dualist. I am what Goetz might call an "antecedent materialist." Although I will leave it to others to decide who among us wins the "ordinary" contest, I do want to comment on two features of Goetz's essay. First, I want to discuss Goetz's claim to be introspectively aware of his simplicity. Then I want to comment on his Simple Argument. I am not convinced that Goetz succeeds in establishing that he is introspectively aware of his substantive simplicity. And the Simple Argument, I believe, is fatally flawed.

## On the Powers of Introspection

René Descartes is the introspective philosopher par excellence, and Goetz follows Descartes in claiming to be introspectively aware of his simplicity, that is, of the substantive simplicity of the soul that is Stewart Goetz. But there is an objection to this Cartesian claim. Might Descartes (and so Goetz) be confusing his failure to be introspectively aware of his substantive complexity for his being introspectively aware of his substantive simplicity? From a failure to be introspectively aware of his substantive complexity, it appears that in the relevant passage of the *Meditations on First Philosophy* quoted by Goetz, Descartes illegitimately infers that he is substantively simple. And the inference to simplicity, so the objection goes, is illegitimate because even if the mind or soul is substantively complex, there is no reason to believe that Descartes (or Goetz) could be introspectively aware of this.

Now Goetz thinks that no such mistake is being made: there is no confusing his (and Descartes's) failure to be introspectively aware of his complexity for his being aware of his simplicity. And so there is no illegitimate inference from the one to the other. I myself remain unconvinced. Here is why. In Descartes's

Sixth Meditation he presents an argument for the real distinction between soul and body that we might dub the Divisibility Argument. Descartes claims that the body is divisible into parts and the soul is not. Since a single thing cannot both be and not be divisible into parts, Descartes concludes that soul and body are two distinct things. The problem is that, as I read Descartes, the reason he believes that the soul or mind is indivisible (or substantively simple) is not because it is unextended and thinking (although he believes it is), but rather because Descartes cannot conceive of dividing the mind into parts. And since he believes that if the mind were divisible into parts he would be able to conceive it, he concludes that it is not divisible into parts.

Conceivability is, for Descartes, a kind of introspective awareness. And what I take Descartes to be arguing is that since he is not introspectively aware of the mind's substantive complexity, the mind or soul is substantively simple. After all, if the mind were substantively complex, Descartes thinks he would be able to conceive it. What I am suggesting here is that Descartes's own Divisibility Argument looks very nearly like an explicit endorsement of precisely what Goetz claims Descartes is not doing—namely, inferring his substantive simplicity from his failure to be introspectively aware of his substantive complexity.

The problem, of course, is that just because Descartes (or any human cognizer) cannot conceive of dividing the mind into parts, it does not follow that the mind is not substantively complex, that is, is not divisible into parts. Here is an illustration. A physical object like a table appears to casual observation to be stable and unitary. But if we are to believe what the physicists tell us, the table is actually made of many things in rapid motion. If the true nature of a physical object like a table is as the physicists tell us, then the true nature of physical objects is not transparent to casual observation. Likewise with the mind. It could be that the true nature of the mind or soul is not transparent to introspection; the mind could be substantively complex but that complexity just not be transparent to introspective observation.

Let me make two more quick points here. First, Goetz might claim that because we are aware through casual observation of an object's spatial extension, shape and solidity, we would be led to believe that the physical object has substantive, though unobserved, parts. Likewise, Goetz wants to claim that in light of his "apprehension" of his soul, not only has he no reason to believe he has unobserved parts, but he has positive reason to believe that he lacks such parts.

I agree that we would be led, in casual observation, to believe in unobserved micro parts of physical objects based on our casual observation of them. But I would contend that we would not infer unobserved parts based solely on what is phenomenologically presented in our perceptual awareness.

It is background beliefs (e.g., the belief that macroscopic objects have unobservable, microscopic parts) coupled with our awareness of extension, shape and solidity that would lead us to believe that, although we are not observationally aware of these tiny parts, they are nevertheless there.

Here is my first point: Even Bishop George Berkeley's metaphysical *Idealism* is compatible with the phenomenological content of a perceptual experience of a table. Since the phenomenology of Berkeley's experience of a table would be no different from the phenomenology of my perceptual experience of a table, and I would bet Berkeley would not infer the existence of unobserved, extended microscopic parts, I conclude that it is not in virtue of the phenomenological content alone that would lead Goetz or me to posit microphysical parts of physical objects. Similarly, I think that it is not the phenomenological content of Goetz's introspective awareness alone that leads him to believe in his simplicity; rather, I suggest that it is his introspective awareness coupled with his antecedent dualism. In my view, Goetz has not succeeded in establishing that simplicity is part of the phenomenological content of his introspective awareness. And that is precisely what he needs to give us good reasons for believing.

My second point is this: Goetz thinks that if the materialist is to undermine the introspective ground for believing one is a simple substance, then he or she must provide a reason for thinking materialism is true. I disagree. The burden of proof is on the antecedent dualist to show that she is not mistaking the lack of introspective awareness of her substantive complexity for her introspective awareness of her substantive simplicity. And, as I have already suggested, there is reason within Descartes's own *Meditations* to suggest that belief in simplicity is based precisely on something like a failure to be introspectively aware of complexity. If Goetz is not making the same sort of mistake as it looks like Descartes is making, it is up to Goetz to give us good reasons for thinking so. The reasons he has given do not strike me as persuasive.

## The Simple Argument

Goetz provides the following positive argument for dualism:

1. I am essentially simple.

2. My body is essentially complex.

3. If I am identical with my body, then whatever is a property of the one is a property of the other.

Therefore, because I have an essential property that my body lacks, I am not identical with my body.

Goetz supposes that someone might begin with the basic belief that she herself is a soul and infer the truth of dualism from the Simplicity Argument. But this, I think, would be a mistake. The reason is that, perhaps surprisingly, the Simple Argument is not an argument for dualism! It is, rather, an argument to the conclusion that one is not identical with one's body. And, as I demonstrate in my own contribution to this volume, one need not be a dualist in order to believe that one is not identical with one's body. So I, for example, think the conclusion to the Simplicity Argument is true (even though I believe the argument is unsound, due to the falsity of the first premise). Here is what I take to be a sound argument to the same conclusion as Goetz's Simplicity Argument:

1. I am essentially a psychological being.

 2. My body is not essentially a psychological being.

3. A single thing cannot both be and not be an essentially psychological being.

Therefore, I am not identical with my body.

Again, this is not an argument for dualism. It is an argument whose conclusion is compatible with both dualism and certain versions of physicalism. For example, it is consistent with the constitution view I shall present in my essay. Even more surprising than the fact that the Simplicity Argument is not an argument for dualism is the fact that one could grant to Goetz the truth of all the premises of his Simplicity Argument, and so commit oneself to the conclusion, without embracing dualism or the constitution view. For one could insist that one is identical with a physically simple object, such as a partless atom in one's brain.

The only argument Goetz endorses for dualism, therefore, does not constitute an argument for dualism at all.[1] And the other arguments he considers— the modal argument and the argument from conceivability of disembodiment—Goetz himself finds problematic. I conclude, then, given the failure of Goetz's Simplicity Argument and the failure of the other arguments for dualism, that Goetz's overall case for dualism still faces difficulties.

---

[1] If each occurrence of the English word *I* in Goetz's Simplicity Argument is to be read as "the immaterial soul that is Stewart Goetz," then quite obviously the constitution theorist cannot endorse the conclusion and my criticism would fail. For then the conclusion comes to this: "Because the immaterial soul that is Stewart Goetz has an essential property that Stewart Goetz's body lacks, the immaterial soul that is Stewart Goetz is not identical with Stewart Goetz's body." And it does seem that one cannot embrace that conclusion without also embracing dualism. Of course, if that is how *I* is to be understood throughout the argument, then the argument seems to me to be completely unmotivated.

Finally, if Goetz desires a materialist argument against his being a simple soul, I offer the following line of argument (inspired by Trenton Merricks):

1. Stewart Goetz sometimes kisses his wife.

2. Stewart Goetz's substantively simple soul never kisses anyone. (It has no lips!)

Therefore, Stewart Goetz is not a simple soul.

## Conclusion

I am at odds with those materialists who believe that dualism is incoherent or can be refuted simply by wrinkling one's nose at it. I think dualism is a coherent view of human beings and compatible with important Christian teaching. But I believe it constitutes a false theory of human nature. If Goetz and Descartes turn out to be right after all, then when I break bread with them in the New Jerusalem I shall humbly admit my defeat. Of course, if Goetz convinces me sooner that he and Descartes are right, I will admit defeat well before the heavenly banquet. As it stands, however, I believe that I have been given no good reason to abandon the constitution view in favor of dualism.[2]

---

[2]Although what I just now said is true, it must be acknowledged that Goetz would not himself believe that he has given reasons that I would recognize as good for abandoning the constitution view. That is because Goetz's task was to begin with the assumption that he is a simple soul and offer grounds for thinking that claim true.

# 3 ON BEHALF OF EMERGENT DUALISM

*William Hasker*

Suppose you believe that a human being is something more than a collection of protoplasm—that it just is not true that everything about us can be explained in terms of the atoms and molecules or, alternatively, the genes and chromosomes, that structure our bodies. Perhaps you think that, in addition to our natural drives to survive and reproduce, we are so constituted that we naturally seek to know the truth about things and that we have in us both a capacity to recognize the good and the right, and some ability and desire (however often frustrated by conflict with other desires) to conform our lives thereto. Perhaps you even believe that we have a capacity for a relationship with God and the possibility of a life beyond the present one, a life that will be the fulfillment of our best hopes and longings. We could summarize these thoughts by saying that you have an aversion to a materialist view of the nature of human beings—particularly, an aversion to a reductive materialist view, one which seeks to explain us entirely in terms of the behavior of the physical stuff of which we are made.

Suppose, on the other hand, that you have come to have doubts about the once popular "dualist" views, according to which a human person consists of a body somehow joined to a soul that is fundamentally totally different from the body and bears no necessary relation to it. You have learned something about the complex and subtle dependencies of our thought processes on the state and functioning of our brains, and you think you might have a hard time making sense of those dependencies if the mind is as separate and different from the brain as traditional dualism has said. You also notice that other animals, while undeniably differing from us, are also similar to us in many ways, and you shrink from the thought that animals, unlike us, are mere physical automata with no souls and no conscious life of any kind. So while materialism strikes you as having little to offer, you find dualism almost equally perplexing.

## The Idea of Emergence

If this description provides at least a reasonable approximation of the state of your thinking about these matters, there is a philosophical idea that you may find intriguing and even helpful. It is the idea of *emergence*. The core idea of emergence is that, when elements of a certain sort are assembled in the right way, something new comes into being, something that was not there before. The new thing is not just a rearrangement of what was there before, but neither is it something dropped into the situation from the outside. It "emerges," comes into being, through the operation of the constituent elements, yet the new thing is something different and often surprising; we would not have expected it before it appeared. Take a mathematical equation of a certain sort, plot it onto a set of coordinates, and a fractal pattern appears—complex, unexpected and sometimes stunningly beautiful. Dissolve some chemicals in water, let the solution stand for a while under the right conditions, and regular, highly organized crystals are formed. When the right numbers and kinds of chemical molecules are arranged in a particular complex structure, we have something new—a living cell. And given a sufficient number of the right kinds of cells, properly organized, there is the wonder of awareness, involving sensation, emotion and rational thought. In each case, what emerges is something qualitatively new—a fractal pattern, a crystalline structure, life, consciousness. But if you view these phenomena in the light of emergence, you will think of this new element not as something "added from the outside," but as something that arises somehow out of the original constituents of the situation.

That this is so is evident in the first two cases. The beautiful and surprising fractal pattern is simply the result of tracing the values assigned by the mathematical equation onto the coordinate grid, and the crystal structure is a straightforward consequence of the way in which the constituent atoms align themselves as a result of chemical bonding. The other two cases, however, have been more controversial. Some have supposed that in order for there to be life there is needed, over and above the physical structure of the cell, some additional component, sometimes called "vital energy" or "life force." This view is now discredited among biologists, but it was taken seriously by some of them as recently as the early twentieth century. And in the final example, the view that the soul is something "added to" the body by a special act of divine creation is seriously advocated today by a number of philosophers. Some believe, indeed, that only in this way is it possible to arrive at a coherent Christian view of the human person. In what follows, I hope to show that this is not the case.

The four examples also serve to highlight the fact that there are different varieties of emergence—or, if you prefer, different senses in which a phenomenon may be said to be "emergent." The fractal pattern is what may be termed a *logical emergent*: for all its complexity and beauty, it is simply a logical consequence of the elements that make up the situation—the mathematical formula, the coordinate system and the convention for matching values of the variables in the formula with positions in the coordinate system. The crystalline structure, on the other hand, is a *causal emergent*: it is a consequence of the causal powers of the constituent atoms, as ascertained by the science of physics, that this new and interesting structure appears. The existence of instances of emergence of these two kinds is uncontroversial, though not everyone uses the language of emergence in describing them.

But now consider the following possibility. An animal or human brain consists of ordinary atoms and molecules, which are subject to the ordinary laws of physics and chemistry. But suppose that, given the particular arrangements of these atoms and molecules of the brain, new laws, new systems of interaction between the atoms, and so on, come into play. These new laws, furthermore, play an essential role in such characteristic mental activities as rational thought and decision making. The new laws, however, are not detectable in any simpler configuration; in such configurations the behavior of the atoms and molecules is adequately explained by the ordinary laws of physics and chemistry. These, then, are *emergent laws,* and the powers that the brain has in virtue of the emergent laws may be termed *emergent causal powers.* Given this much, it is clear that to postulate the existence of emergent causal powers is to make a dramatic, and in fact extremely controversial, metaphysical claim. Many philosophers and scientists strongly resist such a claim, pointing to the immense explanatory success of standard physicochemical explanations in accounting for a broad range of natural phenomena. What has worked so well so often before, they say, should not be abandoned just because at the moment we seem to find ourselves stymied in explaining a particular range of phenomena. Nevertheless, a number of philosophers have felt compelled to assert the existence of emergent causal powers; they hold that crucially important facts about our mental lives cannot be explained in any other way.

Suppose, finally, that as a result of the structure and functioning of the brain, there appear not merely new modes of behavior of the fundamental constituents (as in the case of emergent causal powers), but also a new entity, the mind, which does not consist of atoms and molecules or of any other physical constituents. If this were the case, we would have an *emergent individual,* an individual that comes into existence as the result of a certain configuration of the brain and nervous system but that is not composed of the matter which makes up that physical system. This, clearly enough, represents yet a further stage of emergence, one that is resisted even by those philosophers who acknowledge emergent causal powers. Such an emergence theory would be, in fact, a variety of dualism, in that the emergent mind is an entity not composed of physical stuff. But it would be an *emergent* dualism, unlike traditional dualisms that postulate a special divine act of creation as the origin of the soul. Such is the theory advocated in this essay.

## Emergent Dualism

Having set the stage by this account of emergence, it is time to present the resulting view of the person. The fundamental idea is actually rather simple. As a consequence of a certain configuration and function of the brain and nervous system, a new entity comes into being—namely, the mind or soul. This new thing is not merely a "configurational state" of the cells of the brain (as, e.g., a crystal is a configurational state of the molecules that make it up). The mind, on this view, is a "thing in itself"; it is what some philosophers call a "substance." It is not made of the chemical stuff of which the brain is composed, though it crucially depends on that chemical stuff for both its origin and its continuance. It is this mind—the conscious self—that thinks and reasons and feels emotions and makes decisions; it is the central core of what we mean by a "person."

An analogy I have sometimes used in this connection can be stated as follows. As a magnet generates its magnetic field, so an organism generates its conscious field. Arrange an assemblage of iron molecules in the right way, and something new appears: a magnetic field. Arrange an assemblage of neurons in the right way, and another new thing appears: consciousness, a mind. This analogy can, I believe, be helpful in enabling us to grasp the way in which the mind is produced, but it should not be pushed beyond its limits. It is not the case, for instance, that a magnetic field (or a positronic field) is conscious, in spite of all we have learned from Lieutenant Commander Data in *Star Trek!* Nor are the magnetic field, the gravitational field and the other fields of physics emergent in the strong sense that applies to the conscious mind. The field analogy can be helpful, but we should not try to get from it more than it contains.[1] It is not by any means a proof of the theory's truth.

A strong point of this theory is that it immediately establishes a close connection between the mind/soul and the biological organism, a connection that in some other forms of dualism is far more tenuous. It prevents the splitting of

---

[1]Keith Yandell's critique does press the analogy beyond its proper limits and beyond anything I have said about it. See his "Mind-Fields and the Siren Song of Reason," *Philosophia Christi* 2, no. 2 (2000): 183-95. For my reply, see my "Response to My Friendly Critics," *Philosophia Christi* 2, no. 2 (2000): 197-207.

the person into two disparate entities and cuts off the implication (sometimes found in "Platonic" theories of the soul) that everything of true worth is to be found in the spiritual dimension and that the body is at best a tool, at worst an encumbrance for the soul. In the living of one's life, mind/soul and body form a completely integrated unit; this is, in Charles Taliaferro's expression, an "integrative dualism."[2] The mind/soul is both generated and sustained by the biological organism, and its activities are subserved and enabled by the functioning of the organism. In the living experience of a person, there is no seam that marks the division of mind/soul/spirit from bodily existence. This means, furthermore, that the remarkable ways in which (as we are now discovering) a person's mental life depends on the condition and functioning of the brain—with specific parts of the brain responsible for particular, specialized mental processes—fit quite naturally into the theory of emergent dualism.

So far we have been speaking about human persons, but much of what has been said applies to other animals as well. Humans are animals, after all, and it is a poor strategy if, in our necessary and proper insistence on what separates us from the other animals, we overlook or deny what we have in common with them. If the right configuration and functioning of the human brain and nervous system give rise to consciousness, then surely this must be true of "lower" forms of life as well. How much lower? That is, how far down the scale of biological complexity does consciousness go? That is a good question, but one to which it is difficult to give a clear-cut answer. Most of us think that trees and bushes are not conscious; and on the other hand, we are confident that our pet dogs, cats and birds enjoy a richly varied conscious life. In between, however, there is a broad range of cases about which opinions can reasonably differ. (René Descartes thought it absurd to suppose that oysters might have souls, but then in his view their having souls would have meant they were immortal, which many of us would find hard to swallow—the immortality, that is, not the oysters!) Emergent dualism has no stake in any particular answer to this question; it leaves us free to attribute awareness where the evidence suggests it and to withhold the attribution where the evidence is lacking or inconclusive.

Emergent dualism does not strictly require a theory of biological evolution, but it fits very well with such a theory. This is, in fact, a major advantage of the theory in comparison with traditional dualism. It is also, somewhat surprisingly, an advantage the theory has over most versions of materialism, as we

---

[2]See Charles Taliaferro, *Consciousness and the Mind of God* (Cambridge: Cambridge University Press, 1994).

shall see. The central idea here is that consciousness co-evolves with the organism that generates and sustains it. Gradually more complex neurological structures generate gradually more complex and sophisticated conscious states. The conscious states, in turn, affect behavior, and the entire creature, conscious experience along with physical structure, is subject to the pressures of evolutionary selection. Over time this leads, according to evolutionary theory, to still more complex neurology and states of consciousness.[3] This picture seems so natural, given the ordinary understanding of how evolution works, that it comes as something of a shock that (as we shall see) neither traditional dualisms nor standard varieties of materialism can accept it.

This emphasis on what we have in common with other animals may lead to questions about the ways in which we are unique. How, in fact, are we different from those others? It is clear that we are different from them in many ways, over and above the obvious physical differences. A striking human characteristic is our use of language, something peculiar to humans and distinct from even the most sophisticated systems of communication used by other animals. Along with this is a capacity for reasoning, and in particular for abstract thought, that is quite different from anything seen in animals. (That is not to say, of course, that animals are "mindless automata": the similarities as well as the differences need to be frankly acknowledged.) There is an awareness of moral distinctions, of right and wrong, justice and injustice, which seems to be uniquely human. And there is the capacity for a relationship to the Ultimate Reality, or so at least most humans have believed. The details and precise significance of the differences may be debatable, but that the differences exist is not. (One scientist who worked at teaching sign language to chimpanzees said she was happy to have a conversation with her chimp about a birthday party, but what she would really like would be to discuss the theory of evolution with a chimp. So far as I know, that conversation has not yet taken place!) What emergent dualism says about this is that these differences are somehow grounded in differences in the structure and functioning of the brain and nervous system. And while the details are at present unknown, that there is such a grounding is extremely plausible in the light of the abundant evidence that specific "higher" functions are dependent on the functioning of particular, highly specialized regions in the brain.

---

[3] The emergent dualist has no need to decide whether the increased complexity can be generated by the standard Darwinian processes of random variation and natural selection or whether some special divine guidance and/or intervention is required. Either view is compatible with the theory as set forth here, though I myself find the latter view more credible.

A question that must be faced by any theory of the mind is the possibility of life after death. And here it seems that traditional dualist views have a clear advantage. Most such views, in fact, have held that the soul is "naturally immortal," meaning that it is incapable of dying or of being destroyed by any natural means.[4] Against this it has been pointed out that the Scriptures nowhere speak of the soul in these terms, but rather they point to the resurrection of the body as the believer's hope for an everlasting life. Nevertheless, it seems that a soul would still be needed in order to guarantee personal identity. If there is no soul that survives between death and resurrection, what sense can be made of the claim that it is the *very same person* who once lived, then died and now has been resurrected? These matters will be discussed in more detail later; at present, they are mentioned only in order to set the stage for considering a future life in relation to emergent dualism. What does that theory have to say about this important question?

At first glance, it might seem the implications of emergent dualism do not favor the possibility of a future life. If the mind/soul depends on the brain and nervous system for its continued existence, it would seem that destroying the brain would destroy the mind as well. And the analogy of the magnetic field seems to support this conclusion: destroy a magnet (or, in the case of an electromagnet, turn off the electric current), and the field disappears. But this is far from conclusive. The key point is that, on this theory, the conscious mind is an ontologically distinct entity from the physical brain. Under normal circumstances, the continued existence of the mind depends on support from the body. But to quote the neuroscientist Wilder Penfield, "whether energy can come to the mind of man from an outside source after his death is for each individual to decide for himself. Science has no such answers."[5] Penfield here alludes to the possibility that the mind, while normally dependent on the brain and body for its continuance, might be sustained directly by divine power in the absence of such support. Emergent dualism accepts this, affirming that the continued existence of the person that has died is a miracle of divine power, not a consequence of the soul's "natural immortality."

Upon closer examination, the field analogy also supports this possibility. It has been shown that physical theory implies that a sufficiently intense magnetic field can hold itself together by gravity even if its generating magnet has

---

[4]Christians (and other theists) who are dualists hold that the soul, like all created beings, needs the sustaining power of God in order to continue its existence. The soul, then, would be annihilated should God cease to sustain it, but otherwise it is indestructible.

[5]Wilder Penfield, *The Mystery of the Mind* (Princeton: Princeton University Press, 1975), p. 215.

been removed.[6] A similar point can be made about the black holes that have recently become prominent in cosmology. According to Roger Penrose, once a black hole has formed, it becomes "a self-sustaining gravitational field in its own right" and "has no further use for the body which originally built it."[7] To be sure, it might be unwise to take these ideas as a model for understanding the fate of the emergent mind. To do this might suggest that certain "high-powered" minds could become self-sustaining whereas other, less powerful minds (those of infants and small children, for instance) simply dissipate at death. But the models do underscore the fact that the emergent mind is onto-logically distinct from the organism which generated it, and it is thus a coher-ent possibility that the mind could survive the death of the body.

If the emergent mind can survive the death of its body, it can also be resur-rected in a new or restored body. To be sure, not just any body would do. Du-alists have sometimes supposed that souls could freely exchange bodies, as in John Locke's story of the prince and the cobbler. But a new body for an emer-gent soul would have to be precisely tailored to fit the soul in question; other-wise, the activity of the body in sustaining the soul would clash with the al-ready established character of the latter. (This is just one illustration of the way in which emergent dualism recognizes the complex dependence of mind on body, whereas traditional dualism tends to minimize this dependence.)

A bit more needs to be said about the implications of the concept of emer-gence employed here. Some critics have characterized emergence as "magi-cal," because the emergent properties appear, as it were, out of the blue. This is inaccurate. The emergent powers are in fact among the inherent powers of the basic constituents of the situation, the elementary particles of matter. That is to say, it is an inherent power of ordinary matter that, when combined in the right ways, it produces an entity with the characteristics of the emergent mind. What makes these powers emergent (in the strong sense) is precisely that they are not manifest in any simpler material configurations. They exist but remain latent until the right functional configuration of matter is achieved. That mat-ter—the dust of the earth—should have these remarkable properties is no doubt surprising, even amazing. But if we have learned anything from science, it should be that surprise and amazement are the norm, rather than the excep-tion, as we penetrate further into the mysteries of nature. Certainly, we should

---

[6]See Kip Thorne, *Black Holes and Time Warps: Einstein's Outrageous Legacy* (New York: Norton, 1994), p. 263.

[7]Roger Penrose, "Black Holes," in *Cosmology Now* (New York: Taplinger, 1976), p. 124; see also Thorne, *Black Holes*, p. 30.

not suppose that we now thoroughly comprehend the nature of matter and no more mysteries remain. It is abundantly clear that, in spite of all we have learned about matter, our grasp on its fundamental nature remains tenuous in the extreme. The billiard-ball atoms of early modern science were readily graspable by the intellect, however remote they may have been from the truth about the world. Matter as conceived in quantum mechanics, on the other hand, can be represented in incredibly accurate mathematical formalisms, but we are very far indeed from grasping what it truly is. As Richard Feynman has said, "nobody understands . . . why nature behaves in this peculiar way."[8]

The other consideration to which I would point is found in our faith that this "ordinary" matter is the creation of a God whose wisdom and power far exceed our comprehension. And this God has told us that he created us from the dust of the earth—so we have no choice, really, but to suppose that he endowed that dust with the powers required to enable the rich and various creation that he proposed to fashion from it. It may be that in the end only belief in the power of such a creative God can make emergent dualism a viable and credible hypothesis.

## *Materialism and Reduction*

It is clear, all the same, that there is nothing obvious or self-evident about emergent dualism. It is not the first theory that would occur to anyone! Speaking personally, I found myself led to the theory in large part by observing the difficulties of competing theories—theories that, on the face of it, may seem simpler and more credible than this one. The simplest approaches, arguably, lie at the extremes: materialist theories that explain the mind entirely in terms of the ordinary, known properties of matter at one end, and dualist theories that reject any thought of explaining the mind in terms of matter at the other end. Because of this, the case for emergent dualism must of necessity include a critique of opposing theories—a critique that is also highly relevant to the objectives of the present volume.

Many, perhaps most, materialist theories of the mind are *reductionist* to a greater or lesser degree. In general, the notion of reduction is more or less the polar opposite of emergence. Emergentism holds that, given a particular complex arrangement, something new appears, something that was not there before. According to reductionism, on the other hand, the complex arrangement is really *nothing but* the elements in their interrelationships: there is "really"

---

[8]Richard Feynman, *QED: The Strange Theory of Light and Matter* (Princeton: Princeton University Press, 1985), p. 10.

nothing new there, nothing that was not already present before. That is the general idea, but as in the case of emergence, there are different kinds of reduction or different senses in which a theory can be reductive. Nancey Murphy draws a useful distinction between *ontological* reduction and *causal* reduction. She defines *ontological reductionism* as the view that "as one goes up the hierarchy of levels, no new kinds of metaphysical 'ingredients' need to be added to produce higher-level entities from lower." Specifically, "no immaterial mind or soul is needed to get consciousness."[9] Ontological reductionism is endorsed by all materialists, including Murphy herself. Nevertheless, she terms herself a "nonreductive physicalist" in virtue of her opposition to *causal reductionism*, which she defines as "the view that the behavior of the parts of a system (ultimately, the parts studied by subatomic physics) is determinative of the behavior of all higher-level entities."[10] Murphy is quite emphatic in her rejection of causal reductionism:

> If free will is an illusion and the highest of human intellectual and cultural achievements can *(per impossibile)* be counted as the mere outworking of the laws of physics, this is utterly devastating to our ordinary understanding of ourselves, and of course to theological accounts, as well, which depend not only on a concept of responsibility before God, but also on the justification (not merely the causation) of our theories about God and God's will.[11]

It may be helpful to spell out these objections a bit more fully. If causal reductionism is true, then everything human beings do and say is simply the consequence of the actions and reactions of the elementary particles of matter, operating according to the fundamental laws of physics. What *we* do is simply the result of what *those particles* do—there is nothing there but the particles to "do" anything. It is clear, then, we have no real choice about what we do; even if we have the "experience of choosing," how that choice comes out is wholly determined by the actions and reactions of the fundamental particles. Under those circumstances, it does indeed seem that free will would be an illusion, as Murphy says. And if we have no free will, how can we be responsible? In particular, how can we be responsible before God, as Scripture says we are? There is also the question as to how, if this account is true, we can be rationally justified in any of the reasoning that we do. On this view, our acceptance of certain

---

[9]Nancey Murphy, "Nonreductive Physicalism: Philosophical Issues," in *Whatever Happened to the Soul? Scientific and Theological Portraits of Human Nature*, ed. Warren Brown, Nancey Murphy and H. Newton Malony, Theology and the Sciences (Minneapolis: Fortress 1998), p. 129.
[10]Ibid., p. 128.
[11]Ibid., p. 131.

conclusions is not determined by the fact that those conclusions follow from known truths according to correct principles of logical inference. Rather, we accept those conclusions, and only those conclusions, that we are determined to accept by the particles that make up our brains, acting and reacting according to the fundamental laws of physics. And those physical laws do not in any way have in view the goal of leading us to true conclusions about the world— rather, they are nonteleological; they can be represented by mathematical formulas that have no reference whatever to any human goals or objectives. But to accept that all of our reasoning is determined in this way by nonrational factors is devastating to any reliance we might otherwise have had on our theories and belief systems—including, as Murphy points out, our theories and beliefs concerning God and our relationship with God.

Still another problem with causal reductionism has already been hinted at. Reductive materialist theories of the mind are unable to account for the evolution of consciousness—more specifically, the evolution of rational thought. That this should be so is surprising; materialists typically claim as an advantage for their theory that it is more in tune than are its competitors with current science and, in particular, with evolutionary theory. Yet at this decisive point, the project of reductive materialist explanation fails entirely. Let me explain why.

The central idea of "evolutionary epistemology" is simply that an organism's conscious states confer a benefit in the struggle to survive and reproduce. Such responses as discomfort in the presence of a chemical irritant, or the awareness of light or warmth or food, enhance the organism's ability to respond in optimal fashion. For more complex animals there is the awareness of the presence of predator or of prey and the ability to devise simple strategies so as to increase the chances of successful predation or escape. As the organisms and their brains become more complex, we see the emergence of systems of beliefs and of strategies for acquiring beliefs. Natural selection guarantees a high level of fitness, including cognitive fitness.

Our summary of the reductive materialist version of Darwinist evolutionary theory can be quite concise. It goes like this: Certain complex assemblages of organic chemicals develop a kind of dynamic stability in their interactions with the environment; this stability, combined with a capacity for self-replication, leads us to say they are alive. A variety of random physical forces leads to variations in the self-replicating assemblages, and some of the assemblages are more successful than others in maintaining and reproducing themselves. Over time, some of these assemblages become more complex than the earliest forms by many orders of magnitude, and their behaviors and interactions with the surrounding environment also become more complex. Nevertheless, the entire process is governed by, and explicable in terms of, the ordinary laws of physics and chemistry. Put differently, it is never necessary to go outside of the physical configurations and the physical laws in order to predict the future behavior of these assemblages; this is what philosophers call the "causal closure of the physical domain," and it is a direct consequence of causal reductionism.[12]

It is hoped that the reader will already have spotted the incongruity of these two accounts. It is not merely that the Darwinist account of evolution does not mention the adaptive benefits of awareness and cognition. If that were the only problem, it could easily be maintained that awareness and cognition are among the necessary preconditions for the more successful behaviors and interactions with the environment that are featured in the account. (That, in fact, is exactly what evolutionary epistemology affirms to be the case.) The problem, rather, is that the Darwinist account precludes the kind of role for awareness and cognition that is posited in the epistemological account. It does this by its last two sentences, which affirm the causal closure of the physical domain. Those sentences guarantee that the conscious state of the organism, as such, can have no influence whatever on the organism's behavior and thus on its propensity to survive. The central contention of evolutionary epistemology has been decisively undermined.

These objections could be spelled out in greater detail, but perhaps enough has been said to make the reader aware that there are severe problems with causal reductionism. I believe, furthermore, that Murphy is entirely correct in her objections to this kind of theory. It is extremely unfortunate, then, that Murphy's own view turns out to be a variety of causal reductionism! To be sure, this is a serious charge for me to make and one that needs to be carefully supported. Let me begin by pointing out that secular philosophers also have noted that it is difficult for a materialist or physicalist view to avoid reductionism. A classic statement of this difficulty was given by Jaegwon Kim in his presidential address to the American Philosophical Association, "The Myth of Nonreductive Materialism."[13] I will argue that Murphy's nonreductive physicalism is another version of the same myth.

In addressing this question, it is important to realize Murphy is assuming that the standard laws of particle interaction known to physics govern all such

---

[12]This summary is taken from my article "Theism and Evolutionary Biology," in *A Companion to the Philosophy of Religion,* ed. Philip Quinn and Charles Taliaferro (Oxford: Blackwell, 1997), pp. 430-31.

[13]Jaegwon Kim, "The Myth of Nonreductive Materialism," in *Supervenience and Mind: Selected Philosophical Essays* (Cambridge: Cambridge University Press, 1991).

interactions without exception.[14] (For ease of reference, I shall designate this view as *microdeterminism*.[15]) But given this assumption, it is hard to see how causal reduction can be avoided. The larger entities, after all, are wholly composed of the particles of microphysics, and it would seem that the behavior of all such entities will be exhaustively determined by the behavior of the constituent particles. (It hardly makes sense, for example, to suppose that I could go off in one direction and the particles that constitute my body in another!) And this is the definition of causal reductionism.

Murphy previously thought she could escape this consequence through the use of the philosophical notion of the supervenience of mind on body.[16] More recently, however, she has acknowledged that this defense against the charge of causal reductionism does not succeed.[17] And this means that she needs to look elsewhere if she is to avoid causal reductionism.

The notion Murphy now depends on to stave off causal reductionism is what is known as *downward causation*.[18] To develop this notion, we can start with the idea of reality as organized hierarchically into a number of levels— say, inorganic, organic, mental or conscious, social, and perhaps others. What characterizes the higher levels is not new, additional elements that are added; that is, there are no vital forces or immaterial souls. Rather, we have novel forms of structure and organization, but these novel forms really do make a difference; there really is something new in the world as a result of their appearance. Given this much, we can raise the question of causality. What is it, in this picture of the world, that exerts causal influence? In a great many cases, causality is bottom-up. That is, the behavior of higher-level entities is determined by what happens on the lower levels. The contention that all causality is of this sort is characteristic of causal reductionism. But Murphy would have

---

[14]There may, of course, be laws that are not yet known, or corrections may be needed to some presently accepted laws. This will not matter for our argument, so long as the revised laws are of the same *kind* as those already accepted. (They will not, for example, involve primitive teleology or intentionality.)

[15]This terminology is less than completely accurate, given the element of indeterminacy that is held to exist at the quantum level. This indeterminacy may, however, be unimportant in practice, since statistical laws insure that the behavior of larger-scale objects (including neurons) is effectively deterministic.

[16]Murphy, "Nonreductive Physicalism," pp. 132-38.

[17]See Nancey Murphy, "Response to Cullen," in *Science & Christian Belief* 13, no. 2 (2001): 161-63.

[18]See, e.g., Nancey Murphy, "Giving the Nonreductive Physicalist Her Due: A Response to Hasker's *The Emergent Self*," *Philosophia Christi* 2, no. 2 (2000): 167-73; for my response, see Hasker, "Reply" (cited above). Murphy's approach is spelled out more fully in her article "The Problem of Mental Causation: How Does Reason Get Its Grip on the Brain?" *Science & Christian Belief* 14, no. 2 (2002): 143-58.

us reject this. We must also consider top-down causality, in which wholes that exist at the higher levels exert a downward causal influence on the parts of which they are composed. In this way, then, causal reductionism is avoided. According to Roger Sperry,

> The principle of control from above downward, referred to as "downward causation," . . . says that we and the universe are more than just a swarm of "hurrying" atoms, electrons, and protons, that the higher holistic properties and qualities of the world to which the brain responds, including all the macrosocial phenomena of modern civilization, are just as real and causal for science as are the atoms and molecules on which they depend.[19]

In order to complete the picture, we need to emphasize that, for typical advocates of this view (including Murphy), microdeterminism is strongly affirmed. As Sperry writes,

> The expectation that downward macrodetermination should thus effect reconfigurations . . . in the neuron-to-neuron activity of subjective mental states— or in the micro components of any macro phenomenon—indicates a serious misunderstanding of what emergent interaction is. From the start I have stressed consistently that the higher-level phenomena in exerting downward control do *not disrupt* or *intervene* in the causal relations of the lower-level component activity. Instead they *supervene* in a way that leaves the micro interactions, per se, unaltered.[20]

It is easy to see why this notion of downward causation has seemed appealing. It seems to give everybody what they most want. The physicist keeps the uniformity and universal applicability of the fundamental laws of physics; the antidualist strain in modern thought is appeased through the banishment of souls and their ilk; and yet the psychologist and the theologian are allowed, by invoking upper-level causality, to go their own ways and carry on their business without the frustrating and futile attempt to consider everything in terms of fundamental physics. It is most unfortunate, then, that downward causation so understood is a *seriously confused idea*, one that offers *no legitimate assistance* for those wishing to avoid causal reductionism.

The idea of reality as organized into hierarchical levels, to be sure, is plausible and appealing, and there is no need to reject it. But the terminology of "levels" can easily mislead us into thinking of the different levels as concrete

---

[19]Roger W. Sperry, "Psychology's Mentalist Paradigm and the Religion/Science Tension," *American Psychologist* 43, no. 8 (1988): 609.

[20]Roger W. Sperry, "In Defense of Mentalism and Emergent Interaction," *Journal of Mind and Behavior* 12, no. 2 (1991): 235-36 (emphasis in original).

and as capable of exerting, on their own, distinct kinds of causal influence. It is as though one were thinking of a multistoried building, in which almost everything that reaches the upper stories comes in through the ground floor; but occasionally something comes down from the upper stories—say, a telephone call containing orders or instructions—that makes things on the ground floor go differently than they would otherwise have done. Such a picture is seriously misleading. The higher levels are levels of organization, not concrete entities. The only concrete existents involved are the ultimate constituents and combinations thereof, and the only causal influences are those of the ultimate constituents in their interactions with each other. If the higher-level organization is to make a difference, it can only do this by *affecting the interactions of the constituents at the base level*—but this it is forbidden to do by the thesis of microdeterminism. Causal reduction has in no way been avoided. This diagnosis of the situation is born out by the examples we are given.

> A molecule within the rolling wheel, for example, though retaining its usual inter-molecular relations within the wheel, is at the same time, from the standpoint of an outside observer, being carried through particular patterns in space and time determined by the over-all properties of the wheel as a whole. There need be no "reconfiguring" of molecules relative to each other *within the wheel itself.* However, *relative to the rest of the world* the result is a major "reconfiguring" of the space-time trajectories of all components in the wheel's infrastructure.[21]

It is true, of course, that the wheel's component molecules move differently in relation to the rest of the world because they are part of a rolling wheel than they might otherwise if, for example, they were part of a fragment of metal lying on the ground. But the macroscopic movements of the wheel as a whole are themselves quite thoroughly explicable in the reductionist style, in accordance with bottom-up microdeterminism. The example just does not illustrate the point for which it was invoked. Downward causation, defined as Sperry, Murphy and others have defined it, fails entirely to defeat causal reductionism. And this failure creates a serious situation for Murphy and other advocates of nonreductive physicalism. Unless some new strategy can be devised, the dire consequences of causal reductionism that Murphy previously acknowledged are now staring them in the face.

## Materialism and Emergence

Can there be a materialist view that truly avoids reductionism? Perhaps this is

---

[21]Ibid., pp. 235-36 (emphasis in original).

possible, but if so it will have to take the notion of emergence very seriously. It will have to embrace what Derk Pereboom has termed "strong emergence," in which the microphysical level "is no longer wholly governed by the (ordinary) laws of physics."[22] If this is accepted, then the actions and reactions of the organism can indeed be determined (in part) at the fundamental level by teleological considerations—by the goals the organism is seeking to achieve, including the goal of arriving at the truth about things. Strong emergence also opens the way for the affirmation of libertarian free agency, something which just is not possible, given causal reductionism.[23] A philosopher who has pursued this emergent materialist strategy with considerable care and precision is Timothy O'Connor.[24]

Emergent materialism is not a cheap solution, however; it carries a price tag that will cause most materialists to suffer from sticker shock. It requires us to attribute to the material stuff of the world causal powers that are radically different from those we have learned about from the science of physics. Physics has made amazing progress over the past four centuries by abandoning the idea that the behavior of physical objects is governed by "final causes" or purposes, and by understanding this behavior in terms of formulas which, however subtle and intricate their mathematical structure, have no reference whatever to goals or purposes of any kind. The laws of physics are no respecters of persons! I say this not by way of objecting to this feature of emergent materialism, but simply to point out the radical nature of what is being proposed. Emergent dualism, after all, is precisely similar to emergent materialism in this respect. And the motivation is similar in both cases. As we have pointed out (and as Pereboom confirms), to deny strong emergence is to leave ourselves with no escape from causal reductionism. I would argue, in fact, that emergent materialists have already accepted most of what is needed for emergent dualism and that they had best take just that small step further in order to arrive at a stronger and more defensible position. Emergent materialists, on the other had, will reply that emergent causal powers are one thing, that emergent substances are quite another and that

[22]Derk Pereboom, *Living Without Free Will* (Cambridge: Cambridge University Press, 2001), p. 70. As the book's title indicates, Pereboom is unwilling to pay the price exacted by strong emergence.

[23]"As long as the microphysical level is governed by deterministic laws, all of our decisions will be rendered inevitable by virtue of previous states of the universe, just as their microphysical realizations are" (ibid., p. 71).

[24]See Timothy O'Connor, *Persons and Causes: The Metaphysics of Free Will* (New York: Oxford University Press, 2000). I believe the views of Kevin Corcoran also belong in this category.

we are well advised to content ourselves with the powers and let the substances go![25]

Is there a way beyond this impasse? At this point, I wish to point out two remaining difficulties for emergent materialism—difficulties that, I hope, will motivate the move to emergent dualism. The first of these difficulties concerns the *unity of consciousness*. Gottfried Wilhelm Leibniz points out this problem for materialism as follows:

> In imagining that there is a machine whose construction would enable it to think, to sense, and to have perception, one could conceive it enlarged while retaining the same proportions, so that one could enter into it, just like into a windmill. Supposing this, one should, when visiting within it, find only parts pushing one another, and never anything by which to explain a perception. Thus it is in the simple substance, and not in the composite or in the machine, that one must look for perception.[26]

The difficulty here does not lie, as some have thought, in the fact that Leibniz's example was limited by seventeenth-century technology. If instead of using his "parts pushing one another" we fill the machine with vacuum tubes, transistors or for that matter with neurons, exactly the same problem remains. The problem does not lie in the pushes and pulls but rather in the complexity of the machine, the fact that it is made up of many distinct parts, coupled with the fact that *a complex state of consciousness cannot exist distributed among the parts of a complex object*. The functioning of any complex object, such as a machine, a television set, a computer or a brain, consists of the coordinated functioning of its parts, which, working together, produce an effect of some kind. But where the effect to be explained is a thought, a state of consciousness, what function shall be assigned to the individual parts, be they transistors or neurons? Even a fairly simple experiential state—say, your visual experience as you look at the page on which this argument is set down—contains far more information than can be encoded in a single transistor or a single neuron. Suppose, then, that the state is broken up into bits in such a way that some small part of it is represented in each of the parts of the computer or the brain. Assuming this to be done, we have still the ques-

---

[25]After characterizing the emergent dualist position, O'Connor says, "The present sort of emergence . . . would involve the generation of fundamentally new substance in the world—amounting to creation ex nihilo. That's a lot to swallow" ("Causality, Mind and Free Will," in *Soul, Body, and Survival: Essays on the Metaphysics of Human Persons*, ed. Kevin Corcoran [Ithaca, N.Y.: Cornell University Press, 2001], p. 50).

[26]Gottfried Wilhelm Leibniz, *Monadology* 17, in Nicholas Rescher, *G. W. Leibniz's "Monadology": An Edition for Students* (Pittsburgh: University of Pittsburgh Press, 1991), p. 19.

tion, who or what is aware of the conscious state as a whole? For it is a fact that *I am aware* of my conscious state, at any given moment, as a unitary whole. So we have this question for the materialist: when I am aware of a complex conscious state, what *physical entity* is it that is aware of that state? This question, I am convinced, does not and cannot receive a plausible answer. In spite of this (or perhaps because of it), the question seems an elusive one; it slips away from us before we can fully appreciate its antimaterialist implications. The reason for this, I believe, is that we covertly supply a subject of awareness—a unified consciousness of some sort—that brings together the bits of information separately registered in different parts of the brain and that grasps them as a single, unified experience. Now, I have no doubt whatever that such a unified consciousness does in fact exist. But this consciousness is itself neither a brain, nor any part of a brain. *A person's being aware of a complex fact does not consist of parts of the person being aware of parts of the fact, nor can a complex state of consciousness exist distributed among the parts of a complex object.*[27] Once we grasp this, we see that materialism is in deep trouble.

Yet another difficulty with materialism, for those of us who are Christians, is found in "the life of the world to come." The ordinary, naive believer naturally assumes that if there is to be a future life, there must be a soul that survives after the body has perished. But it has become fashionable, in recent years, to make a sharp distinction, even an antithesis, between immortality of the soul and resurrection of the body, and to claim that it is resurrection rather than immortality which is crucial for Christian faith. This in turn is seen as favorable to materialism, which cannot affirm the immortality of a soul that does not exist, but has no difficulty with the resurrection—or so we are told.

Unfortunately, materialism does confront a severe problem in giving a plausible account of the resurrection.[28] This problem concerns the difficult topic of personal identity. In what sense is the resurrected person the *same individual* as the one who previously perished? In order to see the problem, let me rehearse a pair of truisms. First, my interest in a life to come hinges on the understanding that those who enjoy that life will be the very same individuals as those who previously lived in this world. "I myself will see him with my own eyes—I, and not another," said Job (Job 19:27 NIV), and I hope and believe

---

[27]For a more extensive development of this argument, see my book *The Emergent Self* (Ithaca, N.Y.: Cornell University Press, 1999), pp. 122-46.

[28]For further development of the ideas in this section, see ibid., pp. 211-31.

that this will indeed be the case. And when I hope, by God's grace, to be reunited with my parents and other departed loved ones, it is those very individuals that I expect to meet once again—not other persons extremely similar to them, however close the resemblance might be.

The other truism is slightly more philosophical in flavor but still, I think, clear enough. Identity—in this case, personal identity over time—is a necessary relation, one that, if it holds at all, could not possibly fail to hold. I who am writing these words am the very same individual as one who, quite a number of years ago, entered into marriage with my wife. Assuming this to be true, *I could not* be distinct from that individual, for this would mean being distinct from myself, which is absurd. Furthermore, it is out of the question to suppose that anything true about some *other* individual—someone distinct from me here and now—could have any bearing on whether I am, in fact, identical with the person who took those marriage vows.

I hope you will agree with me that these two propositions—that identity of persons over time is crucial for the resurrection, and that identity is a necessary relation—are indeed truisms. Unfortunately, materialism is unable to honor them. Materialist views of the resurrection typically assert that, at some time after my death, God will recreate an assemblage of atoms (it probably does not matter whether they are the very same atoms or not) which is extremely similar (though probably not exactly similar, for some repairs and improvements will be needed) to me as I was before I died. And, the story goes on, this recreated individual will be I, myself. But suppose that, at the same instant, someone were to create another individual, either exactly like the recreated Hasker or slightly more similar to the Hasker who perished?[29] In either of these cases, the recreated Hasker would not be identical with the one who had died. At best, we would have two presently existing individuals with an equal claim to be so identical; but since both cannot be identical with Hasker-who-died, neither is so. But this means that the identity of Hasker-recreated with Hasker-who-died depends on the nonexistence of another equal or superior claimant to that status, and this violates the necessity of identity. And this, in turn, means that the relation between Hasker-recreated and Hasker-who-died is not identity, but rather some kind of similarity relation. But if it is only *persons similar to us* who shall enjoy the blessings of

---

[29]It is not an answer to this to assert that God, being good, would not (and perhaps *could* not) create such duplicates or near duplicates. What is needed for the objection to go through is only the metaphysical possibility of a situation in which the appropriate atoms are arranged in the right configuration. It is hardly a necessary truth that only God would be able to do this.

heaven, then we should wish them well, but we ourselves have no personal stake in the matter.[30]

## *Cartesian Dualism*

Cartesian dualists (such as Stewart Goetz) will probably welcome all of the antimaterialist arguments that have been deployed in this essay. They will claim, however, that emergent dualism makes unnecessary trouble for itself by a key assumption that it shares with the materialistic views, namely, that mind is ultimately to be accounted for in terms of the nature and properties of the material stuff of the world. Once this assumption is made, elaborate contortions become necessary in order to make it seem plausible that material stuff is able to produce something with the characteristics of mind as we know it to be. How much simpler and more reasonable, the dualists go on to say, if we simply take it as given that minds and matter are two radically different sorts of things and do not try to explain either in terms of the other. In order to complete our case for emergent dualism, we need to say something to ward off this Cartesian counterattack.

I have referred above to Cartesian dualism, so named for the seventeenth-century French philosopher René Descartes. Cartesian dualism is the most commonly discussed, and in my view the most plausible, form of mind-body dualism on the current scene. It has a competitor, however, in the version of dualism derived from the thirteenth-century theologian Thomas Aquinas, who in turn was heavily influenced by Aristotle. The general effect of Thomistic dualism is to establish a closer tie between soul and body than is possible with Cartesian dualism, thus mitigating some of the criticisms that have been leveled against the latter view. Unfortunately, Thomistic dualism suffers from a fundamental incoherence. The key idea, taken from Aristotle, is that the soul is "the form of the body." On the face of it, this seems to say that the soul is a sort of pattern or structure; in Eleonore Stump's helpful phrase, it is a "configurational state" of the body. So understood, this view would really be a kind of materialism; it would be similar to the emergent materialism discussed in

---

[30]It needs to be pointed out that there is a materialist version of the resurrection that is not subject to this objection. Peter van Inwagen has proposed that God, at the time of a person's death, surreptitiously removes either the entire body or some crucial portion thereof (such as the central nervous system) and replaces it with a simulacrum. The resurrection occurs when the body that has been removed is reanimated, at the same time being transformed into its exalted, resurrected state. See Peter van Inwagen, "The Possibility of Resurrection," *International Journal for Philosophy of Religion* 9 (1978): 114-21. So far as I can see, this suggestion is conceptually coherent; but as an account of how God actually proceeds, it leaves a great deal to be desired.

the last section. However, this is not what the Thomistic dualists really want to say. According to them, there are certain mental activities, involving abstract reasoning, that are performed only by the soul, with no assistance from the body or brain. Clearly, this would not be possible if the soul were understood merely as a pattern or structure of the body. Furthermore, the soul is able to continue to exist, after death, separate from the body. And Aquinas and his followers say explicitly that the soul—that is, the "rational soul"—is directly created by God. (According to Aquinas himself, this does not occur until a number of weeks after conception!) None of this fits at all well with the idea that the soul is the "form of the body" in the sense discussed previously. And because of its attempt to combine in a single view these two disparate notions of the soul, Thomistic dualism does not really present a single, logically coherent approach to the mind-body problem.[31]

Cartesian dualism, on the other hand, is completely clear on this matter. The soul is a separate substance, entirely different in its nature from the material body. It has no "physical" properties whatever, not even (on the standard Cartesian view) spatial location.[32] It is directly created by God and during one's lifetime is closely united with the body, but it is capable of existing and functioning on its own in a disembodied state. And since there is no need to explain mind in terms of matter, Cartesian dualists are able to accept that matter is just what the physicists say (and will say in the future) that it is—no more and no less.

Understandably, Cartesian dualism enjoys little favor among naturalistically inclined scientists and philosophers. From a naturalistic standpoint, there is something inherently "spooky" about it; witness Gilbert Ryle's famous description of this view as the theory of "the ghost in the machine." And even if the soul's creation by God is not taken to be an "official" component of the theory, it is very difficult to come up with any other account of the origin of souls that is consistent with the view's fundamental assumptions.

But suppose one does not share in the currently popular naturalistic assumptions. Is Cartesian dualism then worthy of a second look—even, perhaps, worthy of acceptance? I want to say up front that many of the popular objections against dualism are mistaken, unfair or just plain bad philosophy. For instance, the well-worn objection that mind and matter cannot interact be-

---

[31]For more on Thomistic dualism, see Eleonore Stump, "Non-Cartesian Substance Dualism and Materialism Without Reductionism," *Faith and Philosophy* 12, no. 4 (1995): 505-31; and Hasker, *Emergent Self,* pp. 161-70.

[32]Stewart Goetz differs from mainstream Cartesians on this point.

cause they are different kinds of substances has my vote for being the most overrated philosophical objection of all time. (I will leave it to Goetz to explain why this is so!) Still, there really are some serious problems with the theory.

One problem, noted already, is that Cartesian dualism does not fit at all smoothly with the theory of biological evolution. It is ironic that Richard Swinburne entitled his defense of dualism *The Evolution of the Soul*, since the soul, on his view, is precisely what does not and cannot evolve.[33] But it is a puzzle just how the specially (and individually) created souls should be fitted in to the evolutionary story. Is it that, after a new type of organism has evolved, God creates for that organism a soul with enhanced powers, to match the physical development of the organism? Or do the new-model souls come first and exercise a role in the physical development of the organism? Neither view seems particularly attractive or plausible. It may be, of course, that Cartesians have available to them some alternative that is better than either of these. It is hard to tell, because so far they have been reluctant to address the issue.

In these comments I have assumed that biological evolution is a theory worthy of our acceptance, and some readers may have doubts about this. But even apart from evolution, the evident similarities between humans and other creatures make trouble for the dualist. Do all these others—at least, all of the animals—have souls as well? Descartes thought not; in his view all nonhuman animals are mere automata, lacking not only reason but even sensation. For, of course, mere matter cannot by itself give rise to any form of consciousness; that is an essential part of the dualist theory. So when your dog welcomes you home at the end of the day, wagging his tail, barking and jumping all over you, this may create in your impressionable mind the idea that the dog is happy to see you, but really he is just like a wind-up toy, completely unaware and experiencing no feelings or emotions at all. As I tell my students, if you can believe that, you can believe anything!

Since we cannot follow Descartes at this point, we are forced to assert that other animals, too, have souls—but again, which animals? Does God specially create individual souls for slugs, termites and mosquitoes? And what happens to all these souls when the creatures perish? Few of us believe in a mosquito heaven, but does God, then, just annihilate the souls of the creatures not destined for eternal life? Or what? Readers may be inclined to think I am being unfair and that Cartesians have perfectly good answers to these questions. And perhaps they do, but I have been trying for quite some time to find out from them what the answers are, with little success.

---

[33] Richard Swinburne, *The Evolution of the Soul* (Oxford: Clarendon, 1986).

Another group of difficulties for Cartesian dualism results from the facts concerning the dependence of the mind on the brain and its states. To be sure, such dependence is not always a problem for dualism; to some extent it is to be expected, as can be seen in the following quotation from Swinburne:

> A person has a body if there is a chunk of matter through which he makes a difference to the material world, and through which he acquires true beliefs about that world. Those persons who are men have bodies because stimuli landing on their eyes or ears give them true beliefs about the world, which they would not otherwise have, and they make differences to the world by moving arms and legs, lips and fingers. Our bodies are the vehicles of our knowledge and operation. The "linking" of body and soul consists in there being a body which is related to the soul in this way.[34]

According to this, embodiment as such requires that minds depend on brains in at least two ways. They need the brains as sources of information about the environment and also as channels through which to issue instructions for bodily action. So it is readily understandable that brain misfunction (as the result, for example, of a blow to the head) should deprive the mind of sensory information and render voluntary bodily action impossible.

But the observed dependence of mind on brain goes far beyond this. On the dualistic view, why should consciousness itself be interrupted by drugs, or a blow on the head or the need for sleep?[35] And why should reasoning, generally thought of as the distinctive activity of the conscious mind, be interrupted by such physical disturbances? The natural conclusion from Cartesian dualism would seem to be that consciousness should continue unabated during such episodes—deprived, to be sure, of sensory input and the capacity for motor action. There are, furthermore, the well-publicized facts about the effects of mind-altering drugs, as well as the apparently permanent changes in personality and character that can result from brain injuries. By making the mind essentially independent of brain rather than dependent on it, Cartesianism deprives itself of a ready explanation for these kinds of dependence that we actually find.

An especially striking example of dependence is found in the phenomenon

---

[34]Ibid., p. 146.

[35]I am not here insisting on the point that since, according to Descartes, consciousness (or "thinking") is the essential property of the soul, it is metaphysically impossible for the soul to exist without being conscious. No doubt the defining property can be taken to be the potentiality for consciousness, rather than consciousness as such. The problem remains of giving a plausible account, within the Cartesian scheme, of the kinds of dependence we actually find.

of *visual agnosia*.[36] In this condition, persons who have suffered damage to a specific portion of the brain become impaired in their ability to process visual information. These individuals suffer no loss of visual acuity, nor is their general intelligence impaired. But they lose the ability to "make sense" of what they are seeing in ways we ordinarily take for granted. One sufferer from this syndrome found himself unable, after a motorcycle accident, to identify individual faces or to read the expressions on people's faces—obviously, a serious disadvantage for normal social interactions. The point is this: what we have here, as a result of specific damage to the brain, is a disruption not of sensory capacity as such but rather of an extremely subtle and sophisticated type of information processing—just the sort of thing one would expect Cartesianism to assign to the conscious mind rather than to the brain.

A final difficulty is found in the "splitting problem," which asks the dualist to account for what happens when a single organism divides into two. This problem is suggested by the results of the commissurotomy operation, in which the corpus callosum, the thick sheaf of nerve tissue connecting the two cerebral hemispheres, is severed. (This has been done in a number of patients to relieve the symptoms of severe epilepsy.) After this operation the two cerebral hemispheres seem at times to possess distinct centers of consciousness, without direct access to each other.[37] This probably should not be interpreted as one soul becoming two, but there are data from other animals that do suggest that something of the sort has happened. Take, for instance, cloning: before Dolly was cloned, there was nothing there but a single, mature sheep, from which a cell was removed to start the cloning process. But after cloning we have a second sheep, Dolly, with her sheeply consciousness and her sheeply soul. Where did Dolly's soul come from? It cannot have been created by the cloning process itself; Cartesian souls just do not originate in such ways. Perhaps God takes an interest in cloning experiments, as he does in natural reproduction, and created a soul for Dolly ex nihilo. Indeed, I do not know what else the Cartesian dualist can say.

It should not be supposed that this problem is one of recent discovery. According to John Hedley Brooke,

> In the early 1740s, news spread that a freshwater polyp, the hydra, could regenerate itself when cut into pieces. Abraham Trembley's discovery was so astounding that a wave of polyp chopping swept across Europe as scholars repeated the

---

[36]See Neil R. Carlson, *Physiology of Behavior*, 5th ed. (Boston: Allyn & Bacon, 1994), pp. 171-80.
[37]See chapter five of Kathleen V. Wilkes, *Real People: Personal Identity Without Thought Experiments* (Oxford: Clarendon, 1988), for a summary and discussion of the commissurotomy data.

experiment—hundreds of times in the case of R. A. Reaumur, who reported the news to the Paris Academy of Science. The commotion was not simply caused by matter reorganizing itself. If one polyp could become two by artificial division, then indivisible animal souls surely lost their credibility. It was a delight to materialists, who wished to have done with souls altogether.[38]

Cartesian dualists, it appears, have already had a little over 250 years to work out a plausible answer to this problem. Emergent dualism, on the other hand, has a ready explanation. The soul is generated by the organism, and when a new organism is produced, the new soul follows as a matter of course.

All of these difficulties, at bottom, result from one central problem. Cartesian dualism simply creates too wide a separation between consciousness, the mind and the natural world in which that consciousness is embedded. And the answer to the difficulties must consist in bridging that gap and bringing them closer together—exactly what is done by emergent dualism. Consider, if you will, a simple earthworm, as it wriggles across the ground and seeks to escape from the beak of a robin or from the hook on which a fisherman seeks to impale it. Pretty clearly, that worm has some sort of sensation; at least, that is what we will naturally think unless we are in the grip of a philosophical theory. Now ask yourself these questions: Is it plausible to suppose that the earthworm feels pain and pleasure because it has an immaterial soul, directly created for it by God, so that the earthworm is, as Taliaferro once remarked, "Brother Worm"? Or is it more credible that the earthworm's sensations are simply the result of its body being assembled and functioning in the marvelously complex way that it does? If even an earthworm can truly be made of the "dust of the earth," with no supernatural accompaniments, then Cartesian dualism is doomed.

## Conclusion

It is time to recapitulate. We are looking for a credible account of the relationship between the human mind/soul and the human body—one, moreover, that meets the core requirements for a Christian understanding of the human person. Cartesian dualism, while initially appealing in a number of ways, fails because the relationship simply is not close enough; too wide a gap is opened between mind and body and between mind and world. In order to close this gap, mind must somehow arise from the structure and functioning of the biological organism; it cannot be a separate element added from outside. Standard versions of materialism do show mind as arising out of organic function.

---

[38]John Hedley Brooke, *Science and Religion: Some Historical Perspectives* (Cambridge: Cambridge University Press, 1991), p. 173.

But those versions that maintain microdeterminism and the causal closure of the physical domain are unable to do justice to the distinctive characteristics of the mind, including its ability to pursue truth and its exercise of free agency. In order to satisfy these requirements, the materialist must embrace strong emergence, and allow that, on occasion, the behavior of the ultimate constituents of matter is controlled by something other than the mechanistic laws of physics. Even this, however, is not sufficient to account for the unity of conscious experience, nor does it allow for the continuance of the self after the death of the body. What is needed here (so I claim), is to acknowledge the mind/soul/self as an *emergent individual*, one that arises out of the structure and functioning of the biological organism but is a substance in its own right, not a mere system composed of the elementary particles of microphysics.

And this concludes my case for emergent dualism. It is not a simple or obvious theory. But given all we have learned, that is hardly a telling criticism. Whatever the final truth about the world may be, simple and obvious it surely is not! Emergent dualism is an account of the self in its embodiment that seeks to do justice to what we know about the world as well as to the truth that human beings are created by God in his own image, for his glory and our happiness.

# A SUBSTANCE DUALIST RESPONSE

*Stewart Goetz*

Wᴵᴵᴵiam Hasker and I are both substance dualists (dualists). Hence, we share the same view about the nature of the human person. Both of us believe that the soul is a particular entity or substance that is distinct from its physical body and survives death to be reunited with a resurrection body. The explanations for why we are dualists are very similar. Hasker appeals to the self's awareness of its unified consciousness, and I appeal to the self's awareness of its substantive simplicity.

I say that the explanations that Hasker and I provide for our beliefs in dualism are very similar because I am not sure that they are the same. To see why, consider the following argument by a person who thinks it is possible and desirable to supplement my account of belief in dualism with Hasker's. Is it not the case that I am merely unaware of my self as having any substantive complexity and that I need a reason to justify my belief that I am substantively simple? If this is the case, is it not plausible to argue that it is reasonable for me to believe that I am a substantively simple soul because a complex material entity such as my brain cannot be the subject of any of my unified conscious states of which I am aware?

I do not find this line of argument persuasive, for the following reason. Hasker claims that he is aware of his conscious state, at any given moment, as a unitary whole, and maintains that a material object with parts cannot as a whole be the subject of a unified consciousness. For example, no brain as a whole (or no portion of a brain) could be the subject of (have) a thought because a thought cannot be spread equally over all of the parts of that brain. A critic of Hasker's argument from unified consciousness might respond that Hasker is confusing an awareness of the fact that no thought can be spread over all of the parts of a brain with the failure to be aware of how a thought can be spread over all of the parts of a brain. Therefore, if I am merely unaware of my self having any substantive complexity, Hasker's argument will not help because the alleged confusion between an awareness of something and the failure to be aware of something else will be invoked in response to the argument for dualism from unified consciousness.

Setting aside issues of justification, Hasker describes himself as an emergent dualist and me as a Cartesian dualist. I will accept the description for the sake of discussion, though the reader should be aware (as Hasker points out) that I am not a "mainstream" Cartesian dualist insofar as I maintain that the soul is located in space. In that regard, I actually share common ground with philosophers like Thomas Aquinas and Immanuel Kant.

According to the emergent dualist, a substantial soul is brought into and sustained in existence by a certain arrangement and function of the brain and nervous system. According to the Cartesian dualist, God initially causes the soul to exist and subsequently sustains it in existence. Why am I a Cartesian about this issue? Because of my belief about the kind of power that is required to produce a soul and sustain it in existence. For the reason that I briefly gave in my essay, the power involved in creating a soul seems to me to be the power to create ex nihilo. That power, it seems to me, is the greatest kind of creative power. It is what philosophers think of as a great-making property, and it seems to me that such a power is and can only be exemplified by the greatest possible or most perfect being. It is relevant to note that I do not think what I do about this matter because I understand how God can create ex nihilo and have failed so far to figure out how such a power could be a function of a configuration of the parts of a brain. I believe what I do about this matter because of the nature of the power involved. Elsewhere, Hasker has asked why God, if he can do anything that is not self-contradictory, cannot endow matter with the power to generate souls. Is such an idea self-contradictory?[1] If it is not, it does not strike me as intuitively plausible insofar as it implies exemplification of a great-making property by entities whose nature as material is constituted by nongreat-making properties.

For the sake of discussion, suppose that God does create human souls ex nihilo. Hasker points out that it is only natural to wonder whether God also creates souls for slugs, termites and mosquitoes. If God does, what happens to those souls when those creatures die? Does a mosquito go to mosquito heaven? If not, does God simply annihilate the soul of any creature not made for the possibility of experiencing eternal life? Hasker notes that a reader might think that he is being unfair in asking these questions, because a Cartesian dualist might have perfectly good answers to them. He points out, however, that if the Carte-

---

[1] William Hasker, "Reply to My Friendly Critics," *Philosophia Christi* 2, no. 2 (2000): 197-207.

sian dualist does have such answers, he has never seen them.

I do not think Hasker is being unfair in asking such questions. I simply think it is also fair to ask the emergent dualist similar questions. Do the brains/nervous systems of slugs, termites and mosquitoes generate souls for those creatures? If they do, do those souls cease to exist at death, or does God intervene with miracles of divine power to take them to their respective heavens in the same way that he intervenes with miracles of divine power to take human souls to their heaven? Hasker says that it is difficult for the emergent dualist to give a clear-cut answer to a question such as, "how far down the scale of biological complexity does consciousness go?" If this is the case, why can a Cartesian dualist not acknowledge a similar difficulty in answering Hasker's question about whether God creates souls for slugs, termites and mosquitoes? Elsewhere, Hasker says that he takes my protestation of agnosticism about what are the correct answers to these kinds of questions as evidence that I (a Cartesian dualist) am embarrassed about the implication of applying Cartesian dualism to slugs, termites and mosquitoes.[2] I can only say that just as Hasker does not seem embarrassed by the emergent dualist's inability to give clear-cut answers to the kinds of questions at issue, so also I am not in the least embarrassed by my inability to answer these kinds of questions.

Consider now the apparent dependence of the soul and its states on the brain and its states. Hasker acknowledges that, according to Cartesian dualism, the soul's embodiment requires that the soul depend on its brain not only as a source of information about the environment, but also as a channel through which it issues instructions for bodily action. Hence, it is intelligible that brain damage should deprive the soul of sensory information and make voluntary bodily action impossible. The problem is that the soul-body interdependence goes far beyond this. It is natural to expect on Cartesian dualism that reasoning activity should continue unabated after the ingestion of drugs, a blow on the head or the onset of sleep. Yet such activity seems to be interrupted on these kinds of occasions. Moreover, the seemingly permanent changes in personality and character that can result from brain injuries are incongruous with what one would expect on Cartesian dualism. None of these kinds of occurrences, however, are unexpected or incongruous with emergent dualism, which asserts a strong dependence of the soul and its states on the brain and its states.

Despite what Hasker claims, I do not see why a Cartesian dualist cannot acknowledge the kinds of dependencies of the soul on the brain that Hasker

[2]Ibid.

notes.[3] Although some Cartesian dualists might insist on the occurrence of thought without correlated brain processes, there is no need to take this position. Strict soul-brain correlations might exist. All the Cartesian dualist who is also a libertarian about the freedom of the will must insist on is that not all such correlations hold because of a causal dependence of the soul correlate on the brain correlate. When a soul chooses freely to act, the dependence must go the other way in the sense that the occurrence of the brain correlate is causally dependent on the occurrence of the soul correlate.

The kinds of dispute that I have highlighted in commenting on Hasker's emergent dualism are in-house in nature. As I stated at the outset of my response, Hasker and I agree about the big question concerning whether the soul exists. Moreover, we both espouse the existence of libertarian free will. As Hasker clearly and forcefully argues in his essay, it is hard to account for the existence of libertarian freedom on a view like that espoused by Nancey Murphy in this volume. Therefore, despite in-house quibbles, I am glad that I have Hasker on my side when it comes to our general views about the nature of a human person.

---

[3]See Frank B. Dilley, "Critique of Emergent Dualism," *Faith and Philosophy* 20, no. 1 (2003): 37-49.

# A NONREDUCTIVE PHYSICALIST RESPONSE

*Nancey Murphy*

I am grateful to William Hasker for the seriousness with which he has taken my work in his essay for this volume. However, I am puzzled by the extent to which he sees me (primarily) as an opponent, while I see him (largely) as an ally against both the dualists and the reductive materialists.

Let me first explain the extent to which I see us as allies. I write in my essay that, terminologically, I prefer to call my position *nonreductive physicalism*. Substantively, though, I believe it is no different from some forms of emergentist monism. I take it that asserting (some form of) emergentist thesis is equivalent to denying (a correlative form of) reductionism. Hasker agrees. He says that, in general, "the notion of reduction is more or less the polar opposite of emergence." The central issue comes down to what it is that one takes to emerge. Various types of things have been classified in the literature as emergent: laws, effects, events, entities and properties.[1] Hasker's examples include what he calls logical emergence, as well. The difference between Hasker's view and mine, then, is that I am satisfied with asserting, in the case of human beings, the emergence of new causal powers. I would argue that he has simply gone too far (further than one needs to go and further than his arguments warrant) in postulating the mind or soul as an emergent entity.

So my puzzlement is this. Hasker and I agree that nonreductive physicalism (of the causal sort) is in general equivalent to what I shall call *causal emergence*. (This is a different usage from Hasker's own. He uses it for the emergence of crystal structures as a result of the causal processes among the molecules; I shall use it to refer to the thesis that there are emergent causal laws and powers.) If this is the case, then should he not see the nonreductive phys-

---

[1] Achim Stephan, "Emergence: A Systematic View on Its Historical Facets," in *Emergence or Reduction? Essays on the Prospects of Nonreductive Physicalism*, ed. Ansgar Beckermann, Hans Flohr and Jaegwon Kim (Berlin: Walter de Gruyter, 1992), p. 26.

icalist, in general, as an ally? To pursue my speculations I shall speak of two Haskers. Hasker$_1$ is the proponent of *emergent* dualism; Hasker$_2$ is the proponent of emergent *dualism*.

Hasker$_1$ needs causal reductionism to be false. This is because, as he notes, the very concept of emergence is controversial, but there is a gradation: the emergence of fractal patterns and crystalline structures is uncontroversial, although some would not use the term *emergence* here. Emergent causal laws and powers, he says, is an "extremely controversial, metaphysical claim." And the emergence of ontologically different sorts of entities is even more controversial. The pattern of his argument is to motivate acceptance of the strongest claim by building on the weaker and less controversial claims. I argue that the elimination of "emergent causal laws and powers" from the series would put the postulation of the emergence of entities much further out on a limb than it already is.

Without intermediate examples such as the emergence of life (new powers to act—take in nutrients, reproduce, etc., not a new entity), his argument for the emergence of entities depends too much on distant analogies such as the emergence of fields. This analogy actually supports my position. The term *field* does not describe a new entity over and above the magnet. It rather describes the area in which the magnet's causal powers are active. "A field is thus a method of representing the way in which bodies are able to influence each other. For example, a body that has mass is surrounded by a region in which another body that has mass experiences a force tending to draw the two bodies together."[2] I am not convinced that the examples of the "sufficiently intense magnetic field" holding itself together after the magnet is removed or of the self-sustaining black hole support his position. Is it that in these special cases there is a self-sustaining *entity*, or is it rather that the *causal effects* of the magnet or collapsed star continue in time after the original entity is gone? It might be better to describe these as self-sustaining processes.

However, Hasker$_2$ needs to show that nonreductive physicalism fails. That is, if nonreductive physicalism is equivalent to emergentist monism, then there is no need for the more adventuresome thesis of emergent *dualism*.

Hasker$_2$ may be right that my version of nonreductive physicalism falls within Jaegwon Kim's category of the mystical, based as it is on the "seriously confused idea" of downward causation. But Hasker$_2$ is considerably weakening the limb on which Hasker$_1$ is sitting if he succeeds too well in arguing that

---

[2]"Field," in *Concise Science Dictionary*, 2nd ed. (Oxford: Oxford University Press, 1991).

all versions of nonreductive physicalism are doomed. That is, if no version of nonreductive physicalism is coherent, this means that causal reductionism is true. If causal reductionism is true, then there is no such thing as the emergence of new causal powers. In his enthusiastic critique of downward causation, I believe Hasker$_2$ slips into the habits of thought of exactly the modern reductionism that Hasker$_1$ needs to avoid.

So my question is whether Hasker$_1$ can explain to the satisfaction of Hasker$_2$ how it is the case that emergent laws and emergent causal powers come into existence as a result of the configuration of atoms and molecules in the brain. Some perfect examples of such laws are the Hodgkin-Huxley equations that predict the velocity of nerve impulses, what happens when two impulses collide and a variety of other phenomena. These equations are not derivable from physics and apply equally to human brains and (presumably soul-less) squid neurons.[3] Thus, it is not the case (contra Hasker$_2$) that "the larger entities, after all, are wholly composed of the particles of microphysics, and it would seem that the behavior of all such entities will be exhaustively determined by the behavior of the constituent particles." If Hasker$_1$'s explanation is better than those employing the concept of downward causation, then all of us who are struggling to explicate a nonreductive view of the world will be in his debt.

Hasker has two further arguments for emergent *dualism*. Regarding the problem of the unity of consciousness, let me refer to my response to Stewart Goetz's essay (above). On the problem of pre- and postresurrection identity, I refer to my response to Kevin Corcoran (below). I would simply add here that there are equally severe problems in providing criteria for "same soul." Presumably continuity of memory would be essential for Christians' concept of afterlife, yet many in Eastern traditions hold a doctrine of reincarnation according to which the soul ordinarily has *no* memory of past lives. M. R. Bennett and P. M. S. Hacker make a stronger claim regarding René Descartes's concept of a soul, which may apply equally to Hasker's:

> Descartes provided no criteria for identifying a particular spiritual substance and differentiating it from other spiritual substances of the same general kind, [Hasker might want to use "emerged from same body" as a criterion here] or for re-identifying that particular spiritual substance as the same again on a subsequent occasion. So there could be no way to establish that there is one spiritual

---

[3]See Alwyn Scott, *Stairway to the Mind: The Controversial New Science of Consciousness* (New York: Springer-Verlag, 1995), pp. 50-53.

substance "in me," as opposed to a thousand different ones all thinking exactly the same thoughts; or that there is one continuous substance "in me," as opposed to a different spiritual substance each morning to whom the previous one had passed on all its memories (as one billiard ball passes on its momentum to the next one in line which it hits).[4]

---

[4]M. R. Bennett and P. M. S. Hacker, *Philosophical Foundations of Neuroscience* (Oxford: Blackwell, 2003), p. 325.

# A CONSTITUTIONAL RESPONSE

*Kevin Corcoran*

There is much to admire in William Hasker's essay defending emergent dualism. For some years now, and most recently in his book *The Emergent Self*,[1] Hasker has been leveling a devastating critique of what we might call mechanistic materialism, or reductive physicalism, in the philosophy of mind. Personally, I find Hasker's negative arguments wholly persuasive. It is Hasker's positive contribution, his emergent *dualism*, that I cannot embrace. Put simply, on Hasker's view, human persons are the naturally emergent, *immaterial* yet *spatial* substances that result from certain complex configurations of matter, or neural stuff. I believe in miracles, but emergent dualism stretches my powers of belief beyond their limit. Let me, therefore, say a few things about emergentism, and Hasker's own variety of it, and then raise some questions and concerns.

## Emergent Dualism

The basic idea behind emergentism in the philosophy of mind is that consciousness and mentality do not appear until physical systems reach a sufficiently high level of configurational complexity. Just as liquidity and solidity are features that require matter to be suitably arranged before they are manifested, so too with consciousness and the mental. So according to emergentism in the philosophy of mind, the appearance of mentality is dependent on a physical system of appropriate complexity.

Hasker, of course, embraces this modest version of emergentism. He also agrees with another desideratum of emergentists—namely, that mentality is, in some important sense, irreducible. It is with respect to this that mentality is unlike liquidity and solidity. For the latter are nothing over and above organizational/causal features of matter. But the mental is said to be a novel feature

---

[1] William Hasker, *The Emergent Self* (Ithaca, N.Y.: Cornell University Press, 1999).

of the world, something that in a very important sense cannot be reduced to the neurobiological processes that cause it and, furthermore, something that can exert force on the system from which it emerges.

Hasker's original contribution to the philosophy of mind over the years has been to claim that consciousness cannot be an emergent property of the organisms that exhibit it. Why? Because of the unity of consciousness argument. The properties of the mind simply cannot be explained in terms of any combination of properties of, and relations between, the constituent parts of the brain. What is needed is an emergent substance or subject, that is, in the case of human beings, a person. Hasker contends that human souls or minds are just such emergent substances and that they stand to human brains as (say) an electromagnetic field stands to its generating source. A magnetic field is an emergent individual; it normally occupies an area larger than its generating magnet and enters into causal commerce with it. So too with human persons. Human persons emerge when biological systems reach the complex level of organization we normally associate with mature human brains in mature human bodies. And these immaterial, yet spatial emergent substances can bring about changes in the bodies from which they emerge.

Emergent dualism makes it much easier to account for the unity of consciousness and is to be preferred to its materialist alternatives for this and other reasons. At the same time, Hasker's emergent dualism has what he takes to be advantages over standard forms of dualism. For example, according to Hasker, the relation between mind and body is much closer and natural on his view than on the Cartesian view. For consciousness emerges as part of the natural development of human brains in human (and other animal) bodies and is, in fact, dependent on the brain for its emergence.

### Souls and Bodies

Given what I have just said, and what I think Hasker will agree is a fair representation of his view, I find the way he sets up the contrast between his emergent dualism and good old-fashioned Cartesian dualism very odd. Hasker supposes you have come to have doubts about a soul that is "fundamentally totally different from the body and bears no necessary relation to it" (à la Cartesianism). Now one assumes that his emergent dualism will contrast with this feature of Cartesian dualism. But does it? Although the emergent soul is causally dependent on the body for its origin, it bears no metaphysically necessary (i.e., essential) relation to the body. After all, Hasker believes the soul can exist in a disembodied state between death (of the body) and resurrection.

Remember too that the mind or soul is a substance, a concrete particular, on

Hasker's view. What of the body? Is it a substance, too? Given that Hasker refers to his view as "emergent *dualism*," one would think so. But then, does the *dualism* part of Hasker's emergentism not consist just in the fact that the soul is "fundamentally totally different from the body"? If so, then in whatever other ways emergent dualism differs from Cartesian dualism, it does not differ from it in terms of committing itself to two distinct kinds of substance, one material and the other immaterial. Nor does it differ in terms of the soul bearing no essential relation to the body. For, as I mentioned, the soul is capable of disembodied existence.

I find it puzzling, therefore, that Hasker continues to offer as a strength of his theory the claim that emergent dualism establishes a close and natural connection between the soul and the organism. This "close" connection, in fact, is supposed to prevent "the splitting of the person into two disparate entities," says Hasker. I have two problems with this. First, the connection is not so close that the one (the soul) is unable to exist without the other (the body), as we have just seen. If the connection is so close and natural, I would expect the soul to be causally dependent on the body not only for its emergence, but also for its continued existence, in this life and the next. And second, even on Hasker's view, the person—or the human being at least—*is* split into two disparate entities. For we still are left with an immaterial (though spatial) soul and a material body. This is not, of course, to deny the important ways in which emergent dualism does differ from Cartesian dualism; but it is to point out that it does not differ in the ways you might be led to believe given the way Hasker sets up the contrast.

## Reembodied Souls

Hasker claims that identity of persons over time and the claim that identity is a necessary relation are two truisms that materialist views of human persons cannot honor when dealing with the afterlife. Emergent dualism, on the other hand, can accommodate these doctrines, owing to the persistence of the disembodied, and then reembodied, soul. The first thing to be said here is that I have done my best to offer an account of personal identity that honors precisely those doctrines.[2] Granted, Hasker may not find the account I offer very persuasive, but it will not do just to boldly assert that it cannot be done. (I venture to guess that this is an issue Hasker will take me to task on in his response to me!)

---

[2]In addition to my contribution to this volume, see my "Physical Persons and Post Mortem Survival Without Temporal Gaps," in *Soul, Body and Survival: Essays on the Metaphysics of Human Persons*, ed. Kevin Corcoran (Ithaca, N.Y.: Cornell University Press, 2001), pp. 201-17.

Second, I think there is a real difficulty in the doctrine of resurrection for the emergent dualist, one that Hasker has not done enough to address. If what is required for the emergence of a soul is a suitably complex configuration of neural circuitry (or its functional equivalent), then should one not expect the resurrection body God creates to generate its own soul? Or does God prevent the natural emergence of a soul in the next life in order to "add from the outside" the persisting soul of the individual? And if God "adds from the outside" in the next life, is it such a leap to think that God does it here, too (à la Cartesianism)? Perhaps Hasker will insist that the resurrection body is the previously deceased but restored body that originally generated the now disembodied soul. Fair enough. But why, then, does that restored body not generate another soul? Presumably what God does to the body in restoring it is to restore it to soul-favorable conditions. But if God does that, it is natural to think that it will produce another soul and not just be hospitable to the addition of a soul from the outside.

Hasker's response is to suggest that the resurrected body must not, therefore, first be created with its soul-producing powers and then have the disembodied soul added. Rather, "we must imagine the new body created from the very beginning *as the body of this very soul;* the renewed self must be 'in charge' of the resurrection body right from the start."[3] I myself do not understand this suggestion. Either God creates something like a corpse or a husk and infuses the soul into it, or God creates the functional equivalent of a human body. If God does the former, then the "body" will not be hospitable to a soul since souls require the functional complexity of a human body. And if God does the latter, then we are back to our original problem: will the body not produce its own soul? Even if we could make sense out of Hasker's suggestion, is it not open to the Cartesian dualist to say, "Look, if that's how it is with *re*embodied souls, is it really such a stretch to suggest that it is this way too with the initial embodiment of a soul?"

## Materialism, Unity of Consciousness and Spatial Souls
Finally, one of the problems for materialists, which Hasker notes, is the phenomenon of the unity of consciousness. I agree with Hasker that this is a serious problem for materialism, but not for all versions of materialism. Rather, it is a problem for reductive versions. It is not, I contend, a problem for those who embrace a constitution account of human persons. For example, Hasker would have me ask, "When I am aware of a complex conscious state, what

---

[3]See Hasker, *Emergent Self,* p. 235 (emphasis in original).

*physical entity* is it that is aware of that state?" The materialist, assumes Hasker, can put forward nothing but collections or aggregates—the brain or the central nervous system, for example. But I answer, "Me!" I am the physical entity that is aware of my visual field, and I am not a plurality (nor is my body), even though I am composed of many parts. And, I remind you, that I am a wholly physical thing, sharing with my body all of the matter that constitutes it.

Now the idea that there are two things occupying the same region of space (you and your body) may seem deeply mysterious and puzzling. And it must be frankly admitted that this is an entailment of constitution. But is it, I ask, any more puzzling or mysterious than the idea of an immaterial soul that gets generated out of material constituents and has its own spatial boundaries? In correspondence, Hasker's response to my bafflement at the idea of an immaterial yet spatial soul has been to query, "But who made up the rule that only physical things get to be spatial?"—a rhetorically powerful reply, I admit, but it does nothing to assuage my bafflement.

Although the tone of my response has been largely critical, I cannot help but applaud the challenge Hasker has been posing to a mechanistic kind of materialism, the kind of materialism that dominates current debate within the philosophy of mind. Against that target I find his criticisms wholly persuasive. I just happen to believe that emergent materialism *cum* constitution is sufficient to solve the problems posed by reductive materialism. Emergent *dualism*, I believe, is unnecessary.

# 4 NONREDUCTIVE PHYSICALISM

*Nancey Murphy*

In *Freedom Evolves*, Daniel C. Dennett writes,

> One widespread tradition has it that we human beings are responsible agents, captains of our fate, *because* we really are *souls*, immaterial and immortal clumps of Godstuff that inhabit and control our material bodies rather like spectral puppeteers. It is our souls that are the source of all meaning, and the locus of all our suffering, our joy, our glory and shame. But this idea of immaterial souls, capable of defying the laws of physics, has outlived its credibility thanks to the advance of the natural sciences. Many people think the implications of this are dreadful: We don't really have "free will" and nothing really matters.[1]

## Nonreductive Physicalism: What It Is and What It Is Not

Daniel Dennett, with his gift for provocative overstatement, nonetheless points in this opening quotation to two theses that nonreductive physicalists deny. First, physicalism is a denial of dualism.[2] Second, the nonreductive part is the denial of the supposition that physicalism also entails the absence of human meaning, responsibility and freedom.

So it is easy to say what nonreductive physicalists are against. It is more difficult to give a positive account. One complication is that there are a wide variety of positions that go under the heading of nonreductive physicalism. And there are also a number of positions that are quite similar to nonreductive physicalism that go by different names. Bear with me as I sort through some of these terminological tangles.

In philosophy of mind, "nonreductive physicalism" is the most common term for this set of positions, but John Searle calls his view "biological naturalism."[3] I am prepared to argue that the constitution view of the person described by Kevin Corcoran in contribution to this volume is actually very close

---

[1]Daniel C. Dennett, *Freedom Evolves* (New York: Viking, 2003), p. 1.
[2]Christians, of course, deny that the soul is "Godstuff." Yet there is such a close association in many minds between God and the soul that some find it impossible to understand how I could deny the existence of the human soul without also denying the existence of God!
[3]John R. Searle, *The Rediscovery of the Mind* (Cambridge, Mass.: MIT Press, 1992), p. 1.

to the version of nonreductive physicalism I shall describe here. Finally, some thinkers call their position "nonreductive materialism." "Materialism" has been used to refer to a theory of human nature, but also to a worldview or metaphysical system. In the latter case, this involves (in addition) the denial of the existence of God and any other kind of nonmaterial being. Although "physicalism" is sometimes used in this sense, it is a newer term and so does not have the strong atheistic connotations of materialism.

Among scholars who consider the relations between theology and science a common term is "emergent monism."[4] I prefer "nonreductive physicalism" because, while "monism" is a proper contrasting term for "dualism," it means that humans are composed of only one *kind* of substance, but does not tell us whether that substance is physical or something else. Furthermore, while philosophers have done a good job of distinguishing and defining different kinds of reductionist theses,[5] there has (so far) been less agreement about what "emergence" means.[6]

What do nonreductive physicalists believe about human nature? For starters, let me put it this way: For dualists, the concept of the soul serves the purpose of explaining what we might call humans' higher capacities. These include a kind of rationality that goes beyond that of animals, as well as morality and a relationship with God. A reductive view would say that, if there is no soul, then people must not be truly rational, moral or religious; that is, what was taken in the past to be rationality, morality and spirituality is really nothing but brain processes.

The nonreductive physicalist says instead that if there is no soul, then these higher human capacities must be explained in a different manner. *In part* they are explainable as brain functions, but their full explanation requires attention to human social relations, to cultural factors and, most importantly, to God's action in our lives.

In what follows, I shall approach one of these issues, human moral respon-

---

[4]See, e.g., Philip Clayton, "Neuroscience, the Person and God: An Emergentist Account," in *Neuroscience and the Person: Scientific Perspectives on Divine Action*, ed. Robert J. Russell et al. (Vatican City State: Vatican Observatory, 1999), pp. 181-214; Arthur Peacocke, "The Sound of Sheer Silence: How Does God Communicate with Humanity?" also in *Neuroscience and the Person*, pp. 215-48.

[5]Four sorts of reductionist/antireductionist theses are methodological, epistemological, causal, and ontological. My focus is on causal antireductionism, which I take to be equivalent to some emergence theses that focus on the emergence of new causal powers.

[6]However, see the essay by William Hasker in this volume; see also Terrence W. Deacon, "The Hierarchical Logic of Emergence: Untangling the Interdependence of Evolution and Self-Organization," in *Evolution and Learning: The Baldwin Effect Reconsidered*, ed. B. Weber and D. Depew (Cambridge, Mass.: MIT Press, 2003).

sibility, and try to show how it is compatible with a view of humans as entirely physical. I shall end this essay with an account of what I take to be the most serious (additional) philosophical problems facing the nonreductive physicalist. The central issue is, in fact, reductionism itself. Some so-called nonreductive physicalists are in fact reductionists. I believe that showing the flaws in reductionist thinking is one of the most important philosophical tasks of our era. All I can do in here is to explain why reductionist thinking is so appealing and point to some considerations that call it into question.

## From Machines to Organisms

There are two ways of arriving at a physicalist position. One is to begin with a dualist view, such as that of René Descartes, and then simply subtract the mind or soul. Mary Midgley says,

> If certain confusions result from Descartes' having sliced human beings down the middle, many people feel that the best cure is just to drop the immaterial half altogether. . . . The philosophers who favour this programme are known as Physicalists. Sometimes they promote it with brutal zest, sometimes quite apologetically and kindly.[7]

One task of this essay will be to present an alternative to this sort of "Cartesian physicalism." The alternative arises largely from philosophy of biology and, in particular, from the recognition that the natural world needs to be understood as forming a hierarchy of levels of complexity. Quantum physics studies the most basic level (known to date) of this hierarchy; and sciences from atomic physics, through chemistry, and through the various levels of biology add to the picture. The nonreductive physicalist says that as we move up this hierarchy of complexity, we encounter genuinely new entities—atoms, molecules, cells, organisms and finally sentient and conscious organisms.

Cartesian dualism *minus* mind or soul is defective in that it leaves humans as nothing more than machines. Before we can begin to understand human beings, we need to appreciate the differences between machines and complex organisms. Only by recognizing the developments from the levels of physics to the level of the ethological study of the higher primates do we place ourselves in a position to ask intelligently whether a full account of human life requires the postulation of an immaterial mind or soul, and to understand fully what is "left" of a human being if there is no such thing. The task of this section, then,

---

[7]Mary Midgley, "The Soul's Successors: Philosophy and the 'Body,' " in *Religion and the Body*, ed. Sarah Coakley (Cambridge: Cambridge University Press, 1997), p. 53.

will be to consider the difference between organisms and machines. In the following section, I shall address the differences between humans and higher organisms that give humans the capacity for moral responsibility.

The behavior of even the simplest of organisms displays "causal loops" that contribute to their autonomy—that is, to their capacity to detach themselves from causal influences, both biological and environmental. Life first appears when there is a bounded organic structure capable of taking nutrients from the environment for the purposes of self-repair, growth and reproduction. Biologist Harold Morowitz speculates that life began with relatively simple "protocells" capable of replication.[8] The first known organisms are the prokaryotes such as bacteria, capable of very simple forms of metabolism. Somewhere in bacterial evolution motility appeared: flagella rotate and drive the cell forward. Even at the level of single-celled organisms we find a degree of self-direction. Cells in a gradient of nutrients swim toward higher concentrations and in a gradient of toxins swim toward lower concentrations. The mechanism is as follows. Periodically the swimming cells randomly switch directions. In a favorable milieu they change less frequently, and in an unfavorable milieu they change more frequently.[9] Morowitz says that "the behavior looks causal but the end point looks teleological."[10] We have here the first hint of cognition, in that the organism is able to sense its environment and alter its behavior accordingly. Thus, we need to consider the role of information and its relation to causal processes.

Donald MacKay was a physicist who contributed to the development of information theory and then moved into the field of neuroscience. His approach to the understanding of cognition is in terms of information processing systems. In engineering terms, our mobile bacterium is a system governed by a feedback loop. The first mechanical system of this sort was designed by James Watt in the days of steam locomotives. A more familiar example is a thermostatically controlled heating system. All simple self-governing systems can be represented by a diagram as in figure 1.

Here (in figure 1) the action of the effector system, $E$, in the field of action, $F$, is monitored by the receptor system, $R$, which provides an indication $I_f$, of the state of $F$. This indication is compared with the goal criterion, $I_g$, in the comparator, $C$, which informs the organizing system, $O$, of any mismatch. $O$

---

[8]Harold J. Morowitz, *The Emergence of Everything: How the World Became Complex* (Oxford: Oxford University Press, 2002), p. 29.
[9]Ibid., p. 101.
[10]Ibid., p. 102.

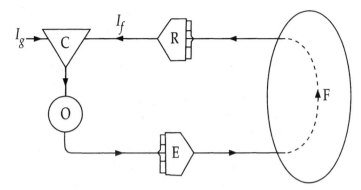

**Figure 1.**

selects from the repertoire of E action calculated to reduce the mismatch.[11]

A crucially important feature of even rudimentary biological activity, then, is action under evaluation. In most cases this is not conscious evaluation, but only a system that is able to correct the routine when feedback from the environment indicates a mismatch between the behavioral routine and the goals, as in the case of the bacterium mentioned above. Different degrees of cognitive power lead to differing degrees of flexibility in responding to the mismatch.

A tremendous leap in complexity occurred when eukaryotic cells developed from prokaryotic cells by incorporating into themselves other types of simple cells. Multicellular organisms became possible with the specialization of cell types. A particularly important cell type is the neuron. Before neurons developed, multicelled organisms sent signals from one part to another by means of the diffusion of chemicals from one cell to others. The speed of such signaling was greatly enhanced by the development of cells with long fibers making a network throughout the body. Morowitz says, "The basic emerging features of animalness are sensory organs, a nervous system, and a digestive tract."[12] "Cephalization" refers to the concentration of the command center for the nervous system in the anterior end of the animal.

By the time we reach the cognitive capacities of insects, we find much more complex activity than that of our mobile bacterium. However, this activity is fixed rather than flexible. A fine example is the *Sphex ichneumoneus*, a type of

---

[11]Donald M. MacKay, *Behind the Eye*, The Gifford Lectures, ed. Valerie MacKay (Oxford: Basil Blackwell, 1991), pp. 43-44.

[12]Morowitz, *Emergence of Everything*, p. 107.

wasp, now beloved insect of the philosophical literature.

> When the time comes for egg laying, the wasp *Sphex* builds a burrow for the pur-
> pose and seeks out a cricket which she stings in such a way as to paralyze but not
> kill it. She drags the cricket into the burrow, lays her eggs alongside, closes the
> burrow, then flies away, never to return. In due course, the eggs hatch and the
> wasp grubs feed off the paralyzed cricket, which has not decayed, having been
> kept in the wasp equivalent of deep freeze. To the human mind, such an elabo-
> rately organized and seemingly purposeful routine conveys a convincing flavor
> of logic and thoughtfulness—until more details are examined. For example, the
> wasp's routine is to bring the paralyzed cricket to the burrow, leave it on the
> threshold, go inside to see that all is well, emerge, and then drag the cricket in. If
> the cricket is moved a few inches away while the wasp is inside making her pre-
> liminary inspection, the wasp, on emerging from the burrow, will bring the
> cricket back to the threshold, but not inside, and will then repeat the preparatory
> procedure of entering the burrow to see that everything is all right. If again the
> cricket is removed a few inches while the wasp is inside, once again she will
> move the cricket up to the threshold and re-enter the burrow for a final check.
> The wasp never thinks of pulling the cricket straight in. On one occasion this pro-
> cedure was repeated forty times, always with the same result.[13]

Thus, the behavior of *Sphex* is fixed in a predetermined pattern in relationship
to specific environmental cues. Her response is hard-wired and cannot be
adapted to devilment by the entomologist.

Mammals exhibit much more flexibility in responding to their environments. They have the ability to suspend the pursuit of one goal, such as getting
a drink of water, for the sake of a more pressing goal, such as avoiding a predator. Animals are capable of learning by trial and error and by imitation. Even
so, our closest animal relative, the chimpanzee, is incapable of the same kind
of flexibility that we see in small children.

Terrence Deacon describes an instructive series of experiments with chimpanzees. A chimp is given the opportunity to choose between two unequal
piles of candy; it always chooses the bigger one. Then the situation is made
more complicated. The chimp chooses, but the experimenter gives the chosen
pile to a second chimp and the first ends up with the smaller one. Children
over the age of two catch on quickly and choose the smaller pile. But chimps
have a very hard time catching on; they watch in agitated dismay, over and
over, as the larger pile of candy is given away.

---

[13]D. Woolridge, *Mechanical Man: The Physical Basis of Intelligent Life* (New York: McGraw Hill,
1968), p. 82.

Deacon says that the task poses a difficulty for the chimps because the presence of such a salient reward undermines their ability to stand back from the situation and subjugate their desire to the pragmatic context, which requires them to do the opposite of what they would normally do to achieve the same end.

Now the experiment is further complicated. The chimps are taught to associate numbers with the piles of candy. When given the chance to select numbers rather than the piles themselves, they quickly learn to choose the number associated with the smaller pile. Deacon argues that the symbolic representation helps reduce the power of the stimulus to drive behavior. Thus he argues that increasing ability to create symbols progressively frees responses from stimulus-driven immediacy.[14]

The experiments with the chimps illustrate a second piece of the autonomy puzzle. What the chimps in the first phase of the experiment are unable to do is to make their own behavior, their own cognitive strategy, the object of their attention. This ability to represent to oneself aspects of one's own cognitive processes in order to be able to evaluate them is what I shall call *self-transcendence*. To represent this capacity we need a more complex diagram, as in figure 2.

Figure 2 represents a goal-seeking system (as in fig. 1) with an added feature: a supervisory system that takes stock of how things are going in the total system. It is represented in figure 2 by two components, the meta-comparator, *MC*, and the meta-organizing system, *MO*. *FF* represents a feedforward part

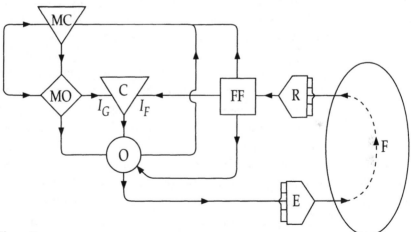

**Figure 2.**

---

[14]Terrence W. Deacon, *The Symbolic Species: The Co-evolution of Language and the Brain* (New York: W. W. Norton, 1997), pp. 413-15.

with feature filters that draw relevant information from sensory input for updating the organizing system.[15] Such a system has the capacity to alter its own goal state in light of its evaluation of how the total system is coping with its environment.

Dennett points out that the truly explosive advance in the escape from crude biological determinism comes when the capacity for pattern recognition is turned in on itself. The creature who is sensitive not only to patterns in its environment, but also to patterns in its own reactions to patterns in its environment, has taken a major step.[16] Dennett's term for this is the ability to "go meta"—that is, one represents one's representations, reacts to one's reactions. "The power to iterate one's powers in this way, to apply whatever tricks one has to one's existing tricks, is a well-recognized breakthrough in many domains: a cascade of processes leading from stupid to sophisticated activity."[17]

## Human Self-Determination and Responsibility

In the previous section, I considered examples of entities that are designed by either humans or natural selection to have a degree of self-direction. Entities such as locomotives running on a governor and simple organisms become causal players in their own right; they are designed to respond to environmental conditions in such a way as to pursue a goal. Appropriate design of mechanical systems makes them teleological. Increasing cognitive abilities in animals give them increasing degrees of flexibility in responding to their own needs and to environmental influences, including the capacity to modify their own goals. I ended the section with the suggestion that *language* and *self-transcendence* are the keys to escaping biological determinism.

The task of the present section is to build a case for moral responsibility that shows it to be compatible with what we know so far about cognition and neurobiology. My method will be to provide a list of the cognitive abilities that are prerequisites for moral responsibility and to sketch some of the ways in which these abilities arise out of our complex neural systems, interacting with the environment, both natural and social.

The analysis of moral responsibility that I shall employ comes from Alasdair MacIntyre's delightful book *Dependent Rational Animals*. He describes action as morally responsible *when it is the product of the evaluation of that which*

---

[15]MacKay, *Behind the Eye*, p. 141.
[16]Daniel C. Dennett, *Elbow Room: The Varieties of Free Will Worth Wanting* (Cambridge, Mass.: MIT Press, 1984), p. 29; referring to D. R. Hofstadter, "Can Creativity Be Mechanized?" *Scientific American* 247 (September 1982): 18-34.
[17]Dennett, *Elbow Room*, p. 29.

*moves one to action in light of some concept of the good.*[18] Now I need to unpack this and show that our capacity for moral responsibility is not *in spite of* the activity of neurons but *because of* our neural complexity.

We take humans, at a point in their cognitive development, to be morally responsible, but in no case do we attribute moral responsibility to animals. MacIntyre has helpfully related his account of morally responsible action to the literature on the behavior of higher animals—his focus is on dolphins—so that we can see precisely what needs to be added in the case of humans. First, what are the relevant capacities of the higher animals?

First and foremost, dolphins exhibit *goal-directedness.* Dolphin goals include food, mates, satisfaction of curiosity, play and affection. MacIntyre argues that their lack of language is no reason to deny that dolphins act for reasons. This means that they have the capacity to make judgments about what actions are likely to produce desired results.

Neuroscientists are investigating the brain systems that enable animals to make judgments about their environments (e.g., their ability to recognize what is dangerous, friendly, useful) and to store these judgments in memory. Joseph LeDoux has focused his investigations on emotions. He writes,

> When a certain region of the brain is damaged [namely, the temporal lobe], animals or humans lose the capacity to appraise the emotional significance of certain stimuli [but] without any loss in the capacity to perceive the stimuli as objects. The perceptual representation of an object and the evaluation of the significance of an object are separately processed in the brain. [In fact] the emotional meaning of a stimulus can begin to be appraised before the perceptual systems have fully processed the stimulus. It is, indeed, possible for your brain to know that something is good or bad before it knows exactly what it is.[19]

Another relevant finding from neuroscience is Antonio Damasio's theory of somatic markers. Damasio has studied victims of damage to the prefrontal cortex who have, as a result, lost the subtle emotional cues that ordinarily move us to do things that are good for us and to resist things that have caused us trouble in the past.[20] So in addition to having inborn goals, we can suppose that the higher animals have the same capacity to learn from experience by means of the development of somatic markers. These subtle emotional cues in-

---

[18] Alasdair MacIntyre, *Dependent Rational Animals: Why Human Beings Need the Virtues* (Chicago: Open Court, 1999), pp. 53, 56.

[19] Joseph LeDoux, *The Emotional Brain: The Mysterious Underpinnings of Emotional Life* (New York: Simon & Schuster, 1996), p. 69.

[20] Antonio R. Damasio, *Descartes' Error: Emotion, Reason and the Human Brain* (New York: Putnam, 1994).

dicate that an immediately contemplated activity is either good to enact or bad to enact.

A great step forward in the ability to evaluate one's own action is the capacity to run behavioral scenarios in the imagination. This allows one to predict the effects of the action without having to go through the costly process of trial and error. Higher animals appear to have some capacity for this. Here is an example from the chimpanzees at the Arnhem Zoo.

> Each morning . . . the keeper hoses out all the rubber tires in the enclosure and hangs them one by one on a horizontal log. . . . One day [a chimp named] Krom was interested in a tire in which the water had been retained. Unfortunately, this particular tire was at the end of the row, with six . . . tires hanging in front of it. Krom pulled and pulled at the one she wanted . . . for over ten minutes, ignored by everyone except . . . Jakie, a seven-year-old male chimpanzee to whom Krom used to be . . . a caretaker. . . .
>
> Immediately after Krom gave up . . . Jakie approached. Without hesitation he pushed the tires off the log, one by one . . . beginning with the front one. . . . When he reached the last tire, he carefully removed it so that no water was lost and carried the tire straight to [Krom], where he placed it upright in front of her.[21]

This scene suggests that Jakie had the ability to imagine a solution to the problem that saved him from the process of trial and error. It also illustrates two additional capacities that we share with animals. The first is Krom's ability to change goals in light of experience indicating that the goal was unachievable or not worth the effort—we might call this the "sour grapes" phenomenon, which Aesop in one of his fables attributed to foxes. Jakie's behavior exhibited another cognitive ability called "a theory of other minds": that is, the ability to recognize the feelings and likely thoughts of another. Children develop this ability anywhere between three and nine years of age.

Human morality builds on these complex capacities. All of the additional requirements for responsibility and morality depend on sophisticated symbolic language. These requirements are, first, a sense of self; second, the ability to pursue abstract goals; and third, the ability to evaluate that which moves one to act.

The term *self* is used in a variety of ways in psychology and philosophy. What is at issue here is not the question of what it means to *be* a self. Rather the issue is that of having a self-*concept*. Such a concept arises, first, from the ability early in life to distinguish between self and nonself and, second, from the de-

---

[21]Frans de Waal, *Good Natured: The Origins of Right and Wrong in Humans and Other Animals* (Cambridge, Mass.: Harvard University Press, 1996), p. 83.

velopment of a theory of mind, mentioned above. This allows for recognition of others in the environment who have bodies of their own as well as thoughts and feelings—and thus recognition of oneself as a member of the class of selves or persons. Leslie Brothers reports on research showing that we come well equipped neurobiologically to develop and use what she calls the "person concept." We have remarkable abilities to recognize faces, and we have neurons that specialize in detecting bodily motions that indicate other actors' intentions.[22]

Patricia Churchland examines some of the multifarious uses of the self-concept and concludes that the issue can profitably be recast in terms of the self-representational capacities of the brain.

> In the brain, some networks are involved in representing things in the external world. . . . Other networks represent states of the body, such as its posture or its need for water. Some networks operate on other representations, yielding meta-representations such as knowing that my need to flee is more urgent than my need for water, knowing that John dislikes me, or remembering that John hit me. Neural networks engaged in integrating such meta-representations are probably the ones most relevant to questions about self-representation.
>
> Self-representations may be widely distributed across brain structures, coordinated only on an "as-needed" basis, and arranged in a loose and loopy hierarchy. We see the slow emergence and elaboration of self-representational capacities in children, and the tragic fading of these capacities in patients with dementia.[23]

Churchland goes on to report on the neural dependencies of some of our self-representational capacities: for example, representation of the internal milieu of the viscera via pathways to the brain stem and hypothalamus; autobiographical events via the medial temporal lobes; and control of impulses via prefrontal lobe and limbic structures. Other capacities involved are the ability to represent a sequence of actions to take in the immediate future and to represent where one is both in space-time and in the social order.

These various self-representational capacities can be teased apart by considering victims of illnesses in which some capacities are intact and others are poor or nonexistent. For example, schizophrenics have good autobiographical memory but difficulty with the self/nonself boundaries, so that they often attribute their own thoughts to an external agent.

---

[22]Leslie A. Brothers, *Friday's Footprint: How Society Shapes the Human Mind* (New York: Oxford University Press, 1997), chap. 3.

[23]Patricia S. Churchland, "Self-Representation in Nervous Systems," *Science* 296 (April 2002): 308-10.

Warren Brown argues that a personal, autobiographical memory forms the basis of a continuous personal identity. Human episodic memory is apt to be of greater scope and complexity than that of animals because of the capacity of human language to preserve detail and because of the remarkably expanded size and complexity of our frontal lobes.[24]

I claimed above that sophisticated animals have the capacity to evaluate courses of action in light of salient goals by means of mental representations. The possession of language clearly augments human ability to do so. In addition to imagining a course of action and depending on past experience to judge whether it will be effective in attaining the goal, humans can consider a much broader range of possible actions due to the ability to describe them in language. Sophisticated language also contributes to our ability to predict consequences. For example, one can consider a whole class of actions—say, acts of aggression—and ask in abstract terms what the usual consequences have been in the past.

One very significant step in the development of responsible action is that language allows us to represent to ourselves and pursue abstract goals, such as justice. Language is the key to this difference, and a great deal of scientific work has been done on the neurobiology of language,[25] although there is much yet to do in order to understand abstract concepts.[26]

MacIntyre argues that moral responsibility depends not only on possession of the capacity for abstract concepts, but also on a high level of syntactical competence. Following Anthony Kenny, MacIntyre states that the ability to pass judgment on one's own judgments is the mark of both rationality and voluntariness.[27] This metalevel judgment requires language with the resources for constructing a sentence that contains as a constituent a representation of the first-order judgment.[28] That is, mature human rationality develops when children attain the ability to consider why they are doing what they are doing and then to raise the question of whether there might be better reasons for acting

---

[24]Warren S. Brown, "Cognitive Contributions to Soul," in *Whatever Happened to the Soul? Scientific and Theological Portraits of Human Nature*, ed. Warren S. Brown, Nancey Murphy and H. Newton Malony, Theology and the Sciences (Minneapolis: Fortress, 1998), p. 116.

[25]For a very brief account, see Peter Hagoort, "The Uniquely Human Capacity for Language Communication: From POPE to [po:p] in Half a Second," in *Neuroscience and the Person: Scientific Perspectives on Divine Action*, ed. Robert John Russell et al. (Vatican City State: Vatican Observatory, 1999), pp. 45-56.

[26]See Deacon, *Symbolic Species*, for an account of the development of the capacity for abstract symbolic reference.

[27]Anthony Kenny, *Aquinas on Mind* (London: Routledge, 1993), p. 82.

[28]MacIntyre, *Dependent Rational Animals*, pp. 53-54.

differently. This requires the linguistic capacity to be able to say something like the following: "I wanted to smoke to impress my friends, but I realized that wasn't a good reason; taking care of my health is more important." Children become independent *moral* reasoners when they can switch from acting in order to please parents or peers to acting on the basis of some abstract concept of the good.[29] MacIntyre says, "In so evaluating my desires I stand back from them. I put some distance between them and myself *qua* practical reasoner, just because I invite the question both from myself and from others, of whether it is in fact good for me to act on this particular desire here and now."[30]

Let us now see how the factors I have suggested as prerequisites for moral responsibility work together. These factors are, first, a concept of self; second, the ability to run behavioral scenarios and predict the outcome of possible actions; third, the capacity for self-transcendence; fourth, sophisticated enough language to make a description of that which moves me to act the subject of evaluation; and, fifth and finally, the ability to evaluate my prior reasons in light of the abstract concept of goodness as such. Here is how MacIntyre relates these capacities:

> As a practical reasoner I have to be able to imagine different possible futures *for me*, to imagine myself moving forward from the starting point of the present in different directions. For different or alternative futures present me with different and alternative sets of goods to be achieved, with different possible modes of flourishing. And it is important that I should be able to envisage both nearer and more distant futures and to attach probabilities, even of only in a rough and ready way, to the future results of acting in one way rather than another. For this both knowledge and imagination are necessary.[31]

So the ability to use sophisticated language makes it possible for social influences in the form of rewards and punishments, and especially in the form of abstract concepts such as *justice* and *kindness,* to exert an influence on one's means-ends reasoning and consequent actions by providing goals against which to evaluate one's plans for action.

Let us consider an example. The fight-or-flight response is prewired in humans, as in other animals. The ability to recognize threatening behavior is apparently built up easily from preexisting perceptual capacities.[32] Thus, a typical series of events can be represented by means of figure 1, MacKay's simplest

---

[29]Ibid., pp. 71-72, 84.
[30]Ibid., p. 69.
[31]Ibid., pp. 74-75.
[32]Brothers, *Friday's Footprint.*

diagram. Let us say that it involves perception of the behavior of another person *(R)*; evaluation of the behavior as threatening *(C)*; selection of response—fleeing, fighting, conciliation—by the organizing system *(O)*; and effecting the response *(E)*. Feedback from the field of operation *(F)* will provide differential reinforcements that actually change the configuration of the brain.

This neurobiological change is an important factor for our enquiry here. The physicalist's worry is neurobiological determinism—that is, the possibility that the laws governing neural processes determine all of human thought and behavior. However, there is also downward causation from the environment to the brain. Neural connections work on a "use it or lose it" principle. Much of the "wiring diagram" of the brain comes about through random growth of neurons and neural connections. Positive feedback makes connections stronger; absence of feedback or negative feedback weakens connections. This is the basis of habit and conditioning. Let us suppose, then, that our agent has developed a habit of violent responses to threats.

Jesuit priest and ethicist G. Simon Harak describes an event that exemplifies such conditioning:

> When I was younger, I studied karate for a few years, going three times a week for practice. One day, two fellow students of theology and I decided to go to a movie. Fran was a former Marine sergeant. John was a bright and articulate student. After we had bought our tickets individually, we regrouped in the lobby. "Did you see that guy on the other side of the ticket booth?" Fran asked me. "Yeah," I replied. "He sure was cruisin' for a bruisin', wasn't he?" "You know," Fran said, "the look on his face . . . I was just waiting for him to try something," and he put his fist into his left palm. I started to say, "If he made a move on me, I would've. . . ." But John interrupted us by saying, "What guy?"
>
> The facts are these: Fran and I saw this young man, and were ready even to fight with him. John, a bright and alert person, didn't even perceive him. Why? The key lies in our respective backgrounds. In our history, Fran and I shared a training in violence. It was, significantly, a *physical* training which *disposed* us to "take things in a certain way." Specifically, we were "looking for trouble." And we found it. John, with no such training, didn't even perceive the "belligerent" young man.[33]

Now, MacIntyre's account of moral development involves self-transcendence—that is, becoming aware of and evaluating that which moves one to action. In Harak's case this evaluation happened as a result of the contrast between his and John's responses. He says, "I could see my deficiency precisely

---

[33]G. Simon Harak, *Virtuous Passions* (New York: Paulist, 1993), p. 34.

because of my association with John and others like him in another community."[34] The other community was the Jesuit order, and, in due course, he realized that he needed to give up his practice of martial arts and adopted a pacifist ethic.

This story fits MacIntyre's account of the emergence of moral responsibility. Harak became conscious of what moved him to action and then evaluated it, first, in light of the norms of other community members and, finally, in light of an abstract conception of the good.

To represent this process in information-engineering terms, we need the more complex diagram I presented as figure 2. Notice that in figure 1, $I_g$, the goal state of the system, is set by something outside the system: in the first instance it was set by natural selection. In figure 2 the goal state itself is set by higher-level processes within the system. In the case of our pacifist, the meta-comparator places a higher value on nonviolent resolution of conflict than on survival. The meta-organizing system then adjusts $C$'s priorities accordingly. $C$'s job will now be to evaluate threatening behavior not in terms of threats to survival, but in terms of threats to the peace of the community. A different repertoire of skills and norms will have to be developed in $O$. As this system develops, the $FF$ path, which selects relevant features of sensory input, will be affected by action and reactions of the environment. As Harak points out, virtuous behavior effects changes in the agent's perceptions.

Notice that in figure 2 there is feedback from the field of operation to the meta-comparator. This represents the fact that, in the case in question, the moral principle is subject to readjustment in light of the effects produced by acting in accordance with it. For example, it is often supposed that pacifist responses increase others' aggression. The pacifist might reevaluate his commitment to this principle if this turned out to be true.

So figure 2 represents a system in which first the social environment and then an abstract moral concept exercise what we might call downward causal efficacy on an individual's behavior, and the change in behavior will have an effect in reshaping neural connections in such a way that the new behavior becomes habitual. Thus, we have a dynamic interplay between neurobiology and environment.

A worry arises, though, regarding the pacifist's moral responsibility. What if his acceptance of pacifism was *socially determined*, for example, because of a strong need for social conformity? Notice that if this worry occurs to Harak, it provokes another level of self-transcendence. That is, it engages once again his

---

[34]Ibid., p. 35.

ability to make himself the object of his reflections and evaluations. This means that as soon as the suspicion of social determination arises for the agent, he is able to transcend that determination. In this case, he may invoke a higher-level evaluative principle to the effect that all genuine moral commitments must be accepted on the basis of autonomous rational examination, not on the authority of one's community. Representation of this second act of self-transcendence requires a more complex diagram in which a higher-level supervisory system has been added that evaluates the meta-comparator of figure 2. In figure 3, the supervisory system, *SS*, represents the cognitive capacity to evaluate in light of a still more abstract goal the whole complex of motives and principles that, up until then, have moved him to act.

There is no limit, other than lack of imagination, to the ability of the agent to transcend earlier conceptions. For example, our pacifist may take a course in philosophical ethics and become persuaded that MacIntyre's tradition-based approach to ethics is better argued than his previous Kantian position. He then comes to see his bid for moral autonomy as both unrealistic and culturally determined. So a higher level of meta-ethical evaluation overturns (or, alternatively, could have reinforced) his earlier ethical program.[35]

What I have been doing in this section and the previous one is calling atten-

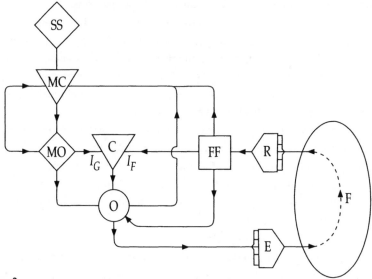

**Figure 3.**

---

[35]This section and the previous one are adapted from the Scottish Journal of Theology Lectures, which I presented in Aberdeen in March 2003.

tion to obvious facts about how animals differ from machines and how adults differ from both animals and small children. Along the way I have very briefly mentioned biological and especially neurological theories about the underlying physical processes that make these capacities possible. I employed MacIntyre's analysis of moral responsibility and have suggested (all too briefly) that it is our complex neurobiological equipment that enables us to participate in the world of moral action and evaluation. The reason for pursuing this issue, of course, is the assumption Dennett criticized in my opening quotation: the view that if humans have no souls, then they cannot be morally responsible agents.

Some readers will be entirely unsatisfied with my approach, and so it is time to address some of the most potent challenges to nonreductive physicalism.

## Outstanding Problems

In this section I shall mention what I take to be the main philosophical challenges facing a physicalist account of human nature. I acknowledge that there are challenges of other sorts. For example, there are biblical texts that are hard to square with physicalism, as well as theological problems such as the Catholics' and Calvinists' doctrine of the intermediate state.[36] Here are the main philosophical issues, as I see them.

First, there is an epistemological question: what are the grounds for thinking that physicalism is true? Philosophical arguments for dualism and against dualism, for physicalism and against, seem to be interminable. Recent successes of the neurosciences in studying mental capacities as brain functions have provided strong motivation for physicalism. However, science can never *prove* that there is no soul, a soul whose capacities are simply well *correlated* with brain functions.[37] I have argued (elsewhere) that the best way to view the contest between dualism and physicalism is to treat each position not merely as a philosophical thesis but as the "hard core" of a scientific research program.[38] This approach to philosophical problems via science represents a view

---

[36] For a treatment of the biblical issues, including texts that are taken to support the doctrine of the intermediate state, see Joel B. Green, "Eschatology and the Nature of Humans: A Reconsideration of the Pertinent Biblical Evidence," *Science & Christian Belief* 14 (April 2000): 33-50; see also Joel B. Green, ed., *What About the Soul? Neuroscience and Christian Anthropology* (Nashville: Abingdon, 2004), chaps. 4-7.

[37] For a recent example of such an account, see Richard Swinburne, *The Evolution of the Soul*, rev. ed. (Oxford: Clarendon, 1997).

[38] See my "Nonreductive Physicalism: Philosophical Issues," in *Whatever Happened to the Soul? Scientific and Theological Portraits of Human Nature*, ed. Warren S. Brown, Nancey Murphy and H. Newton Malony, Theology and the Sciences (Minneapolis: Fortress, 1998), pp. 127-48; esp. 139-42.

of the nature of philosophy quite different from that of the analytic philosophy represented in other contributions to this book.

Second, if humans have no souls, what accounts for traditional views that humans have a special place among the animals? In what does human distinctiveness lie? It has been common for Christians to argue that, while the human body may have evolved from animal predecessors, humans have a special place in God's eyes because they alone possess immortal souls. I take this approach to human distinctiveness to be based on poor exegesis of the creation stories in Genesis and would argue that our special place in God's plans has to do with our capacity to know God and enter into conscious relationship with God.[39]

So a related problem is that of religious experience. For centuries it has been supposed that it is humans' possession of a soul that enables them to interact with God. The physicalist response is to say that all human experience is mediated by the nervous system and so religious experience must be as well. This suggests that, in addition to God's influencing our thoughts and feelings through other people, there must be some occasions when God acts directly on a person's neural system. Is this a problem? It might be, were it not for the fact that Christians have traditionally understood God to be able to act on *any* part of creation, physical or otherwise.[40] I have argued (elsewhere) that religious experience requires *on the human side* nothing more than our ordinary cognitive and emotional capacities, and these are a product of neural complexity and culture.[41]

Fourth, if there is no soul, what accounts for personal identity over time? This topic is a difficult one in any case, but Christian expectation of bodily resurrection adds complications; we have to ask, what accounts for pre- and post-resurrection identity? I believe that the constitution view of human personhood (discussed in Corcoran's contribution to this book) provides abundant resources for addressing this problem.

A final issue is less tractable, namely, the problem of reductionism. If humans are purely physical—that is, if it is the brain that does the work once attributed to the mind or soul—then how can it *not* be the case that all human thought and behavior are simply determined by the laws of neurobiology? This is the general problem, but it leads to a variety of more specific issues. One is

---

[39]See Brown, "Cognitive Contributions."

[40]An exception to this view is that of the Protestant liberalism that takes its cue from Friedrich Schleiermacher (and others). These theologians reject the notion of divine "intervention" in the world of nature. The reasons are largely based on the assumption of causal reductionism, discussed below.

[41]See Murphy, "Nonreductive Physicalism," pp. 143-48.

the problem of moral responsibility, as noted above. Another is the problem that philosophers address under the heading of mental causation: how does reason get its grip on the brain? Most difficult of all is the problem of free will.

I noted at the end of the previous section that some readers were bound to be dissatisfied with my treatment of moral responsibility. If humans are purely physical, then their behavior *must* be determined by the laws of nature and therefore they cannot be morally responsible. The philosopher Ludwig Wittgenstein noted that we necessarily conceive the world by means of conceptual paradigms or pictures. Yet "we do not judge the pictures, we judge by the pictures. We do not investigate them, we use them to investigate something else."[42] Wittgenstein took it to be a clue that one was in the grip of such a picture when one says "but it *must* be this way."[43]

I have put a "must" on my objector's lips because I believe that modern thinkers have been in the grip of a picture or conceptual paradigm. Stewart Goetz makes a helpful distinction between "past-to-present determinism" (the view that a past state of the universe and relevant causal laws together entail the occurrence of one course of events) and "bottom-to-top determinism." He attributes the latter to present-day naturalists, who adhere to the hierarchical view of reality (described above) along with the thesis that the lowest level of reality determines all the properties of the higher levels.[44] In other words, our commonsense view that macroscopic objects (rocks, horses, people, for example) exert causal effects on one another is only a manner of speaking. All macroscopic past-to-present causation is in fact by means of micro-to-micro-causal processes. All of the real causal work is done at the lowest level.

I have (above) endorsed the model of the hierarchy of complex systems and the corresponding hierarchy of sciences, but why should it be assumed that causation or determinism is always and only bottom-up? This reductionist view has predominated throughout the modern period (although many now, both naturalists and theists, have called it into question).

The Copernican revolution was one of the factors involved in the transition from the medieval worldview to the modern. Emphasis is usually placed on the fact that this new view of the universe displaced humans from the center,

---

[42]Ludwig Wittgenstein, *Remarks on the Foundations of Mathematics*, trans. G. E. M. Anscombe, ed. G. H. von Wright, Rush Rhees and G. E. M. Anscombe (Cambridge: Cambridge University Press, 1978), 4.12.

[43]Brad J. Kallenberg, *Ethics as Grammar: Changing the Postmodern Subject* (Notre Dame, Ind.: University of Notre Dame, 2001), p. 199.

[44]Stewart Goetz, "Naturalism and Libertarian Agency," in *Naturalism: A Critical Analysis*, ed. William Lane Craig and J. P. Moreland (London: Routledge, 2000), pp. 156-86 (esp. pp. 167-68).

but a much more significant effect was the necessity of abandoning Aristotelian physics: if the Earth is not the center of the universe, then the falling of objects composed of the element earth cannot be understood in terms of their seeking their natural positions. Aristotle's theory was replaced by an even more ancient account of matter, Democritus's atomism. On this account, commonsense entities came to be seen as ontologically secondary when contrasted with the primary ontological status of the atoms.[45] If we combine the two assumptions of atomism

1. all entities are (nothing but) arrangements of atoms, and

2. atoms have ontological priority over the entities they compose,

with the further assumption

3. the laws of nature are deterministic,

it seems necessarily to follow that

4. the behavior of complex entities is determined by the behavior of their parts,

or perhaps equivalently,

5. the laws of physics determine the behavior of all complex entities.

This is the source of the causal-reductionist thesis. William Hasker expresses it well: "The only concrete existents involved [in putative cases of downward causation] are the ultimate constituents and combinations thereof; the only causal influences are those of the ultimate constituents in their interactions with each other."[46]

If I am right that this is a worldview issue—a picture or conceptual paradigm in Wittgenstein's terms—then it is very difficult to mount an *argument* against it. It is so deeply ingrained in modern thought that it serves as a measure against which arguments are tested. Wittgenstein's recommendation in such cases is to "look and see." *Must* it be this way?

We cannot "look and see" whether human behavior is entirely determined by the laws of physics or neurobiology.[47] So let us look at simpler cases. First,

---

[45]Edward Pols, *Mind Regained* (Ithaca, N.Y.: Cornell University Press, 1998), p. 64.

[46]William Hasker, *The Emergent Self* (Ithaca, N.Y.: Cornell University Press, 1999), p. 176.

[47]That the question can be phrased in term of either physics or neurobiology is instructive. The degree to which quantum phenomena play a role in the brain is an open question, so it is unlikely that many serious thinkers believe that human behavior is governed directly by basic physics. In fact the Hodgkin-Huxley equations that govern nerve impulse dynamics cannot be reduced to the laws of physics. (See Alwyn Scott, *Stairway to the Mind: The Controversial New Science of Consciousness* [New York: Springer-Verlag, 1995], pp. 52-53.) If neural function cannot be derived from physics, why should we assume that human behavior can be derived from the laws of neurobiology?

what does it mean to say that the lowest-level entities (the "atoms" in the philosophical sense of being "uncuttables" rather than in terms of current science) have "ontological priority"? One wants to say that it is only the atoms that are *really* real and everything else is *merely* a construction or arrangement of atoms. But what work is being done by the italicized words in the previous sentence? Consider two children playing with Lego bricks. One (the antireductionist) says, "Look there's a house and a car and a dog and plane." The other (the reductionist) says, "No, all there *really* is, is Lego bricks." Is there any way to resolve this dispute? I suggest that there are two factors that weigh in on the side of the antireductionist. One is the extent to which the "new entities" are tightly interconnected and stable.[48] If all there is on the table is an outline of a house made of disconnected blocks, we might tend to agree with the reductionist. But if the house is solidly constructed and can be picked up and moved, we might tend to agree with the antireductionist.

The second factor is causation. If the new structures have causal capacities that the blocks alone do not have—if, for instance, the toy plane could fly—then, again, we might agree with the antireductionist. A typical answer to the philosophical question of how we decide what is real is to say that real things or properties are just the ones we have to take account of in our causal interactions.

Of course a plane built only of Lego bricks cannot fly, and this brings us back to the question of whether there are things with genuinely new causal powers or whether, if we understood well enough how dogs and people are built, we would see that their causal powers, like that of a real plane, are simply the product of the mechanical functioning of their parts, which in turn are determined by the laws of physics.

Consider first a typical watch. It is designed so that its behavior is, as strictly as possible, determined by the behavior of its parts. Good watches are shockproof and waterproof and are now not even dependent on the wearer's remembering to wind them. Consider, though, a different kind of watch. I have one that resets itself every so often by picking up signals from orbiting satellites. It has been designed specifically so that its behavior is subject to readjustment by causal factors *from outside* the system.

Consider now a paper airplane. Its parts are the cellulose and other molecules making up the paper. These "parts" only serve the function of providing mass and rigidity. They do not do anything except be there. The behavior of the plane is almost entirely governed by two things. One is its shape, a holistic

---

[48]See Nancey Murphy and George F. R. Ellis, *On the Moral Nature of the Universe: Theology, Cosmology and Ethics* (Minneapolis: Fortress, 1996), chap. 2.

property of the plane. The other is environmental factors: the hand that throws it and the air currents that affect its flight path. This ever-so-simple device shows that the atomist-reductionist thesis is simply false in some cases.[49]

I suspect that there are readers who are wanting to say, "Yes, but the plane still obeys the laws of physics, so causation is still all bottom-up." My reply is, first, to agree that the flight of the plane, once released, is determined by the laws of physics. Recall, though, that the question we were addressing is not the universal rule of the laws of nature, but rather the more specific question of whether the behavior of an entity is determined by the laws governing the behavior of its parts. All that I mean to show by this example is the falsity of this latter claim. What we find instead is evidence for three contrary points. First, the holistic property of the shape of the plane is crucial. Second, its behavior is a result of how this holistic property enables it to be affected by its environment, in ways that none of its parts alone could be. Third, although the flight of the plane is a result of air pressure, we might want to say that there are higher-level laws in effect (the laws of aerodynamics) which, while still counted as part of physics, are *emergent* in the sense that before there were things that fly or glide, there were no such regularities in the universe.[50] They are also emergent in the sense that they cannot be derived from quantum physics.

So what I am arguing for here is the applicability of the concept of downward or top-down causation. Accounts that consider only bottom-up causation—that is, the effect of the parts on the whole—are often inadequate. We also need to consider features of the whole as a whole, as well as the downward effects of the environment. Downward causation is a controversial idea. The sense in which I intend it here is parallel to the claim that there are emergent entities (e.g., birds) with new causal powers. This is not to say that there are new causal *forces*, but rather that there are new complex entities with the ability to use lower-level causal forces (e.g., air pressure) in new ways to do new things (e.g., to fly). This does not involve overriding lower-level laws, but rather *selection* among lower-level causal processes.[51]

To see the crucial role of selection consider an example from chemistry. Suppose it were the case that the largest molecules in the universe could have no

---

[49]So I should not have conceded above that the causal powers of a real plane are *simply* a product of its parts.

[50]I recognize that this raises the question of the *nature* of the laws of nature. Are they merely descriptive of regularities in the universe or are they in some sense preexistent and prescriptive?

[51]The best account of downward causation is that of Robert Van Gulick, "Who's in Charge Here? and Who's Doing All the Work?" in *Mental Causation*, ed. John Heil and Alfred Mele (Oxford: Clarendon, 1995), pp. 233-56.

more than 112 atoms. The laws of chemistry permit the construction of $10^{110}$ different compounds. This number (10 followed by 110 zeros) is equal to the mass of the universe measured in units of the mass of a hydrogen atom times the age of the universe measured in picoseconds ($10^{-12}$ sec.).[52] What explains the fact that the universe contains only a tiny fraction of all of these possible molecules? There will be some bottom-up explanations, such as the rarity of certain elements. But most complex molecules are biochemicals (e.g., proteins). To explain why only *these* proteins exist we need to look at the functions they play in living organisms and at the higher-level causal processes (such as selective reproduction) that have resulted in the emergence of these organisms.

## Retrospect and Prospect

So is the behavior of an organism more like that of an ordinary watch or my satellite-adjusted watch; more like a paper airplane, or a jetliner flying on autopilot? Or is it different from all of these? Consider one more example. The laws of biology, chemistry and physics determine much of what a horse can do—how far and fast it can run, how high it can jump. Do these laws also explain why horses of certain breeds are often found to run counterclockwise in circular or elliptical paths? Clearly not. The explanation has to involve the human practice of horseracing and the conventions of the race track. Is this another and even better example of the failure of causal reductionism? Our antireductionist will say, "Yes." Our reductionist will say, "No, because if you knew the states of the neurons in the brains of the people who decided that races should be run in a counterclockwise direction, then you *would* have a biological account of why the horses run that way." Notice, though, that this argument, as do the horses, runs in a circle. The reductive physicalist says that all decisions are determined by biology. The nonreductive physicalist says that we cannot answer this question on the basis of neurobiological evidence and so instead challenges the *general* assumption that it *must* be this way by looking at simpler cases. When we look at the world we find that some things, like ordinary clocks, *are* determined by (the laws governing) the behavior of their parts, but these are in fact special cases. Indeed, in this essay we have drawn attention to how very different a simple organism is from a clock and how very different conscious organisms are from simple ones.

I do not expect to convert the reductionists among my readers. I am convinced that this is a well-entrenched assumption about how the world works, based on a (not very clear) philosophical dogma regarding the "ontological

---

[52]See Scott, *Stairway to the Mind*, pp. 21-22.

priority" of atoms. But because it is one of those "pictures" that we use to judge reality by, it cannot be defeated by a few pages of argument. What is required is something akin to a *Gestalt* switch or paradigm change that allows us to see the world once again in a commonsense way. In the playroom it may in fact be "nothing but Lego bricks," but in the real world there are clocks and organisms and intelligent beings that act for reasons, both moral and otherwise.

I have not of course addressed here the philosophers' problem of mental causation—how do *reasons* play a role in physical organisms?—and shall not attempt to do so here.[53] A final and very challenging problem is free will. This is actually a nest of more or less closely related problems, but the one physicalists have to address is that of neurobiological determinism. My questioning here of the ontological priority of the parts and of bottom-up determinism is, of course, relevant to the problem of neurobiological determinism but is far from sufficient. The one contribution I would like to make here to the free-will debate is this: Philosophers' debates center on the distinction between "compatibilist" and "libertarian" accounts of free will. The former term represents the view that the very meaning of "free will" is such that it is (conceptually) compatible with determinism, and the latter represents the claim that if determinism is true then no one can have free will in the proper sense of the term. I do not know how this debate about the meaning of "free will" can be settled. However, it may be possible to set it aside by showing that determinism versus indeterminism is not the crucial issue. The crucial issue is instead the more specific question of whether bottom-up determinism is (always) true. If not, then it is plausible to say that the whole person has downward causal effects on her own parts.[54]

---

[53] A prior question is how language can be meaningful if it is instantiated in brain processes. For a first attempt at these questions, see Nancey Murphy, "The Problem of Mental Causation: How Does Reason Get Its Grip on the Brain?" *Science & Christian Belief* 14 (October 2002): 143-57; idem, *Human Nature at the Intersection: Theology, Science and Philosophy* (Cambridge: Cambridge University Press, forthcoming).

[54] These suggestions represent work in progress. Warren Brown and I hope to publish a book (tentatively titled *Did My Neurons Make Me Do It? Neurobiological and Philosophical Perspectives on Moral Responsibility*) that will deal with the issues of meaning, rationality and free will. I thank him for innumerable contributions to my thinking on all of these issues.

# A SUBSTANCE DUALIST RESPONSE

*Stewart Goetz*

As I stated in my essay, I start with my belief that I am a soul, where that belief is based on introspective awareness of my self. I do not arrive at this belief by argument. Hence, contrary to what Nancey Murphy suggests, as a dualist I do not postulate the existence of the soul for the purpose of explaining the existence of the higher capacities (e.g., capacities for rationality, morality and a relationship with God) of human beings. I agree with Murphy, however, that philosophical argumentation for and against dualism, and for and against physicalism, seems to be interminable. I would add that few, if any, people ever seem to be moved by such argumentation, which leads me to think that what people believe about these matters is not really a function of argument. Indeed, my argument for dualism (the Simple Argument) presupposes belief in the soul's existence (the "I" which is the subject of the first premise is "the soul that I am") and will not convince anyone who does not share that belief. I also agree with Murphy that it is a mistake to argue on the basis of the creation stories in Genesis that humans have souls and, thereby, a special place in God's eyes. My agreement with her is based on the position that I set forth in my essay, which is that Scripture as a whole does not teach that the soul exists. Scripture simply presupposes the existence of the soul because its existence is affirmed by the common sense of ordinary people.

In opposition to what ordinary people believe, Murphy defends nonreductive physicalism, which is the view that consciousness, sentience, mentality and religious experience are all higher-order features of the physical world that cannot be reduced to microphysical constituents (e.g., atoms, molecules, cells, quantum events) and their relationships. As I explained in my discussion of dualism and free will, I have not been convinced by any physicalist's (reductive or nonreductive) argument that dualism is either false or so problematic that it is necessary to look elsewhere (e.g., to nonreductive physicalism) for a more plausible view of human nature. Moreover, I briefly suggested in that section that nonreductive physicalism (emergentism) does not avoid any of the problems of causal interaction that physicalists typically maintain undermine dualism. If causal interaction is a problem for dualism, it is just as much of a problem for nonreductive physicalism. Murphy endorses the constitution view of human personhood to account for personal identity over time in this life and with respect to pre- and postresurrection existence. I have expressed my thoughts about the constitution view vis-à-vis the issue of personal identity in my response to Kevin Corcoran (below).

I stated that I am not convinced by arguments for nonreductive physicalism. Murphy says there are two ways of arriving at a physicalist position. One begins with a dualist view and simply drops out the soul. The other, which is the one Murphy prefers, starts with the philosophy of biology and the recognized need to understand the natural world as forming a hierarchy of levels of complexity with sentient and conscious organisms at or near the top. In her brief for nonreductive physicalism, Murphy focuses on the concept of autonomy, which is an organism's capacity to detach itself from causal influences so as to act. The idea is that the higher the complexity of the organism and the more sophisticated its ability to stand back from its situation and conceptualize alternative courses of action, the more flexible it is in responding to its environment. An organism that can employ symbolic representation not only of alternative courses of action but also of itself and its cognitive processes and representations, possesses the ability of self-transcendence. With the capacity for self-transcendence, an organism is able to evaluate courses of action in light of some concept of the good and be morally responsible for its behavior. Moral behavior that is governed by the concept of the good is goal-directed or teleological in nature. What Murphy believes supports physicalism is the fact that mental capacities such as those for self-transcendence and moral behavior depend on neural complexities of various kinds.

Murphy is well aware that a dualist can acknowledge the existence of correlations and two-way causal interactions (dependencies) between higher order capacities and neural complexities but maintain that the capacities and complexities are properties of different substances—namely, a soul and its body (brain) respectively. It is important to point out that a dualist is not being hardheaded in affirming substance dualism in light of the noted correlations and dependencies. What often goes unmentioned by physicalists is that the seemingly substantive simplicity of the self is presupposed by, and sets the agenda for, an interesting issue in brain science known as the binding problem. The binding problem originates with first-person experience and the unity of our conscious lives.[1] Neurobiologists wonder about how this unity relates to the workings of the complex brain. For example, scientists are aware that the visual system has cells and regions of the brain that are especially responsive to stimuli originating from properties (e.g., color, lines, angles, shape and movement) of physical objects. When we see a physical object, however, we have a unified experience of a single object. The neurobiologist is interested in discovering where in the brain all of the effects of these diverse stimuli are bound together into a single, unified visual experience of an object. In other words, in light of the unified nature of our first-person visual experience, the neurobiologist searches for a corresponding single point in the brain which in virtue of its singularity captures the nature of our first-person experience.

The binding problem also encompasses different modes of perception. For example, because I am currently hearing voices in the distance, feeling the keys of this computer, smelling the odor of brewing coffee and seeing words on the screen, the neurobiologist is interested in locating the singular spot in the brain wherein all of the effects of corresponding stimuli are bound together. So far, scientists have failed to find what they are looking for. My point, however, is not that the failure to find a point of binding in the brain is evidence for the existence of the soul as the substance in which the binding is located. Rather, it is that the mere fact that the binding problem exists is confirmation of the reality of the apparent substantive simplicity of the self. It is confirmation that practicing scientists themselves take seriously our experience of ourselves as unified, simple subjects. And it is because I take seriously my experience of myself as a simple substance that I remain convinced that the dualist view of the self is true.

I close my response to Murphy with some very brief comments about her treatment of free will. As I suggested in my essay, there is a close link between belief that the soul exists and belief that we possess libertarian freedom. (According to a libertarian, a choice cannot be simultaneously free and determined.) Those who espouse a physicalist view of the self tend to deny that we have libertarian freedom and instead endorse compatibilism. (According to a compatibilist, a choice can simultaneously be free and determined.) Murphy says she does not know how the debate about the meaning of "free will" can be settled, and she suggests that the determinism-indeterminism issue is not the crucial issue that so many have claimed it is. Instead, the more crucial issue

---

[1]See John R. Searle, "The Mystery of Consciousness: Part I," in *The New York Review of Books*, November 1995, pp. 60-66. William Hasker emphasized the unity of consciousness in his contribution to this volume.

is whether bottom-up determinism (always) obtains, with the implication being that perhaps both bottom-up and top-down determinism obtain. I beg to
differ with Murphy's assessment of the importance of the determinism-indeterminism issue. It seems obvious to me that I cannot be morally responsible
for a choice that I was determined to make, regardless of whether that choice
was bottom-up or top-down determined. Indeed, I am inclined to think that
any event that is determined cannot even be a choice. Hence, if determinism is
true, I cannot be morally responsible for anything. Murphy does not tell the
reader what she thinks about these issues. It would have been nice if she had.

# AN EMERGENT DUALIST RESPONSE

*William Hasker*

From where I stand, the most interesting part of Nancey Murphy's paper comes near the end, when she defends her view against the objection that it is reductionist. This section is more crucial for her overall strategy than one might suppose. She has acknowledged the devastating consequences of causal reductionism (see the quotation in my essay), so if she cannot successfully defend her view against this charge, the whole project comes crashing to the ground. It is this defense, then, that I propose to examine in my comment.

Murphy makes several interesting moves in the few pages she devotes to this topic. There is a Ludwig Wittgenstein-inspired discussion about the importance of the "pictures" we have in our minds when we are thinking about the question of causal reductionism. She then produces an argument that might be used by the reductionist to support his or her point. It is a bad argument, but she does not bother to refute it. Rather, the argument is a diagnostic aid, a device that may help us to grasp the peculiar (and distorted) way the reductionist is viewing the situation.[1] Next we are treated to a series of examples, examples which are supposed to address the question "whether there are things with genuinely new causal powers or whether, if we understood well enough how dogs and people are built, we would see that their causal powers, like that of a . . . plane, are simply the product of the mechanical functioning of their parts." Finally, she sums up her discussion by invoking the concept of "downward causation." Each of these moves is interesting in its own right, and there is a lot that needs to be said about them.

Murphy's appeal to Wittgenstein is especially interesting. According to her, the picture that guides and distorts the thinking of reductionists is the atomistic world-picture of early modern science. She implies that reductionists are "in

---

[1]Throughout her discussion, Murphy refers to her opponent as a reductionist. As the reader will recognize, I am no reductionist; rather, I am quite critical of reductionism. I also tend to be critical of views that claim to avoid reductionism but in fact fail to do so.

the grip" of this picture and have never reflected on it critically. (I wonder how many actual reductionists that is true of?) Now Wittgenstein himself was resolutely opposed to metaphysics; he believed that the traditional problems of metaphysics—and indeed the problems of philosophy in general—would simply disappear if one thought about them in the right way. Most of us have long since given up on that idea, and I presume Murphy has too, since she is proposing a metaphysical hypothesis of her own. But this invites the question, what is the picture that guides (and perhaps distorts) Murphy's own thinking on this topic? (This assumes that it is not only her opponents who have such pictures!) I made a suggestion about that in my paper (above): I proposed that advocates of "downward causation" were thinking of the different "levels" in their hierarchy as like the stories of a multistoried building. I do not know whether that is right, but it would be interesting to have her comments on the notion.

Actually, I would deny that my thinking about this topic is based on a picture. Instead, it is based on the conception of the world as understood in contemporary physics, a conception which in many respects is unpicturable. An argument based on this conception as Murphy herself understands it shows that her position is reductionist—or so I would claim. Here is the argument:

1. All entities in the natural world consist of the elementary particles of physics and nothing else.

2. Anything that happens to these entities must consist in the actions and interactions of their elementary parts, including their interactions with other objects in the environment.

3. All of these actions and interactions occur in accordance with the fundamental laws of physics and are determined by those laws (with allowance for quantum indeterminacy).

But this conclusion is equivalent to causal reductionism, which Murphy herself has defined as "the view that the behavior of the parts of a system (ultimately, the parts studied by subatomic physics) is determinative of the behavior of all higher-level entities."[2] This argument is not at all circular, as Murphy suggests. It is a straightforward, linear argument based on premises I think she is committed to accept.

To Murphy's exasperated question, "*Must* it be this way?" the answer is, "Of course not!" As an emergent dualist, I reject all three of the propositions

---

[2]Nancey Murphy, "Nonreductive Physicalism: Philosophical Issues," in *Whatever Happened to the Soul? Scientific and Theological Portraits of Human Nature*, ed. Warren Brown, Nancey Murphy and H. Newton Malony, Theology and the Sciences (Minneapolis: Fortress, 1998), p. 128.

given above. Emergent materialists, such as Kevin Corcoran and Timothy O'Connor, accept the first two but reject the third. (Their "emergent causal powers" mean that the fundamental laws of physics are not all-determining.) But which proposition can Murphy reject? The first proposition is implied by the "ontological reductionism" that Murphy explicitly endorses. If the first proposition is true, so must be the second: if everything there is consists of those elementary particles, then whatever happens has to happen *to* the particles; there is nothing else there for it to happen to.[3] That does not mean, of course, that when Murphy is in a good mood her elementary particles are in a good mood; that sort of reductionism would be silly. But there must be something going on with the particles, in virtue of which she is in a good mood; otherwise nothing would be happening at all. Finally, if the second proposition is true, so is the third; Murphy explicitly rejects any modifications in the physical laws according to which the elementary particles behave. So I do not see that she has any way out; if she thinks she does, she needs to explain what it is.

But I have been overlooking her examples, one of which allegedly "shows that the atomist-reductionist thesis is simply false in some cases." What is this example? A paper airplane! Let us look at Murphy's support for her claim. She asserts that "the holistic property of the shape of the plane is crucial." She also affirms that the plane's "behavior is a result of how this holistic property enables it to be affected by its environment, in ways that none of its parts alone could be."[4] True enough, but neither of these points has any bearing on the avoidance of causal reductionism as defined by Murphy. The "holistic property of the shape of the plane" is a straightforward consequence of the configurations in which the elementary particles that make up the plane are arranged; there is nothing antireductive about that. Even more interesting, however, is the point (and she makes this same point with regard to several other examples) that the plane's behavior is a "result of how this holistic property enables it to be affected by its environment." It becomes apparent here that what Murphy is refuting is the claim that the behavior of a complex object is determined by the behavior of its parts *without considering its interactions with the environment.* Now that is indeed egregiously false, but can Murphy give a single example of a reductionist who has actually held such a view? If

---

[3] This is not to say that composite things "do not really exist" or are "not really real"—whatever those locutions might mean. It is simply to say that the composite things are wholly composed of the particles that make them up.

[4] A third point is that the laws of aerodynamics are emergent. This may be true in some sense of *emergent* (a word that, as I have pointed out, has many different uses), but not in any way that is relevant to the avoidance of causal reductionism.

not, why all the fanfare about "refuting" a view that no one holds?

Murphy concludes this part of her argument by invoking the concept of "downward or top-down causation." She claims to have shown that

> there are emergent entities (e.g., birds) with new causal powers. This is not to say that there are new causal *forces*, but rather that there are new complex entities with the ability to use lower-level causal forces (e.g., air pressure) in new ways to do new things (e.g., to fly). This does not involve overriding lower-level laws, but rather *selection* among lower-level causal processes.

Well, birds can fly, and that is new all right, but both the fact that birds fly and the way they fly are, on her view, merely the consequences of the basic laws of physics. Such terms as *using* and *selection* suggest, misleadingly, that there is some higher-level entity exercising intentional control in the situation. In fact, however, the "using" and the "selection" are themselves entirely the consequences of the operation of the (so-called) lower-level laws. There is nothing here that any sensible reductionist needs to worry about.

In conclusion, here are some thoughts about Murphy's final word, concerning free will. She suggests that "determinism versus indeterminism is not the crucial issue," and that the real question is "whether bottom-up determinism is (always) true." That is an interesting question, all right, but it cannot stand in for the question of determinism and free will; there are plenty of deterministic views that do not involve exclusively bottom-up causation. To say that once higher-level causation is in place, determinism does not make any difference is to say that, theologically, the difference between Calvinism and Arminianism makes no difference. And that just cannot be taken seriously.

# A CONSTITUTIONAL RESPONSE

*Kevin Corcoran*

**M**y response to Nancey Murphy's essay consists in what I take to be a sort of friendly critique, for there is much in her essay with which I agree. For example, Murphy and I both agree in our rejection of dualism. We agree, too (though I do not discuss it in my essay), that reductionism in the philosophy of mind is to be rejected. So, for example, we both want to preserve moral responsibility even while dispensing with immaterial souls. I think we also share a skepticism of philosophical arguments as having the power to convince, for example, dualists to become physicalists or reductionists to become nonreductionists. When it comes to viewing and interpreting the world, "pictures" or "frameworks" as foundational to human experience as dualism or naturalism do not easily fall to the power of syllogism; something more like conversion—a *Gestalt* shift, as Murphy says—is often necessary. So, as I say, I see in Murphy an able ally in the ongoing discussion over the nature of human nature.

That said, a response in a text such as this just would not pass muster without calling attention to those places in our accounts of human nature where we differ. And, in the words of Gomer Pyle, USMC, "Surprise, surprise, surprise!" There are differences between us! I want to focus, then, on three issues: (1) the idea of reductionism in the philosophy of mind, (2) the issue of so-called top-down causation as a way to escape reductionism, and, finally, (3) the subject or agent of moral responsibility. For it seems to me that the notion of top-down causation cannot, by itself, free Murphy's nonreductive physicalism from reductionism. The result, as I see it, is that on Murphy's view we are left to wonder *who* or *what* is the subject or agent of moral responsibility. Even so, supplementing her nonreductive physicalism with a metaphysics of constitution and with a robust sort of property or capacity emergence, can, I believe, help alleviate the pressure toward reductionism and secure for Murphy the moral agent or person.

## Reductionism

Murphy is an enthusiastic adherent to what I want to call the "scientific world-view."[1] According to this worldview, all the big and middle-sized objects in the natural world, such as planets and galaxies, pianos and geraniums, are composed of smaller objects that are themselves composed of even smaller objects, until we arrive at the level of molecules, which are composed of atoms, which are composed of subatomic particles.

If we take collections of objects whose boundaries are set by internal causal relations and call those collections "systems," what emerges is a picture of the natural world according to which cats, cabbages and combustion engines are all "systems." The metaphor that suggests itself here is that of a multilayered universe where each system is made up of subsystems which are, in turn, made up of still smaller systems. Organisms, for example, are made up of subsystems called cells. Some such cellular organisms develop subsystems of nerve cells. And some cellular organisms with appropriately developed nerve cells are capable of producing complex, symbolic languages that enable the systems to evaluate their own behavior in terms of abstract goals and principles.

The philosophically interesting question raised by this tiered view of the objects and entities constitutive of the natural world concerns the relationship that is asserted to hold between different levels. Since entities or systems of one level are decomposable into parts and systems that belong to the nearest lower level, an obvious question is just how the higher-level parts, properties and systems stand in relation to the lower-level parts, properties and systems. One possible answer to this question is that the relation is the reducibility relation: higher-level properties and systems are reducible to lower-level ones.

Murphy rejects this answer. More specifically, she rejects *causal* reduction, the view that the microphysical goings on of a system causally *determine* the higher-level, macrophysical goings on of a system. For example, I believe in God the Father almighty, maker of heaven and earth. And if reductionism is true, this belief of mine is nothing more than the causal upshot of the microphysical goings on in my brain, goings on which obey the same physical laws that govern falling apples and the trajectory of baseballs as they fly off baseball bats. And the latter two macroevents (apples falling and baseballs flying) are

---

[1]Obviously, I do not mean to imply by this that she is not also an enthusiastic adherent to a *theistic* or even *Christocentric* worldview. The two are not, contrary to popular opinion, non-overlapping and exclusive.

wholly determined by the microphysical goings on of those objects' constituent elements and the laws governing their behavior.

The problem is that, as William Hasker points out in his essay, Murphy seems to be hoisted by her own petard. If he is right about that, Murphy would not be the first. As I have argued elsewhere, John Searle, who also claims to reject reductionism, is guilty as well.[2]

So what, exactly, is the problem? Well, the problem is that, on the one hand, while Murphy believes the micro goings-on of a thing make a significant causal contribution to the macro goings-on of that thing, she believes the micro goings-on do not wholly determine those macro goings-on. On the other hand, it is hard to see how she can hold that view and embrace the scientific worldview. Put it this way: There seem to be two claims Murphy would like to embrace: (1) causal reductionism is false, and (2) the mental and other morally significant properties of human beings are causally dependent on the microphysical parts, properties, and behaviors of human brains. The problem is, absent some sort of robust emergent power or even a substance emergence view of the mind, it is hard to see how to escape microdeterminism. For according to the scientific worldview, what is there to apples, baseballs and human organisms other than their microphysical constituents? Sure, there are the equally natural environments in which they are embedded, but it is hard to see how that helps to avoid causal reductionism.

## *Top-Down Causation*

We can use the very notion Murphy employs to escape reductionism to help illustrate the problem. There are, in fact, two worries here. First, there is what philosophers call the problem of *causal overdetermination*. We can illustrate the problem by way of so-called mental causation.

A mental property, D—my *desire* for mint chocolate-chip ice cream, say—is caused by an instantiation of a certain biological or neural property, B. Now assume that D has the power to cause other properties to be instantiated. Presumably there are two possible scenarios. The properties D can cause to be instantiated are other mental-properties (mental-mental causation), or the properties D can cause to be instantiated are physical properties (top-down causation).

Consider the first scenario. D causes another mental property, D* to be instantiated—my *desire* for ice cream causes a numerically distinct *desire* to go to

---

[2]See my article "The Trouble with Searle's Biological Naturalism," *Erkenntnis* 55 (2001): 307-24.

the market. But now $D^*$, like $D$ itself, is caused by a lower-level, biological/ neural phenomenon, an instantiation of some biological/neural property $B^*$. So $D^*$ has two distinct *sufficient* causes, one a mental phenomenon $(D)$ and the other a biological/neural phenomenon $(B^*)$. Thus $D^*$ is causally *overdetermined*. Here is a picture:

$$D \rightarrow D^*$$
$$\uparrow \quad \uparrow$$
$$B \quad B^*$$

Notice it will not do to solve the problem by claiming (as some are wont to do) that $D$ and $D^*$ are themselves biological phenomena, even if mental. For $D$ is either identical with $B^*$ (or some other lower-level biological phenomenon) or not. If it is identical with one of those, then the mental property of desiring ice cream is a lower-level biological/neural phenomenon. And if $D$ is not identical with one of the lower-level biological/neural properties, then $D^*$ is still causally overdetermined. For some lower-level biological phenomenon, $B^*$, and some (higher) biological phenomenon, $D$, will be the sufficient cause of $D^*$. So the claim that both $D$ and $D^*$ are biological would be of no help. That is one worry.

## Moral Responsibility and the Problem of the Subject

The second worry I mentioned is brought out by Murphy's use of examples to illustrate moral evaluation and goal setting as instances of top-down causation. The worry is this: each of Murphy's examples are in terms of physical systems—and in the case of human organisms, those "systems" performing various kinds of self-evaluation and self-correction—in light of abstract moral principles or goals. One wants to know, however, who or what it is that is performing these evaluations and setting these goals. Is it the "system"? But systems are collections of parts and parts of parts. As Hasker has pointed out, we cannot take the metaphor of the multilayered universe too literally; the higher "levels" are not concrete particulars or individuals; they are instead structural or configurational features of constituent elements. But "structures" or "arrangements" of elements are simply not the right sort of things to count as agents or subjects of moral responsibility. What is needed are individuals— persons. The worry is that on Murphy's view there is no individual agent or subject of moral responsibility.

As I noted at the beginning, I do not think all of this need count as a devastating critique of Murphy's view. For in her essay she begins to flirt with precisely what she needs to escape reductionism—namely, a robust emergent power or capacity, emergence of the sort Timothy O'Connor has been defending.[3] And as for needing an individual to serve as the agent of moral responsibility, Murphy comes close to a solution when she says we need to take into account "new complex entities with the ability to use lower-level causal forces . . . in new ways to do new things." I suggest supplementing Murphy's nonreductive physicalism with a metaphysic of constitution. This could deliver an individual human person constituted by a human organism who can serve as the agent.

---

[3]Murphy's near embrace of a robust emergent view of the mind makes one wonder why she prefers the "nonreductive physicalism" nomenclature over that of emergence. For the philosophically significant work that will enable her to escape reductionism is, at the end of the day, done by an emergent capacity or power. And it ought to be pointed out that the robust sort of emergence needed to escape reductionism would require Murphy to embrace an additional belief—namely, a belief in modification of the microlaws. I assume, given Murphy's comments, that to the extent that she is prepared to embrace a robust emergent power, she is, to that same degree, prepared to embrace modifications in the microlaws.

# 5 THE CONSTITUTION VIEW OF PERSONS

*Kevin Corcoran*

In 1968 I lost my father to cancer. I was four years old. I can still remember the funeral home. And I can remember that as I looked into the casket, my mother told me that my father was now with God in heaven. I recall being perplexed by what my mother said. After all, for all appearances my father was lying lifeless before me. How could my father be with God in heaven? Now I understand that my mother believed what many Christians have believed down through the centuries—namely, that we human persons are *immaterial* souls. On this view, my father's lifeless body may have been lying before me, but not my father. Although we human persons may be contingently and tightly joined to human bodies during the course of our earthly existence, so the view goes, we can, and in fact one day will, exist without them.

The question this essay is most interested in answering is the metaphysical question that Saint Augustine ponders in book 7 of his *Confessions* and that René Descartes poses in his Second Meditation: *What kind of thing am I?*[1] Am I an immaterial substance or a material substance? Am I a compound substance? Are there alternatives to these views? In this essay I am going to tell you why I believe that I am a physical thing even if the physical thing I am is not—perhaps surprisingly—the biological body that constitutes me. I will conclude by considering some important issues related both to ethics and to the Christian doctrine of resurrection.

Let me begin first with a confession. This essay is an exercise in *Christian* philosophy. As a Christian, I have certain theological commitments. What I try to do in this essay is to explore how some of these fit together with a particular philosophical or metaphysical view of human nature that I also hold. For example, as a Christian I am committed to the doctrine of the resurrection of the body, and one of the issues I will explore in this essay is just how the materialist view of human nature I embrace meshes with this Christian commitment.

Let me be very clear, though. Considering things like the doctrine of the res-

---

[1] For the relation of Augustianism to Cartesianism, see Stephen Menn, *Descartes and Augustine* (Cambridge: Cambridge University Press, 1998).

urrection and the metaphysical nature of human persons is difficult business. Whatever the truth, it is not transparent and obvious. Whereas some philosophers who consider these issues are prepared to speak in bold and authoritative terms, I myself am hesitant to so speak. I have thought long and hard about these matters and am committed to the truth of the views I hold. However, it is conceivable to me that I should one day learn, perhaps in heaven, and certainly to my chagrin, that it is not my view but one of the views I reject that is the truth about our nature. Then I should be like Ptolemy, who did his level best to seek the truth and weigh the evidence about the heavenly bodies, but who, for all of that, was nevertheless mistaken.

## Dualisms

My mother, as I have suggested, is a dualist about human persons. Try as I might, I cannot bring myself to believe what my mother believes, and what many Christians down through the ages have believed, about the metaphysics of human persons. It is not that I do not understand the view. I do. It is rather like someone telling me that the natural world is the product of blind, mechanical processes operating over large stretches of time on matter cooked up in some primordial soup. I understand the story of evolution by natural selection, where the primary mechanism of natural selection, genetic mutations, is to be understood as blind, random and mechanical. Try as I might, however, I simply cannot believe that what I see around me is the outcome of blind and random processes. So too with the traditional way of understanding the nature of human persons. I simply cannot believe that I am an immaterial thing. I can believe that some kinds of persons are immaterial—for example, nonhuman, divine persons like God and the angels. But not *human* persons like me. That I cannot believe. (Here is an exercise for the reader: Close your eyes right now and try to will to believe that you are, instead of reading this essay, on a Ferris wheel at a carnival. I am not asking you to try to *imagine* that you are on a Ferris wheel at a carnival. I am asking you to will to *believe* it. I do not think you can. The fact of the matter is that many, if not most, of your beliefs are not actually "up to you." Most are like your belief that you are reading this essay now. You cannot help but believe it and, try as you might, you cannot believe that you are on a Ferris wheel now—unless, of course, you *are* on a Ferris wheel now. If that is the case, however, you should put the book down and enjoy the ride!)

Have I then no reasons for discounting this brand of dualism? I do. For one, if persons (or souls) and bodies are as distinct as Descartes and Augustine seem to have thought them to be, then I would not expect to find the level of causal dependence of the one (the mind) on the other (the body) as we in fact do find. For we can alter or even (apparently) eliminate consciousness by altering or destroying certain regions of the brain. Moreover, that we human beings are immaterial souls seems to introduce an unnecessary and inelegant cleavage into the natural world—something I would not expect to find within creation. In other words, that human beings are not of a piece with the rest of nature, which would be the case if human beings of all the animals are the only creatures endowed by God with souls, strikes me as odd. Call it a Calvinist fondness for order, efficiency and elegance, if you want. But I would expect the natural world, as a product of divine creation, to be elegant and seamless. In any event, these are just two, albeit controversial, reasons for why I find dualism about persons problematic. But, truth be known, before I ever thought very hard about the problems associated with Cartesian dualism, I could not bring myself to believe it.

The kind of dualism I have been considering is known as *substance* dualism because of its claim that the natural world consists of two kinds of finite substances, one kind immaterial (soul) and the other kind material (body). As a theist, quite obviously I do not reject dualisms of all kinds. For I believe both that God and the angels are immaterial and that there is a dualism of Creator and creature. What I reject is substance dualism. There are, however, other versions of dualism which deny that human persons like us are identical with immaterial, substantial souls. According to one such alternative, human persons like us are a compound of soul and body or, as defenders of such views might prefer to put it, a compound of *form* and *matter.* Saint Thomas Aquinas, for example, is believed by many to have held a view of this sort. I do not believe this view either. But unlike the case with the previous sort of dualism, which I understand perfectly well, I simply do not understand Thomistic dualism. And it is not all my fault either. Aquinas was not himself altogether clear in articulating the view. Today the range of logically incompatible views of human nature that travel under the banner of Thomism is dizzying. So my failure to believe Thomistic dualism is at most only partly a function of my own failure of imagination. In any case, it seems to me that I am not only physical but essentially[2] and wholly physical: that is, if there should be an immaterial person

---

[2]When I use the term *essential* and its cognates, I have a special meaning in mind. For starters, distinguish between substance and properties. Think of substances as individual things and properties as ways those things can be or fail to be. For example, being six feet tall, being green or weighing 200 pounds are examples of properties. Some things have those properties and some do not. Now some properties are had by the things that have them *contingently,* and others are had *essentially.* If a substance has a property essentially, then that sub-

in the future who claims to be me, that person is mistaken, and necessarily so. For, as I see it, I cannot exist and fail to be physical. And the physical thing I am, I believe, has no immaterial parts such as a soul.[3]

## Materialisms: Animalism and Constitution

One materialistic alternative to dualism is to identify human persons with the physical objects that are their bodies. On such a view, we human persons are identical with human *animals*. According to animalism you and I are essentially animals and only contingently persons, which is to say that while we could not exist and fail to be animals, we could exist (and in fact at one time did) without being a person. In other words, according to animalism, the property of being a person is like the property we have of being married or single. During some stages of our existence we may be married, while during other stages of our existence we may be single. Well, during our fetal lives we were not persons; now we are. If things should go badly for us, we may end up once again as nonpersons. For example, if the upper part of my brain should suffer traumatic damage such that I completely lack the capacity for a psychological life, but the lower part of my brain remains intact such that the biological functions necessary for biological life continue, then I should continue to exist but cease to be a person. But, so the view has it, I could never end up as a nonanimal; for an animal is what I am essentially.

What many find surprising about my view is that while I do not identify myself with an immaterial soul or a compound of soul and body, neither do I believe that I am identical with the physical object that is my biological body. But how can that be? If I am neither an immaterial soul nor a compound of soul and body, how could I possibly be a physical object if I am not the physical object that is my body? I will now attempt to explain what I realize sounds like an odd claim indeed.

---

stance cannot exist and fail to have that property. If a substance has a property contingently, then that substance can exist without having that property. For example, you may have the property of weighing 200 pounds. But surely you could exist without weighing 200 pounds. You may either gain or lose that property without ceasing to exist. But take a particular dog, say, Lassie, for example. Lassie has the property of being a canine. And Lassie could not exist without being a canine. So we say that Lassie is essentially a canine. If Lassie should cease to be a canine, Lassie would cease to exist.

[3]Whether to categorize Aquinas as a dualist is a matter of debate. Although it is true that he did not identify human persons with immaterial substances or souls, he did think that the form of a human body (i.e., a rational soul) could exist apart from any body. And that makes me agree with those who locate him among dualists. But again, he is not a *substance* dualist because he did not think that the rational soul was a substance. It was, in his terms, a "subsistent."

The view of human persons I defend is known in the literature as the *constitution view*. According to it, we human persons are constituted by our bodies without being identical with the bodies that constitute us. To claim that human persons are constituted by bodies without being identical with the bodies that constitute them is not to make any special pleading for human persons. I believe lots of medium-sized physical objects stand in constitution relations. For example, statues are often constituted by pieces of marble, copper or bronze. But the statues are not identical with the pieces of marble, copper or bronze that constitute them. Likewise, dollar bills, diplomas and dust-jackets are often constituted by pieces of paper. But, none of those things are identical with the pieces of paper that constitute them. Why do I say this? Because there is a very good test for determining whether some thing, $x$, is identical with a thing, $y$. Ask yourself, are there any properties that the one has but the other lacks? If so, then $x$ and $y$ are not identical. Are there any changes that $x$ could undergo without ceasing to exist but which $y$ could not undergo without ceasing to exist, or vice versa? If so, then $x$ and $y$ are numerically distinct things. Even if $x$ and $y$ possibly differ, then $x$ and $y$ are not identical.

Outside philosophy we use the term *identical* or the phrase *the same as* in a loose and nontechnical sense. We might say, for example, that your book is "the same as" mine or that we have "identical" computers. What we mean is that our books or computers are phenomenologically indistinguishable: that is, they look exactly alike. When philosophers use the term *identical* or the phrase *the same as*, they do not have in mind phenomenological indistinguishability. Instead, they are thinking in terms of number, the number *one*. And with respect to number, of course, you and I do not have the same book or computer; you have one and I have one, and one plus one makes *two*. It is the distinction between *numerical sameness* and what we might call *qualitative sameness* that led me to say a moment ago that, if some thing, $x$, could survive a change that would destroy some thing, $y$, then $x$ and $y$ are numerically distinct. What I meant was that $x$ and $y$ are two things and not one.

Consider, for example, Saul of Tarsus, that scoundrel, persecutor of Christians, and the apostle Paul, the faithful follower of Jesus. Are Saul and Paul the same person? Well, could Saul of Tarsus exist without the apostle Paul existing? If so, then they are not numerically the same person. Since Saul cannot exist without Paul existing, nor can Paul exist without Saul existing, we ought to say that Saul of Tarsus is the apostle Paul: that is, they are numerically the same person.

When I use this example with my students they usually protest, saying, "But we can conceive that Saul may never have met Jesus on the road to Damascus. If so, Paul never would have existed, but Saul would have. So Saul is *not* Paul." "Plus," they say, "didn't Paul say in 2 Corinthians 5:17 that if anyone is in Christ, there is a *new* creation: everything old has passed away; see, everything has become *new*"? This much is certainly true: Saul may never have met Jesus on the Damascan road, and Paul is a new creature in Christ. What is not true is that Saul could have existed without Paul (or vice versa) or that at some time on the Damascan road one person (Saul) ceased to exist and a numerically distinct person (Paul) replaced him. Think about it this way. Did Paul experience a conversion? Certainly he did, we say. Well, if there is a conversion, then there must be a single thing that survives or undergoes the conversion. There must be some single thing that radically changes. To say, "I am a completely different person since I met Christ," is to say that I was once one way and now I—the same I—am quite a different way. So in the numerical sense, Saul is Paul (there is just one guy), but that one guy has radically changed.[4] It is not that God annihilated one person (Saul) and replaced him with a numerically distinct person (Paul). No, there is one guy in the story and his life has been radically altered.[5]

So if anyone is in Christ, there is a new creation: everything old has passed away; see, everything has become new!

Let us now consider the case of a particular copper statue. Is the piece of copper numerically the same as the statue? I think not. For it is possible that the copper could survive changes that would terminate the existence of the statue. For example, extreme heat or repeated blows with a sledgehammer

---

[4]It was, I am told, the custom for Jewish people in the diaspora to have two names—one Jewish and the other Greek/Roman. So, really, the Saul/Paul problem, as I have set it up, assumes the mistaken view that the two names track the pre- and post-Christ experience of Paul (Saul). Even so, you get the point. The same point about numerical sameness could be made by using Cassius Clay and Muhammad Ali, Samuel Clemens and Mark Twain, or Clark Kent and Superman. In each case, we have a single individual picked out by different names. And in the first and last cases we have the different names signaling radical change in the individual, just as it is often assumed to be the case with Saul/Paul.

[5]So what are my students imagining when they claim to be imagining Saul existing without Paul existing? What they are imagining is some description not being true of Paul (Saul). They are imagining that Paul (Saul) never met Jesus. But that is not to imagine Saul existing without Paul existing. It is only to imagine that a certain description does not apply to Paul (Saul). I can imagine that Samuel Clemens never wrote a single book. That is not, however, to imagine Mark Twain not existing. It is only to imagine a certain description not being true of the one guy both names happen to pick out. The same is true for Cassius Clay and Muhammad Ali. I can imagine Cassius Clay never having converted to Islam. But that is not to imagine Cassius Clay existing without Muhammad Ali existing. Again, it is just to imagine a certain description's (e.g., having converted to Islam) not being true of the one guy both those names in fact pick out.

might destroy the statue but not the copper. Why not the copper? Because we can imagine the surviving piece of copper being hammered flat, say, but not the statue. Well, a single thing cannot both survive and fail to survive through the same changes. So if the piece of copper can survive through changes that would destroy the statue, the piece of copper is not identical with the statue! Similar distinctions apply to dollar bills, tables, physical organisms of various kinds and the things that constitute them.

So according to a metaphysics of constitution, two material objects will be said to stand in constitution relations one to the other just in case those objects are spatially coincident and belong to different kinds. To say that two material objects are "spatially coincident" is just another way of saying that the objects share the same matter. Every atom that composes the one composes the other. The statue and the piece of copper share the same matter. (This is why defenders of constitution want to say that constitution is as close as you can get to identity *without* identity. Since two objects that stand in constitution relations share all the same matter, you cannot pull them apart.) But pieces of copper and statues are, pretty obviously, objects of different kinds. Indeed, as we have seen, an object of the one kind can survive through changes that would terminate the existence of an object of the other.[6] So that is the general shape of the constitution relation. Although I would never claim that Aristotle himself held a constitution view of medium-sized physical objects, I would suggest that the constitution view bears certain similarities to Aristotle's metaphysics of substance. I say this to highlight the fact that the constitution view did not drop down from on high in the twenty-first century with no historical antecedents. Elements of the view are, I believe, there in Aristotle and John Locke, for example.

Now, to apply the constitution view specifically to human persons. On a constitution account, human persons are constituted by bodies but are not identical with the bodies that constitute them. Why say so? First consider what it is in virtue of which some object is a *person* and what it is in virtue of which some object is a *body*. Though it is difficult to state conditions that all and only persons satisfy, I think we can say with some confidence that persons (human or otherwise) are, minimally, beings with a capacity for intentional states: believing, desiring, intending and so on. I say "minimally" because, of course, there are things that satisfy the condition that pretty obviously are not persons:

---

[6]For those who prefer bells and whistles, here is a characterization of the relation using logical notation. $x$ constitutes $y$ only if: *(i)* $x$ and $y$ wholly occupy the same space and *(ii)* there are different sortal properties $F$ and $G$ and an environment $E$ such that *(a)* ($Fx$ and $x$ is in $E$) and ($Gy$ and $y$ is in $E$) and *(b)* ($\forall z$) [($Fz$ and $z$ is in $E$) $\supset$ ($\exists w$) ($Gw$ and $w$ is in $E$) and ($w \neq z$)].

for example, dogs. But if something does not so much as have a capacity for intentional states, it seems equally obvious that that thing is not a candidate for personhood. So if a being lacks a capacity for intentional states, then that being, whatever it is, is not a person. Persons are also the only sort of thing that has what Lynne Baker calls a first-person perspective. A first-person perspective is more than just a perspective on the world or a locus of consciousness, as lots of nonpersonal creatures have that. A first-person perspective is the capacity to think of oneself as oneself, without the need of a description or third-person pronoun. For example, I can think of myself as myself without thinking of my-self as Kevin Corcoran, without thinking of my self as the father of Shannon and Rowan Corcoran, or without thinking of myself as the sole Irishman in the philosophy department of Calvin College. When I wonder, for example, whether I will live long enough to see my children graduate from college, I am thinking of myself from the first-person perspective. Finally, on my view, not only are human persons essentially bodily beings, insofar as they are now con-stituted by biological bodies,[8] but human persons are *essentially* constituted by the biological bodies that do in fact constitute them. Therefore, if my body should ever cease to exist, I would cease to exist.[9]

By biological body, I mean a physical organism. And according to a consti-tution account of physical organisms, they are themselves constituted objects being constituted by masses of cellular tissues. Moreover, by "physical organ-ism" I mean a "living animal," and by "life" I have in mind an individual bio-logical process of a very special sort—a sort that is remarkably stable, well in-dividuated, self-directing, self-maintaining and homeodynamic.

One reason for denying that human persons are identical with the physical organisms that constitute them is that the kinds "person" and "physical organ-ism" have different identity conditions. For example, there is nothing in the criterion of identity for an organism that involves having intentional states.

---

[7]See Lynne Rudder Baker, *Persons and Bodies: A Constitution View,* Cambridge Studies in Phi-losophy (Cambridge: Cambridge University Press, 2000), esp. chap. 3.
[8]Here I reveal my commitment to the plausible claim that material objects are *essentially* ma-terial. Take my son's baseball mitt, for example. I do not believe that that very mitt can exist and fail to be a material object. This plausible claim is, for all its plausibility, not uncontro-versial. Some philosophers think that some material objects are merely *contingently* material. Someone who believed that my son's baseball mitt was only contingently material believes that though it in fact is material, it could exist without being material. I do not believe that.
[9]It should be pointed out that the constitution view of persons is a metaphysical view of the relation between a human person and his or her body. It is not a theory of the mind and the relation between mental events (e.g., being in pain) and physical events in the brain (e.g., the firing of neurons). As I understand the view, it is neutral with respect to so-called reductive and nonreductive theories of mind.

Therefore, there is no conceptual impossibility involved in thinking about the physical organism that is my body existing while completely lacking a capacity for intentional states; if what I said above is true, however, then there is such an impossibility involved in the idea of *my* existing while lacking all capacity for intentional states. For I am a person. And this is why I believe that while I am constituted by my body, I am not, strictly speaking, identical with it. Indeed, I believe that my body came into existence before I did and that it is conceivable that my body should outlive me. I am therefore not my body, since I cannot possibly have come into existence before I did, nor can I conceivably outlive myself.

Elsewhere I have done about as much as I can to defend this view against some potent philosophical objections.[10] What I want to do here is defend the view against some important theological and moral objections. For I have been criticized for putting forth a view of human nature that is (1) incompatible with Christian teaching concerning postmortem survival and (2) at cross purposes with a robust ethic of life. So let me take each of these in turn.

## After Life, Life!

I have heard it said that the constitution view is ill-equipped to deal with the afterlife, unlike its handsome cousin dualism, which, in any of its many guises, is much more hospitable to this key Christian belief. The criticism is usually put like this. Bodies peter out and eventually cease to exist. And on any plausible materialist account of persons, one's body is necessary for one's own existence. How can a body that peters out and ceases to exist somehow turn up in the New Jerusalem? Worse, if the deceased immediately join the Savior in heaven, then how can that fact possibly be squared with the apparent fact that the corpse is often right before our eyes? Dualists do not have such problems to embarrass them, since immaterial souls are not subject to the vagaries of bodily demise.

If the issue is simply one of postmortem survival, then I admit that dualists have a much easier time accommodating such a doctrine. But if one is both a dualist and a *Christian*, then it is plausible to believe that such a dualist faces at least one of the very same problems as the Christian materialist, namely, how to make sense of the Christian doctrine of resurrection of the body.[11] For

---

[10]See my "Persons, Bodies and the Constitution Relation," *Southern Journal of Philosophy* 37 (1999): 1-20.

[11]By "Christian materialist" I mean someone who confesses Christ and who also believes that human persons are wholly material beings. I most emphatically do not mean someone who confesses Christ and also believes that if something exists, then it must be made of matter. For no Christian can coherently believe that!

it is precisely that doctrine that needs to be addressed by *Christian* dualists. None of the ecumenical creeds of the church, for example, confesses belief in a doctrine of "soul survival." The Christian doctrine has been understood as the doctrine of *bodily resurrection*. Contemporary dualists seem to have forgotten this in a way that our ancient dualist ancestors did not. Most, if not all, orthodox Christian theologians of the early church were anthropological *dualists*. And it was these dualist-minded theologians who struggled in systematic ways to make sense of the Christian doctrine of *bodily* resurrection.[12] Telling a story of how a body that apparently suffered a martyr's death can be numerically the same as a body that enjoys resurrection life is not the special preoccupation of twenty-first-century Christian materialists. This has been, at least until very recently, a concern for dualists too.

Aquinas, for example, recognized the need to provide an account of the resurrection of the body. And like the dualists who preceded him, his view seeks to account for the numerical sameness of the resurrection and earthly body. What accounts for the fact that a body once dead can nevertheless enjoy resurrection life is, according to Aquinas, the further fact that the human soul continues to exist, temporarily disembodied, between death and resurrection. That soul, Aquinas believed, organizes both the matter that composed the body before death and the matter that will compose the body after death. Same soul; therefore, same body.

Aquinas's view of the soul, however, is not without difficulties. Some of the difficulties center on Aquinas's ambiguous use of the term *soul,* using it sometimes in the sense of a particular thing and at other times in the sense of "form" or kind of "state" a body is in. Perhaps most important, however, is how, given the rest of Aquinas's metaphysics of substance, a soul can plausibly be said to survive the death of the body.

In any case, it is plausible to believe that providing an account of the identity between the resurrected and earthly body is constitutive of an account of resurrection of the body. For the Christian doctrine is not the doctrine of reincarnation or the doctrine of the acquisition of some body or other, any more than it is the doctrine of soul survival. Consider, for example, 1 Corinthians 15:42-43, where we read, "So it is with the resurrection of the dead. What is sown is perishable, what is raised is imperishable. It is sown in dishonor, it is

---

[12]For fascinating reading on the importance of bodily continuity and numerical sameness in patristic and medieval reflections on the resurrection, see Caroline Walker Bynum, *The Resurrection of the Body in Western Christianity, 200-1336* (New York: Columbia University Press, 1995).

raised in glory. It is sown in weakness, it is raised in power. It is sown a physical body, it is raised a spiritual body." It is reasonable to believe that it is numerically the *same* body which exists before and after death, although after
death that body is glorified and radically changed. For this reason, I think providing an account of the sameness of resurrected and earthly bodies ought to
be of interest to all Christians, dualists no less than materialists.[13] Moreover,
given the fact that the Christian tradition has historically understood the doctrine of resurrection as involving numerically the same body, any putatively
Christian view of the afterlife that departs from tradition at least owes us an
explanation for why we should understand the doctrine in a way that explicitly or implicitly departs from that tradition.[14]

So the first thing to see is that dualists and materialists alike owe us an ac-

---

[13]I say this in full recognition that it is, surprisingly, a minority view. Apparently most contemporary philosophers of religion do not think numerical sameness even a plausible view
of the resurrection. See, e.g., Bruce Reichenbach, *Is Man the Phoenix?* (Grand Rapids: Eerdmans, 1978): "The language of resurrection is misleading when it suggests that the very
thing which died will be raised again. . . . [This] seem[s] generally contrary to any factual
possibility, given the disintegration of bodies upon death and the dispersal of their constituent elements" (p. 181). See also John Hick, *Death and Eternal Life* (New York: Harper & Row,
1976): "A human being is by nature mortal and subject to annihilation at death. But in fact
God, by an act of sovereign power, either sometimes or always resurrects or reconstitutes
or recreates him—*not however as the identical physical organism that he was before death*" (p. 279,
emphasis added). And John Cooper, although he does not come right out and say it, seems
to think that the resurrection bodies we human beings will enjoy in the afterlife are not the
same numerical bodies we had in our preresurrection existence (*Body, Soul and Life Everlasting: Biblical Anthropology and the Monism-Dualism Debate* [Grand Rapids: Eerdmans, 1989],
pp. 185-95).
[14]See Bynum, *Resurrection of the Body*. I also want to point out why I believe that it is permis-
sible to depart from tradition in believing the constitution view but do not believe we
should depart from tradition here. I believe we should only depart from tradition when it
seems to us that the tradition is mistaken about some matter that is not essential to ecumenical orthodoxy and we believe we can account for how that mistake may have come about.
So, for example, I believe the tradition found itself wedded to a dualistic anthropology because it could not conceive any other way to account for the difference between humans
and nonhuman animals, except by attributing to us immaterial souls. The constitution view,
however, provides an account of human persons that distinguishes us from nonhuman animals, but without positing immaterial souls. I do not see the tradition's insistence that the
resurrected and earthly bodies must be identical as a mistake. If others do, then it is they
who owe us an account of why it is a mistake and how that mistake may have come about.
Cooper suggests that the biblical writers came to believe in an immaterial soul on the basis
of their belief in an intermediate state of existence between death and resurrection (*Body,
Soul*). This may be so. Again, I would suggest that this is a mistake likely made because the
biblical writers could not conceive how there could be such a state without an immaterial
soul. However, there is an option equally compatible with belief in an intermediate state,
namely, intermediate bodies. In the following sections, I show how the constitution view is
compatible with belief in immediate survival.

count of the resurrection of the body. The trick, of course, both for materialists and dualists, is to say just how a body that has passed out of existence can turn up in the New Jerusalem. Think about it this way. The apostle Paul died many years ago. If Saint Paul's *body*, which existed in A.D. 45, 55 or 65, exists in the hereafter, then a physical object numerically identical with Saint Paul's body exists in the hereafter. But how could that be? There appear to be obviously good reasons for denying that St. Paul's body could exist in the hereafter. Even if his body survived for sometime as a fairly well-preserved corpse, the odds are that it has undergone radical decay over the years and has long since passed out of existence. How can a physical object that exists in the hereafter be numerically identical with a physical object that has either radically decayed or passed out of existence under more gruesome circumstances?

## The Same Body

One way of explaining how the body Saint Paul had in (say) A.D. 50 could be numerically identical with a body that will exist in the New Jerusalem is first to offer an account of the persistence conditions of human bodies. Persistence conditions tell us the sorts of changes a thing can undergo without ceasing to exist. For example, a thing like a banana, which we might imagine is yellow on Monday, can survive through changes such as those that result in a brown banana on Friday. But a thing like a banana cannot survive through changes such as those involved in making banana bread. In other words, things like bananas can survive through color changes, but they cannot survive through smashings and mixings. After offering an account of the persistence conditions for human bodies, one would then need to show how, appearances to the contrary, Saint Paul's body survives, alive and well, through the biological processes which end in death. Such an approach seems especially necessary if one believes that immediately upon death we go to be with the Lord.

Although I myself do not believe in immediate survival (at least for the vast majority of us human beings), I do believe that there is an account of the persistence conditions of things like human bodies that can accommodate belief in immediate survival—and this despite the fact that many deaths leave behind a corpse. In the next section, I present that account.

## The Importance of Causation to Survival

What are the persistence conditions for bodies? It is often thought that continuity through time and space is, if not sufficient, at least necessary for the persistence of bodies. Yet there are good reasons for claiming that spatiotemporal continuity is neither necessary nor sufficient for the survival of physical organisms. First, it seems possible that an evil genius could totally annihilate a body during a certain interval of time and that God could replace it with a newly created molecular duplicate during precisely the same interval, and in precisely the same place as the place once occupied by the original body at the time of its annihilation. The picture is that of the gradual top-down annihilation of one body and the replacement of it with a numerically distinct duplicate—the replacement body exactly filling the human-body shaped receptacle created by the annihilated body. In other words, the same interval of time would mark the end of one body's existence and the beginning of a duplicate's existence, while the spatial region originally filled by the annihilated body would come to be wholly filled by a body numerically distinct from it. This seamless replacement of one body with another seems to suggest that continuity through space and time is not enough for the persistence of bodies.[15] Again, it is not enough because the example appears to present us with a case in which there is spatiotemporal continuity *without* persistence.

There is also some reason to believe that spatiotemporal continuity is not even necessary for the persistence of bodies. Reflection on such thought experiments as those graphically portrayed on *Star Trek* suggest as much. Occupants of the transporter seem to disappear at one time and from one place only to re-emerge at another time and in a different place. One interpretation of what happens to those who enter the transporter is that they are able to skip over intervening times and spaces en route to their future destination. What imaginative scenarios like this have suggested to some philosophers is that spatiotemporal continuity is normally merely a consequence of persistence and not its ground.[16] In other words, there must be something else that secures persistence. And it has been thought that a really good candidate for what grounds cases of persistence is some kind of causation. If the computer monitor before me has persisted into the present, then it seems that its existence in the immediate past must be causally relevant to its existence now. So too with human bodies. It seems that if a human body sitting before me at 9:00 a.m. is not causally connected with one that was sitting before me at 8:59 a.m., then it is plausible to think that the human body before me at 9:00 a.m. is not a continuation of the body that was before me at 8:59 a.m., but rather is a numerically distinct replacement, even if there is spatiotemporal continuity between the 9:00 a.m. and 8:59 a.m. bodies

[15]The idea of "smooth" replicas or "immaculate" replacements can be credited either to Sydney Shoemaker ("Identity, Properties and Causality," in *Identity, Cause and Mind* [Cambridge: Cambridge University Press, 1984], pp. 234-60), or David Armstrong ("Identity Through Time," in *Time and Cause*, ed. Peter van Inwagen [Dordtrecht: Reidel, 1980], pp. 67-78).
[16]See, e.g., Armstrong, "Identity Through Time," p. 76.

and even if the bodies are phenomenologically indistinguishable.

Causal considerations, therefore, seem especially pertinent to the giving of persistence conditions for material objects of any sort. Of course, the kinds of causal dependencies relating an object at earlier and later stages of its career will very likely differ according to the kind of object whose career we are tracing. Different kinds of persisting things will have different persistence conditions. What it is in virtue of which a human body persists is different from what it is in virtue of which a computer monitor persists. But even so, it is causal considerations that are relevant to the persistence of each.[17]

When it comes to the persistence of bodies, I suggest we think this way. Human bodies are like storms. A tornado, for example, picks up new stuff and throws off old stuff as it moves through space. Human bodies are like that. They are storms of atoms moving through space and time. They take on new stuff and throw off old stuff as they go. And a body persists in virtue of the atoms that are caught up in a life-preserving (causal) relation at one time passing on that life-preserving causal relation to successive swarms of atoms at later times. My body has persisted into the present just in case the swarm of atoms that are caught up in the life of my body now have been bequeathed that life-preserving causal relation from the swarm of atoms that were caught up in its life a moment ago.[18]

We can name this condition on the persistence of human bodies the *immanent causal condition*. I say the causation involved is immanent. In immanent causation, a state $x$ of thing $A$ brings about a consequent state $y$ in $A$ itself, whereas in cases of causation of the sort we normally think of, a thing $A$ brings about state-changes in a numerically distinct thing, $B$. For example, the state or event of the rock's hurtling through the air brings about state changes in the window it hits. The immanent causal condition makes it a requirement on the persistence of an organism that immanent causal relations hold among the different stages of an organism's career.[19]

---

[17]See Chris Swoyer, "Causation and Identity," *Midwest Studies in Philosophy* 9 (1984): 593-622.

[18]To put it more technically: If an organism $O$ that exists at $t_2$ is the same as an organism $P$ that exists at $t_1$, and $P$ persisted from $t_1$ to $t_2$, then the (set of) simples that compose $P$ at $t_1$ must be causally related to the (set of) simples that compose $O$ at $t_2$.

[19]See Dean Zimmerman, "Immanent Causation," *Nous*, Supp. vol. (1997) (*Philosophical Perspectives, vol. 11, Mind, Causation and World*): 433-71; also idem, "The Compatibility of Materialism and Survival: The 'Falling Elevator' Model," *Faith and Philosophy* 16 (1999): 194-212. Zimmerman offers the definition of "temporal stage" for objects in general; I have taken the liberty to make the relevant substitutions so that the definition applies to organisms in particular.

Technically, we can put it this way: A human body $B$ that exists at $t_3$ is the same as a human body $A$ that exists at $t_1$, *in virtue of persisting from $t_1$ to $t_3$*, just in case the temporal stages leading up to $B$ at $t_3$ are immanent causally connected to the temporal stage of $A$ at $t_1$.

Here then is one way of fulfilling this condition in the case of Saint Paul (or us), if, as some do, one wants to maintain a belief in immediate survival. First, we must suppose the account just given of the persistence conditions for human bodies. It seems possible that at the moment just before Saint Paul's death, each of the smallest building blocks composing his body (let us call them "simples") could be made by God to fission such that the simples composing his body are, at the very next moment, causally related to two different, spatially segregated sets of simples.[20] One of the two sets of simples would immediately cease to constitute a life and come instead to compose a corpse, while the other would continue to constitute a body in heaven.[21] In other words, the set of simples along one of the branching paths at the instant after fission fails to perpetuate a life, while the other set of simples along the other branch does continue to perpetuate a life. Here then is a view of immediate survival of the body that is congenial to both dualism and materialism and meets the immanent causal condition on the persistence of bodies.

This view of immediate survival, like most others in the neighborhood, does not come without a price. At least part of the cost involves giving up the assumption we might have that material continuity is necessary for the persistence of physical objects. Moreover, whereas we may be willing to allow physical organisms in particular to gradually replace some or all of the matter that constitutes them, we may not be willing to allow for an all-at-once replacement like that entailed by the fissioning model of survival. We may think that is too high a price to pay. However, if what ultimately matters for the persistence of organisms is the holding of immanent causal relations among successive temporal stages of an organism's career, giving up the assumption about material continuity is not a cost incurred by the view, but rather an entailment of it.

There is a more serious metaphysical problem with the fissioning model of survival, however: namely, it seems to violate what one philosopher calls "the only *x* and *y*" principle. According to this principle, whether or not some microscopic objects *x* and *y* compose some macroscopic object *F* should have nothing to do with events involving numerically distinct microphysical ob-

---

[20]Dean Zimmerman was the first to suggest this view in a paper presented at the American Philosophical Association's Pacific Division meeting in 1994. I take up the view in "Persons and Bodies," *Faith and Philosophy* 15 (1998): 324-40. Zimmerman develops it further in "Compatibility of Materialism and Survival."

[21]We will assume not only that persons are essentially persons, but also that being alive or conscious is a necessary condition for human personhood. Therefore, there is after the fissioning only one possible candidate for a person-constituting object since the surviving corpse is not a living organism and so is not capable of subserving consciousness.

jects spatiotemporally segregated from *F*. But in the account of immediate survival just suggested, it looks as though whether a body persists into the afterlife has everything to do with what happens to the other fission product, namely, that it immediately perish. I believe this objection can be met, and since I have suggested elsewhere just how to meet it I will not take it up here, except to say that I think there are good reasons for believing that it can never be the case that there be a competitor for identity with my body.[22]

The reason I myself do not believe in immediate survival, however, is a theological reason. The Christian doctrine is *resurrection* of the body. Yet the account just offered is not an account of resurrection; it is an account of *survival*, to be sure, survival *without death*. But the Scriptures seem to take death much more seriously than this view does. For there death is portrayed as a terrible foe, an enemy finally conquered in the resurrection of Christ. But on this account of survival, bodies do not actually die; they remain intact through death (i.e., the death of the cellular tissues that once constituted them).

So for reasons having mostly to do with biblical interpretation, I am of the opinion that death marks a real and tragic end to our existence.[23] This, of course, presents us with an apparent puzzle. If I am committed to the aforementioned account of our persistence, as I am, then how can I maintain belief in an afterlife? The answer is simple. In the words of a 1970s disco hit, "I believe in miracles. . . . *(You sexy thang!)*"

---

[22]See my "Physical Persons and Post Mortem Survival Without Temporal Gaps," in *Soul, Body and Survival: Essays on the Metaphysics of Human Persons*, ed. Kevin Corcoran (Ithaca, N.Y.: Cornell University Press, 2001), pp. 201-17.

[23]For illuminating discussion of death and eschatology in biblical perspective, see Joel B. Green, "Eschatology and the Nature of Humans: A Reconsideration of the Pertinent Biblical Evidence," *Science & Christian Belief* 14 (2002): 33-50; idem, "What Does It Mean to Be Human? Another Chapter in the Ongoing Interaction of Science and Scripture," in *From Cells to Souls: Changing Portraits of Human Nature*, ed. Malcolm A. Jeeves (Grand Rapids: Eerdmans, 2004), pp. 177-98. I must hasten to point out that I am beginning to have serious doubts about what I say here. Of all the things the tradition has had disagreement over, never, so far as I know, has there been disagreement about the communion of saints. Probably not until late-fifteenth-century Protestantism do we find the belief questioned, and then often on the mistaken understanding that it involves petitioning the departed saints in the same way we petition God. But the fact of the matter is that in the devotional life of believers, the communion of saints functions very much like the Bible study of which I am a member. Just as I might ask a fellow member to pray for me, so I might ask a departed saint known for his or her mercy, kindness, devotion, fidelity or generosity to pray for me as I seek to cultivate those same virtues in my own life. But there can be no communion of saints if there is no conscious existence between death and the general resurrection. And this is leading me to believe that a commitment to an intermediate state of bodily existence does not soften the tragedy of death. It is leading me back to a belief in immediate (bodily) survival.

### The Miracle of Resurrection: Reassembly, Re-creation and Retreat to Ignorance

The first thing to recognize here is that the immanent causal condition on our persistence is a condition that applies during any temporal stretch during which we exist. If our existence can have gaps in it (i.e., if we can exist, cease to exist and then begin again to exist, as I believe is possible) then, quite obviously, the account does not apply during the gap (i.e., during the temporal stretch during which we do not exist). The condition is a condition for our persistence or continued existence.

Some philosophers hold that it is impossible for a material thing to have *two* beginnings (i.e., that a material thing like an organism cannot begin to exist, cease and then begin again to exist). As I say, I am not among those philosophers. For I see no a priori reason to reject the possibility of gappy existence. I admit, however, that, absent a miracle, the prospects for gappy existence look pretty bleak. I am a Christian theist, however, and, as I say, I believe in miracles. Indeed, I can conceive several different ways God could bring it about that I come back into existence after ceasing.

The first way is via *reassembly*. The traditional reassembly view of resurrection has it that at the resurrection, God gathers together all the bits (or all the most important bits) that made up one's body at death and causes them to be propertied and related just as they were at the moment immediately preceding death. Since the post-gap body is composed of all the same bits, propertied and related exactly as they were in the pre-gap body, the resulting object, on this view, is the previously existing, *living* body.[24] And lest resurrection by reassembly be facilely rejected, it ought to be noted that there are analogies to resurrection by reassembly in common experience. When your lawnmower is taken in for repairs, thoroughly dismantled, cleaned and later reassembled, what you are inclined to say is that the lawnmower returned to you is numerically the same as the lawnmower you took in for repairs. True, the lawnmower did not persist through its disassembly and cleaning, but its constituent parts did. The lawnmower received after repairs, on this view, is the same as the one taken in for repairs because it has all the same parts propertied and related in exactly the same way. On the traditional reassembly view of resurrection, so too with human bodies.

Although it is true, on the standard reassembly view, that the bits in the

---

[24]If you think this presents a problem because the body, once brought back into existence, will immediately die (again!), then you are forgetting that God can, and no doubt would, immediately heal the body of whatever defects led to its initial demise.

resurrected body are the way they are because the atoms in the body just before death were the way they were, it does not appear to be the case that the two stages of the "body's" existence are immanent causally related. Instead, on the standard reassembly view, the causal chain runs through God. God reassembles the original bits based on their arrangement immediately before death.

In the past, I have voiced the concern that the standard reassembly view of resurrection fails to meet the immanent causal requirement for the persistence of bodies, precisely because the causal chain runs through God.[25] For it has seemed to me that there is no immanent causal contribution made by the dying bits to the bits that make up the resurrection body. However, Dean Zimmerman has convinced me that the reassembly view can be made compatible with the immanent causal condition. For what the immanent causal condition rules out is that there be some state or event that is both present during the temporal gap during which the body is not present and that is itself causally sufficient for the later stage of the body's existence. That requirement, however, would not be violated if God were to issue a decree of the following form— "Let there be a resurrected body that is composed of the same parts, propertied and related just the same way, as the parts that composed Saint Paul's body just before his death"—followed by the appearance of said body. God's decree, in other words, though causally necessary for the reappearance of Saint Paul's body, is not causally sufficient for its appearance and, therefore, would not transgress the immanent causal requirement.[26]

I now agree that the divine decree version of the reassembly view can be made compatible with the immanent causal condition. I would, however, still maintain that the parts that compose the post-gap body must be the way they are at least partly in virtue of the causal contribution of the pre-gap parts (and their properties and relations). I would also suggest that there are aesthetic reasons for preferring a view of the resurrection that involves God on the front end of the gap, perhaps even at the beginning of creation, bestowing on the simples that compose bodies a capacity for passing on causal "umph" across temporal gaps and issuing a general decree, also at the beginning of creation, to the effect that when the requisite conditions obtain, capacity is exercised. Such a view, I think, would be preferable to any reassembly view according to which the mere presence of the parts of a body (and their properties and rela-

---

[25] I voiced this concern during the presentation of papers at several conferences.

[26] Such a view has been suggested in Zimmerman, "Compatibility of Materialism and Survival."

tions) at death are, together with God's decree, causally sufficient for the reappearance of the body after death.

One might wonder whether it is plausible to believe that immanent causal relations can cross a temporal gap. I think it is, for the following reasons: First, we know from revelation that God promises resurrection. And experience seems to teach us that bodies cease to exist. Now if it is true that for some future body to be numerically the same body as one that previously existed but ceased, then the last stage of the pregap body and the first stage of postgap body must stand in immanent causal relations to one another. And this would require that immanent causal relations cross the temporal gap. But can they? The Christian believer has reason to think so. In fact, here is an argument to that conclusion.

1. Bodies cease to exist.

2. The Scriptures teach that my body is going to be raised.

3. If some future body is going to be numerically the same body as one that previously existed but ceased, then the last stage of the pregap body and the first stage of postgap body must stand in immanent causal relations to one another.

4. Therefore, immanent causal relations can cross temporal gaps.

Assuming that a requirement for my body to exist after ceasing is that the two relevant stages of its existence (the last stage of the pregap body and the first stage of the postgap body) be immanent causally related, it must be true that immanent causal relations can cross gaps! The challenge for the Christian who embraces the immanent causal condition (dualist or materialist) would be to seek to understand just how that might work. But regardless, insofar as one believes the argument is sound, it provides one with good reason for believing that gappy existence is compatible with the controversial claim that immanent causal relations can cross temporal gaps.

I must admit, however, that I have no clue how this might work. The problem is that it is completely opaque (to me at least) as to how the atoms or simples that compose the pregap body can pass on a life-preserving causal relation across the gap to the atoms or simples that will compose the postgap body. So let us suppose, for the sake of argument, that it is not possible for this to happen. Does it follow that resurrection life is therefore impossible? No! For one could argue that the immanent causal condition is a diachronic condition: that is, it applies across time, connecting earlier and later stages of, in this case, a single organism. But take the first instant of my body's pregap existence. At that instant there are no stages to be immanent causally connected. But it is that body which God causes to exist. If God causes that body to exist once, why could God not cause it to exist a second time? Perhaps like the first time, once it is brought into existence what will make it the case that some later stage is a stage of the same body is that immanent causal relations link those stages. But what makes the first stage of the postgap body a different stage of the same body that perished is just that God makes it so.

That is one thing that could be said. But another thing that could be said is that if one insists that if any two stages are to be different stages of the same body, then those stages must be immanent causally connected. The "must" need not be a *metaphysical* "must" (i.e., a "must" that applies in every possible situation). It could be a *nomological* "must": that is, it could be what must occur *given the laws of nature that obtain in the world we inhabit.* In other words, one could argue that the immanent causal condition is not a *metaphysically* necessary condition on the persistence of bodies, but a *nomologically* necessary one. And since it is reasonable to believe that the "natural" laws that govern the postmortem world of the New Jerusalem might be quite different than those governing this world, it may not be the case that immanent causal connections unite the last stage of the pregap body and the first and succeeding stages of the postgap body. Even so, all of those stages could be stages of the same body.

So much for worries over the resurrection. It should be apparent by now that the constitution view has no trouble accommodating belief in the afterlife. I want now, before drawing this essay to a close, to answer an important ethical objection to the constitution view.

### Ethics at the Edges of Life

According to the constitution view of human persons, human persons are essentially physical *and* essentially psychological. One implication of the constitution view is that no early term fetus constitutes a person. Another implication is that any entity once possessing, but having lost all capacity for, the relevant kinds of psychological states also fails to constitute a person; and, therefore, some human organisms in so-called persistent vegetative states (PVS) no longer constitute persons. Among the objections to the constitution view is that such a view is defective because it lacks the metaphysical resources to generate moral obligations or moral expectations to protect life in either its early or late stages.

The intuition behind such an objection can be formulated as a claim about a necessary condition for grounding our obligations to the unborn and other vulnerable human lives. Call it N.

*N:* A necessary condition for grounding our obligations to the unborn and other vulnerable human lives is a commitment to human persons as having immaterial souls.

Supplementing *N* with

*S:* The constitution view of personhood denies that human persons have immaterial souls.

delivers what admittedly would be, if true, a defect in the constitution view of persons, namely,

*O:* A constitution view of personhood lacks the requisite resources for grounding our obligations to the unborn and other vulnerable human lives.

The idea that N attempts to capture is, I think, that there is a very tight connection between personhood and moral status such that anything lacking personhood lacks a moral status sufficient to guarantee a prohibition against its killing. Given that intuition, and accepting *N* and *S*, seems to commit the defender of constitution to the view that we have no moral obligations or responsibilities with respect to protecting the life of nonperson constituting human organisms.

The problem, however, is that although the move to *O* from *N* and *S* is valid, *N* is neither intuitively known nor self-evidently true. Not only is it not obviously true, it is, I believe, demonstrably false. Indeed I want to show that not only is dualism not *necessary* for generating obligations and responsibilities to fetuses and PVS patients, but also it is, in fact, compatible with the belief that no abortion ends the existence of a human person.

Consider first the claim that human persons are at least partially composed of immaterial souls, which are connected as intimately as you like to human organisms. On all such dualist views currently on offer by Christian philosophers—be that dualism of the Cartesian variety or of the Thomistic variety advocated by J. P. Moreland and Scott Rae,[27] be it emergent dualism or creationist dualism—it is metaphysically possible for the soul both to continue in existence after the demise of the organism it animates and to carry with it the identity of the person. On such views, therefore, abortion ends the life of an object that is such that if it ceases to exist, no person will cease to exist as a result. For this reason not only it is plausible to think that abortion never ends the existence of a person, but it in fact is an entailment of many brands of du-

---

[27]See J. P. Moreland and Scott B. Rae, *Body and Soul: Human Nature and the Crisis in Ethics* (Downers Grove, Ill.: InterVarsity Press, 2000).

alism. And if an abortion never ends the existence of a person, then, for dualists, any prohibition against abortion cannot be because destroying the fetus destroys a person.[28]

Of course, dualists can still oppose abortion. A dualist, might, for example, offer the following as support for a prohibition against abortion: (1) God intends every human person to be a soul-body composite, and (2) abortion is the wrenching apart of what God intends to be joined. Notice, however, the metaphysics of dualism does not alone support the moral conclusion that the life of a human fetus ought to be protected. Instead, it is an appeal to God's intentions that, coupled with the metaphysics, supports the prohibition. But an appeal to God's intentions as a justifying reason for protecting human fetuses is no less congenial to materialist views of persons. Indeed, this is exactly how I propose we ground the prohibition against killing human fetuses. For I have argued elsewhere that every human fetus is created by God with the ultimate intention of coming to constitute a person, and on the basis of God's ultimately good intentions for it, the life of the fetus ought to be protected.[29] The same holds for human organisms in persistent vegetative states. It is plausible to believe that God intends every human organism to constitute a person, and in view of this there is a prima facie obligation not to kill a PVS patient. So even defenders of views like the constitution view are not without the moral and theological resources to argue for the moral wrongness of abortion, some varieties of euthanasia and so on.

I believe that this brief discussion is sufficient to demonstrate that neither a metaphysics of dualism nor a metaphysics of naturalism about persons alone settles the moral issues at stake by either entailing or precluding an ethic of life. I conclude, therefore, that although it is true that a constitution view of persons lacks the metaphysical resources either necessary or sufficient to generate moral obligations or moral expectations to prohibit the taking of human life, this is also true of dualist views of persons.

There is one final issue I wish to consider. Someone might wish to argue that the same relevant moral or theological principles can be invoked to prohibit the taking of canine life and that a moral problem with my view of persons is that it does not preserve the moral difference between human and nonhuman lives. The problem can be presented like this. I have been using the

---

[28]If the dualist objects that a living human fetus is a person in virtue of being ensouled, then I do not understand how a thing (a person) can become identical with a part of itself (i.e., a soul).

[29]Corcoran, "Persons and Bodies."

term *person* in the sense of "individual with a capacity for certain kinds of psychological states." But there are different senses of the term *person*. Suppose that instead of using the term in the sense of "individual with a capacity for certain kinds of psychological states" we use the term in the moral sense of "an entity deserving protection under an ethic of life," that is, an entity possessing inherent value. Now if we embrace a thesis like

> *MB:* Only human persons are moral beings (i.e., entities deserving protection by virtue of possessing inherent value)

it might be thought that we can grant that, while we may have obligations toward nonpersons, our obligations toward moral persons differ in important respects from our obligations toward nonpersons. For example, obligations toward moral persons are correlated with moral rights, and in virtue of this we might think that our obligations toward persons are weightier than those toward nonpersons. If we are committed to something like *MB*, then it is right to think that views like the constitution view, which denies human personhood to human fetuses and PVS patients, cannot generate moral obligations that carry anything near the same weight as those generated by views that do count human fetuses and PVS patients as persons.

There are several ways to respond to this important objection. One obvious way would be simply to deny *MB*. But we need not do that. One thing I want to say in response is that a virtue of grounding value in something like God's ultimately good intentions for God's creation is that one need tell only one story that obligates us to protect the life of created, living things whereas alternative views need to tell two stories—one of them yielding obligations to persons and another yielding obligations to nonpersons. Second, a single story grounding value in theistic intentions is compatible with there being different degrees of moral weightiness. Our obligations toward moral persons might be weightier than our obligations toward nonpersons based on God's intentions for each kind. But it is plausible to believe that our obligations toward *human* nonpersons are, for the same reason, weightier than our obligations to *nonhuman* nonpersons. For example, because God intends every human organism to constitute a human person and human persons have a privileged role in God's economy, our obligation to human fetuses and PVS patients is weightier than our obligation to nonhuman entities, so much so as to prima facie prohibit the killing of either the human fetus or the PVS patient. I believe, therefore, that materialist views of human persons like the constitution view can grant *MB* without there following any dire ethical consequences.

## Conclusion

I wish to return to a point I made many pages ago about the boldness and authoritativeness with which some philosophers speak about the metaphysics of human persons. I said then that I cannot so speak. Do I believe that the constitution view is true? Yes. To my lights, and on most days, it seems to me it is. But I am of aware of both the philosophical costs the view involves as well as the theological and ethical worries that attend the view. I have addressed the latter here, and the philosophical objections to the view I have addressed in various other places. In any case, I cannot say I hold the constitution view with anything like the same degree of firmness as, say, I hold to the claim that God was in Christ reconciling the world to himself. Nor, of course, do I hold the view with anything like the same degree of firmness as I hold the view that $2 + 2 = 4$. But dualism has never seemed compelling to me. Nor has animalism, the claim that I am numerically identical with a human animal. Constitution seems to me a plausible alternative to animalism, on the one hand, and dualism, on the other. For now, and until I am convinced that there are insuperable problems with the view, I will continue to defend the constitution view.[30]

---

[30]There are many people who provided helpful comments and suggestions on various drafts of this essay. First, I would like to thank members of the Tuesday afternoon colloquium at Calvin for characteristically helpful and incisive criticism of an early draft of this essay. John Hare and Del Ratzsch deserve special mention in this regard. I would also like to thank two of the most gifted and eager philosophy students I have ever had the pleasure of working with, Josh Armstrong and Michael Grant-Schweiger. These two provided me with invaluable suggestions for improving the essay. I also wish to thank the editors of this volume for providing helpful feedback on an earlier draft of the essay. Finally, a special thanks to Jeremy Johnson, who completed an independent study with me on issues related to this essay shortly after its completion. It was Jeremy's insistence that the communion of saints must be taken seriously by anyone who wishes to take Christian tradition seriously that has led me to rethink my commitment to gappy existence.

# A SUBSTANCE DUALIST RESPONSE

*Stewart Goetz*

Kevin Corcoran informs us that in contrast to his mother, who is a substance dualist (dualist, for short), he is a physicalist (materialist). Corcoran goes on to tell us that the metaphysical view that he holds as a philosopher about what we are fits well with the theological doctrine of the resurrection of the dead, which he holds as a Christian. He believes that if the issue of the afterlife were simply that of postmortem survival, then the dualist would have a much easier time than the physicalist accounting for life after death. For the Christian, however, the issue is the resurrection of the dead, for which survival of the soul is not sufficient. Corcoran concedes that dualism is not incompatible with the doctrine of the resurrection of the dead. (If it were, most, if not all, orthodox Christian theologians of the early church would have believed something false, because they were dualists.) But he claims that all Christians, dualists and materialists, must address and make sense of the doctrine in question. Though Corcoran does not explicitly state that he thinks a physicalist of his kind—one who advocates the constitution view of human persons—can do a better job than a dualist at making sense of the resurrection, one gets the impression that a dualist account of the resurrection just cannot measure up because it cannot provide a convincing Christian account of the idea of a body's being the numerically same body, an idea that Corcoran believes is at the heart of the doctrine of the resurrection of the body.

Does belief in the resurrection of the body require belief that one will have the numerically same body in the afterlife? Do the writers of Scripture answer this question? Not that I can find. Saint Paul, who has more to say about the resurrection body than anybody else, never talks in terms of numerical versus qualitative sameness. Indeed, he talks in terms of a sown seed that dies with one kind of body and grows to have a different type, which is hardly the talk of a philosopher seeking to impart logical clarity about the idea of sameness. If anything, Saint Paul seems intent on emphasizing the dissimilar natures and, thereby, the lack of numerical sameness of the pre- and postresurrection bodies. For example, he stresses that flesh and blood cannot inherit the kingdom of God, and he believes that a mortal and perishable body that is ensouled in this life will be replaced by an immortal and imperishable body that is (in addition to being ensouled) enlivened by the Spirit of God. Like Scripture, the Apostles' Creed does not address the issue of numerical sameness. A confessor of it affirms only that he or she believes in the resurrection of the body and the life everlasting. Moreover, I am not aware of any other creed that either requires a confessor to affirm the numerical sameness of the pre- and postresurrection bodies or addresses the issue of what constitutes the numerical sameness of a human body.

If what I have said in the previous paragraph is true, then on what grounds does Corcoran claim both that it is reasonable to believe that it is the numerically same body which exists before and after death and that any supposed Christian view that departs from this position owes us an explanation about why we should understand the idea of the resurrection of the dead in a way that does not involve numerical sameness of body? Consider, first, the claim that it is reasonable to believe that it is the numerically same body which exists before and after death. What is presupposed by such a claim about the concept of the numerical sameness of a human body? To help answer this question, it is interesting to consider Augustine's discussion of the calumnies of unbelievers who made fun of the Christian belief in the resurrection.[1] As a way of ridiculing the idea that the resurrection of the dead required the numerically same body, these unbelievers asked the following kinds of questions: What will be the size of our resurrection bodies? Will deformed bodies be reassembled with the same deformed parts? Will resurrected bodies be infant or adult in nature? What will happen if a person's body at, say, age thirty, which will be resurrected, had a part that was also a part of another person's body of the same age which will be resurrected? Which body will get that part? What questions like these indicate is that in the minds of these unbelievers, if a person is going to get the numerically same body in the resurrection life that he had in his earthly life, then there must be numerical sameness of parts in those bodies. Given this concept of numerical sameness, these unbelievers thought it would not take long for a person to conclude that the idea of the resurrection of the body, if it requires numerical sameness of body, is a joke. At this point, there are two general options for the believer.

First, believers can accept the unbeliever's concept of the numerical same-

---

[1] Augustine *The City of God* 22.12.

ness of a human body and rethink whether the doctrine of the resurrection requires the numerical sameness of the pre- and postresurrection human bodies.
Believers who are Kierkegaardian in disposition can affirm that the resurrection does require numerical sameness of body and revel in any resulting ab-
surdities. If they are more rationally disposed, they can deny that the resurrection of the body requires the numerical sameness of the body.[2]

Second, the believer can reject the unbeliever's concept of numerical sameness of a human body and explain the doctrine of the resurrection according
to some other account of the numerical sameness of such a body. Because of
the kinds of problems raised by the unbelievers and because of his commitment to the view that the resurrection of the body requires the numerical
sameness of pre- and postresurrection body, Corcoran opts for this second alternative.[3] What then is involved in numerical sameness of a human body, according to Corcoran? The unbelievers of Augustine's day, and apparently Augustine himself, would be surprised to learn that it does not require the
numerical sameness of any parts. The resurrection body can be the numerically same body as the one that went to the grave, even though they do not
share any parts in common and even though there was a temporal gap between their existences during which neither existed. What supposedly makes
this numerical identity possible is an immanent causal relation (an immanent
causal condition), the details of which are found in Corcoran's essay. I would
suggest to readers who are inclined to embrace Corcoran's view—that the numerical sameness of a human body over time and even temporal gaps does not
require any sameness of constituent parts—that a dualist can provide an
equally, if not more, plausible account of the numerical sameness of the pre-
and postresurrection body. Instead of an immanent causal condition, the dualist can invoke the soul as the explanation of the numerical sameness of a human body. The dualist can do this while maintaining that the soul is a particular substance or entity and not, as Thomas Aquinas suggested, a form or
universal. On this dualist view, an organism like a human body can undergo
the loss and acquisition of parts in a regular and controlled way and remain
the numerically same body because it is a structure whose changes are caused
by the soul on which it depends for its existence. On this account, the soul and
not an immanent causal condition is what controls and limits the kinds of part
substitution that are consistent with the human body's remaining the numer-

---

[2]This is the view I would advocate.
[3]On the problems raised by the unbelievers, see Kevin Corcoran, "Dualism, Materialism and
the Problem of Post Mortem Survival," *Philosophia Christi* 4, no. 2 (2002): 395-409.

ically same body. The best defense of this kind of view in the recent literature is J. P. Moreland and Scott B. Rae's *Body and Soul*.[4] Of course, Corcoran is not attracted to this dualist account of the numerical sameness of a human body because he begins with the conviction that he is a physical thing. Is there any way that Corcoran and I can find common ground for discussion, even though we start at such radically different positions? As I said in my essay, in response to a comment by Peter van Inwagen about what he finds when he enters most deeply into himself, I find that as a soul I seem to occupy the space occupied by my physical body. If Corcoran also finds that he seems to occupy the space occupied by his physical body, then we have some common ground upon which we can begin a conversation. That conversation, however, will have to wait for another time and place.

---

[4]J. P. Moreland and Scott B. Rae, *Body and Soul: Human Nature and the Crisis in Ethics* (Downers Grove, Ill.: InterVarsity Press, 2000).

# AN EMERGENT DUALIST RESPONSE

*William Hasker*

K evin Corcoran finds it impossible to believe in mind-body dualism. He is right in saying that none of us have very much direct control over what we do and do not believe. (We can exercise some indirect control over this by managing properly the process of reflection by which we come to believe many of the things we do believe.) But he also gives reasons for his rejection of dualism—namely, that the observed dependence of mind on brain is not what we would expect if dualism were true, and also that dualism introduces "an unnecessary and inelegant cleavage into the natural world." I would recognize these reasons (especially the first) as good reasons to have reservations about traditional (Cartesian) dualism. Emergent dualism, on the other hand, comes up well on both counts, as readers of my essay will already have learned!

If we are going to be materialists, it would seem the natural view to take is that a human person is identical with a certain living human body. Corcoran, however, dissents from this, holding instead that persons are constituted by, but are not identical with, their bodies. I agree with him that the constitution relation is an important one, and he does an excellent job of explaining it. It is indeed true that bronze statues are constituted by, rather than identical with, the lumps of bronze of which they are made, and I would agree with some of his other examples as well. But I do not believe it is plausible to suppose that human beings are constituted by their bodies, *even if we are already committed to materialism.* Why not simply say we are animals, albeit a rather special and complex sort of animal?

So far as I can see, Corcoran gives two reasons for preferring the constitution view to animalism. One is that it is impossible for a person to continue existing while he or she lacks the capacity for intentional states. But is this really impossible? If someone goes into a coma, we do not normally say that person has ceased to exist. Now suppose we learn that the coma is permanent and irreversible. Do we then say that the individual who previously existed no longer exists? What many of us will say, rather, is that the person who previously existed is still alive, though tragically she or he is no longer a person (or at least, cannot function as a person). And in saying this, we are in agreement with animalism, not with the constitution view.

Where the shoe really pinches for the constitution theorist is at the beginning of life. According to the constitution view, Corcoran's daughter Shannon *did not exist at all* during the first few months of her mother's pregnancy. It is not merely that she existed but was not yet a person; many people are willing to say that, though others will find it to be controversial. But the truth is (according to the constitution view) that *there simply was no such individual as Shannon Corcoran* during those first few months; that individual first came into existence only when the developing fetus first attained the capacity for intentional mental states. My guess is that I will not be the only one who finds this strange and hard to believe

The other reason given for preferring the constitution view, according to Corcoran, is that this view provides an account of human persons that distinguishes us from nonhuman animals but without positing immaterial souls. My response is that a Christian animalist is perfectly able to do this as well.[1] Such a person will emphasize the special rationality of human beings, our capacity for moral discernment and our capacity for a relationship with God as what decisively sets us apart from other animals.[2] (More about this in my essay, above.)

Lynne Baker claims another advantage for the constitution view—namely, that persons can change bodies while remaining the same individuals.[3] Corcoran rejects this (rightly, in my opinion), and so he has the difficult task of showing how the resurrection body can be the identical body that was formerly

---

[1]Admittedly the phrase *Christian animalist* has an odd ring to it. "Animalist" suggests a view according to which we are *merely* animals, no different (or not much different) from the rest of the beasts. In this context, however, "animalist" implies that we are animals, but a very special kind of animals, in view of the important differences between humans and other sorts of animals.

[2]Actually, it is not clear that the constitution view has anything of its own to offer on this point. According to that view, a new individual (a person) comes into existence when a fetus becomes capable of intentional mental states. But many animals also have intentional states (my dog is chock-full of beliefs and desires), so why is there not a new individual in this case also? If there is, the metaphysical difference between humans and other animals has disappeared.

[3]See Lynne Rudder Baker, "Material Persons and the Doctrine of Resurrection," *Faith and Philosophy* 18, no. 2 (2001): 151-67. For a critique of Baker's arguments, see my article "The Constitution View of Persons: A Critique," *International Philosophical Quarterly* 44, no. 1 (2004): 23-34.

alive, in spite of the well-known facts about the decay and disintegration of corpses. Corcoran argues, to be sure, that mind-body dualists also have this problem, in view of the Christian tradition that it is the very same bodies that previously died that will be raised on the last day. Maybe so, but there are options that may provide some leeway for the dualist here, options not open to the materialist. The view of Thomas Aquinas, that the body is the same because it is "organized" by the same soul (whether or not the matter is the same), is not obviously incoherent, but it is not available to the materialist, who denies the existence of souls. It could be that, in resurrecting us, God gathers up the available matter from the premortem body (that which has not been annihilated or used by some other person), adds additional matter as needed, shapes the stuff into an appropriately transformed resurrection body, and causes that body to be animated by the soul that survives from our earthly life. Many would say that such a scenario gives us something "close enough" to count as the same body, but this scenario also is unavailable to the materialist. The materialist has to come up with a view that provides strict identity of the resurrection body with the earthly body and do this without benefit of a soul that carries the personal identity of the individual who previously lived. And that is a tall order.[4]

Has Corcoran succeeded in providing such a view? I do not think so, mainly for the reason detailed in my essay. As with other materialist views of the resurrection, he is unable to show how the resurrection body can be identical (*necessarily* identical—anything less is not identity) with the body that died. He offers no fewer than three different scenarios for our consideration. (Is that not already a reason to wonder about his "solutions"?) One, the "body-splitting" view, is unique to Corcoran himself; since I have discussed this elsewhere, I will not comment on it further at this point.[5] The second scenario is a version of the "reassembly" view, with the additional wrinkle that "immanent causal connections" are said to be able to cross temporal gaps. Corcoran admits, however, that although he thinks it may be possible that they can do this, he has no idea *how* it is possible. So he proposes yet a third option, in which

---

[4]It strikes me as odd that Corcoran finds the idea that the resurrection body may not be strictly identical with the body that died to be a more serious deviation from the tradition than his own view of the soul's nonexistence. It is not easy to decide how much deference should be paid to tradition on such topics, but I believe most of us would consider the rejection of dualism to be the more momentous alteration.

[5]See my book *The Emergent Self* (Ithaca, N.Y.: Cornell University Press, 1999), pp. 222-32. It should be noted that Dean Zimmerman, the codeveloper with Corcoran of this view, is a dualist who does not himself endorse the view. He proposes it as the best a *materialist* can do, but regards it as ultimately unsatisfactory.

the resurrection body is identical with the body which previously died simply because God decrees that this shall be so. The notion that God can make two things identical by decree strikes me as wholly incredible; but there is no space here to construct an argument against it.

Having said all this, let me acknowledge that the search for an acceptable and coherent materialist view of the resurrection is bound to continue. Many Christian thinkers are strongly motivated to embrace such a view; like Corcoran, they are simply unable to believe in dualism. And they will not be deterred by objections such as the ones raised in my essay. I wish them well in their endeavor—though even were they to succeed, my other main objection to materialism, based on the unity of consciousness, would still remain. Up until now, though, I do not think they have come up with a view that gets the job done.

# A NONREDUCTIVE PHYSICALIST RESPONSE

*Nancey Murphy*

I am quite sympathetic to Kevin Corcoran's view of human nature. Thus, my responses here will amount only to a bit of tinkering with his terminology and emphases.

My primary concern will be to suggest a slightly different way of dealing with the problem of pre- and postresurrection identity. There is a rich philosophical literature on personal identity. One longstanding argument is between those who stake personal identity on spatiotemporal continuity of the body and those who tie it to continuity of memories. It is a fact about us in this life that continuity of memory depends on temporal continuity of our brains and thus of the rest of our bodies. So these two criteria are essentially related. However, there is more to continuity of consciousness than a bundle of memories. This is the ability to recognize my conscious self over time, which is so unproblematic most of the time (e.g., when I wake up in the morning) that it may go unnoticed. An obvious case of failure is the phenomenon of split personality. Its absence is also striking in certain sorts of the misidentification syndrome, in which patients believe they are being transformed into someone else's psychological identity. Although we might speculate that this is the effect of reading too much philosophy of mind late at night, such patients show either localized or diffuse brain damage.[1]

Recognition of oneself as oneself over time and after interruptions of conscious experience may have been presumed to be part of what philosophers have been referring to all along as the memory criterion, but I want to highlight it; I will call this additional criterion the "continuity-of-consciousness criterion."

I now want to argue that the combined memory-consciousness criterion is still too narrow, in that memory and continuity of consciousness together do not capture all of what we need in order to secure personal identity. Given the

---

[1]Leslie A. Brothers, *Friday's Footprint: How Society Shapes the Human Mind* (New York: Oxford University Press, 1997), pp. 3-10.

moral and social character of the kingdom of God, we need to add "same moral character" to our criterion. I propose that identity of persons depends as much on character identity as it does on memory/consciousness and bodily continuity. That is, a replica or transformed version of my body with all my memories intact would not be me unless she possessed my virtues (or vices), affections and moral perceptions.[2]

Another factor that needs to be taken into account in understanding personal identity is our relationships. It is clear that a great deal of what makes us to be the persons that we are is our relations with other people, and particularly with God.

I need now to introduce a helpful philosophical clarification. David Wiggins has shown that to say "$x$ is the same as $y$" or "$x$ is identical to $y$" requires the specification of what he calls a covering concept; that is, one needs to be able to answer the question, "the same *what* as $y$?" This solves many traditional philosophical puzzles, such as whether one can step into the same river twice. The puzzle is due to failing to distinguish between "same body of water" and "same mass of water molecules." Criteria of identity need to be tailored to fit the relevant covering concept.[3] Consequently, in discussing personal identity, it is necessary to ask specifically what are the identity criteria for the covering concept *person*, and to expect that these be different from identity criteria for a material object or even for a human body.[4]

The identity criteria for an ordinary material object clearly involve spatiotemporal continuity. How do I know that this pencil is mine, even though it is now three inches shorter than when I bought it? The answer is that it has been in my possession all along. What about identity criteria for "same body"? Here spatiotemporal continuity still matters, and this makes up for the fact that the body changes qualitatively from birth to death and even for the fact that most of the matter of which it is made is replaced after about seven years.

So what are the criteria for "same person"? And what is there about you that seems to be necessary so that on the day of resurrection you will happily recognize yourself to have survived? I have argued that the criteria include

---

[2]Brian Garrett broadens the memory criterion to a "psychological" criterion that includes memory together with other features such as well-entrenched beliefs, character and basic desires. He also argues that the bodily and psychological conditions need to be taken together ("Personal Identity," in *The Routledge Encyclopedia of Philosophy*, ed. Edward Craig [London: Routledge, 1998], 7:305-14).

[3]David Wiggins's solution is to require covering concepts to be *sortal* concepts, which serve to pick out individuals. Thus, *mass of water molecules* is not an appropriate covering concept. See his *Identity and Spatio-Temporal Continuity* (Oxford: Clarendon, 1967).

[4]Ibid., pp. 1, 35-36, 50.

continuity of memories, continuity of consciousness itself, continuity of moral character and continuity of relationships. I especially want to emphasize continuity of one's relations to others in the body of Christ and to Christ himself. Thus, I concur with those who emphasize that God's remembering, recognizing and relating to me are essential to my postresurrection identity.

What about bodily continuity? It is a fact that on this side of resurrection all of these other criteria are tied to the same body in the sense of same material object. But what if, given our faith in the resurrection, we revise our concept of personal identity accordingly and define "my body" as that which provides the substrate for all of these personal characteristics? It is that which allows me to be recognized by others; that which bears my memories; and that whose capacities, emotional reactions and perceptions have been shaped by my moral actions and experience. It is these characteristics that make me who I am. So any body that manifests all of these is in fact Nancey Murphy.

This recognition allows us to avoid tortuous attempts, as in the early church, to reconcile resurrection with material continuity. Early theologians raised gruesome questions such as the problem of chain consumption: What if you die and a fish eats your body and then someone else eats the fish? Who gets the matter in the end? These attempts are based on failure to distinguish the covering concepts of same person and same collection of particles. The contemporary dualist who takes the concepts of body and person to be the same is importing a reductionist view of persons and is making the same conceptual mistake as these early writers.

Corcoran is not, of course, making the reductionists' error. I believe that the difficulty he encounters in dealing with postresurrection identity is exacerbated by the self-imposed necessity of applying the immanent causal condition as a requirement for the persistence of an organism. I would like to try out some slightly different but related terminology. In some of my earlier writings I have used the now popular concepts of *supervenience* and *realization* for purposes comparable to Corcoran's.[5] *Supervenience* was first used as a technical term to describe the relation between moral properties and nonmoral characteristics. The property of being a good person supervenes on properties such as being generous, truthful and so on. I argue (contrary to the most common usage) that the lower-level (subvenient) properties constitute the higher-level properties, given certain suitable conditions. For example, giving all one's

[5]See my "Nonreductive Physicalism: Philosophical Issues," in *Whatever Happened to the Soul? Scientific and Theological Portraits of Human Nature*, ed. Warren S. Brown, Nancey Murphy and H. Newton Malony (Minneapolis: Fortress, 1998), pp. 127-48.

money to the poor may or may not constitute goodness, depending on whether one has a family to support. Supervenient properties are "multiply realizable." That is, there are a variety of different life patterns that constitute goodness.

So what if we say that this physical body constitutes me now, but in the next life my personhood will be realized by a very different kind of body, yet one that still embodies all of the characteristics I have mentioned above as necessary for personal identity?

I am experimenting with language here. It is important to remember two things: First, the specification of identity criteria is difficult and controversial in all sorts of cases. (If I gradually replace all the parts of my car but keep the old ones and put them all together, which is the original car?) Second, language regularly falls short of giving adequate expression to theological realities, and the realm of theology where our language is most inadequate is eschatology, the doctrine of last things. Our language of bodies is all based on the physical features of this world. We know that the next world—not just our bodies, but all of creation—will be as different as the resurrected Christ was from the bruised body laid in the tomb.

# LIST OF CONTRIBUTORS

**Kevin Corcoran** (Ph.D., Purdue University) is associate professor of philosophy at Calvin College. He is the author of over a dozen articles in professional journals and editor of *Soul, Body and Survival: Essays on the Metaphysics of Human Persons* (Cornell University Press, 2001). He is also the author of *Material Beings: Human Nature at the Margins of Life* (Baker Academic, forthcoming).

**Stewart Goetz** (Ph.D., University of Notre Dame) is professor of philosophy and chair of the Department of Philosophy and Religion at Ursinus College. He is the author of numerous articles on the philosophy of mind and free will in professional philosophical journals and books, and he was recently awarded a grant by the John Templeton Foundation for a project entitled "Developing Non-Supervenience Views of the Mental."

**Joel B. Green** (Ph.D., University of Aberdeen) is vice president of academic affairs, provost and professor of New Testament interpretation at Asbury Theological Seminary. He serves on the editorial board of *Science & Christian Belief* and is the author or editor of twenty books, including *What About the Soul? Neuroscience and Christian Anthropology* (Abingdon, 2004).

**William Hasker** (Ph.D., University of Edinburgh) is professor emeritus of philosophy at Huntington College. He is the author of numerous philosophical articles and several books, including *The Emergent Self* (Cornell University Press, 1999) and *Providence, Evil and the Openness of God* (Routledge, 2004). He currently serves as editor of the journal *Faith and Philosophy*.

**Nancey Murphy** (Ph.D., University of California, Berkely; Th.D., Graduate Theological Union) is professor of Christian philosophy at Fuller Theological Seminary. She is the author of nine books and coeditor of eight, including (with R. J. Russell et al.) *Neuroscience and the Person: Scientific Perspectives on Divine Action* (Vatican Observatory, 1999).

# AUTHOR INDEX

Wright, G. H. von, 133
Wright, John P., 12, 18, 33–34
Wright, N. T., 33–34
Woolridge, D., 120

Yandell, Keith, 78

Zimmerman, Dean, 38, 60,
166–67, 170, 183